Plays of Passion, Games of Chance

Jerzy Kosinski and His Fiction

Barbara Tepa Lupack

Wyndham Hall Press

THE RHODES-FULBRIGHT INTERNATIONAL LIBRARY

PLAYS OF PASSION, GAMES OF CHANCE

Jerzy Kosinski and His Fiction

by Barbara Tepa Lupack

§ *The punctuation and footnoting style used in this book have been adapted by the Publisher from the Past Masters Series of the Oxford University Press.*

Jerzy Kosinski photo by Scientia

Permission granted for cover use by V. Marshall

Library of Congress
Catalog Card Number
────────────

ISBN 1-55605-063-1 (paperback)
ISBN 1-55605-064-X (hardcover)

THE RHODES-FULBRIGHT INTERNATIONAL LIBRARY became available in the spring of 1986, and is intended as a repository and showcase of research in the humanities and the social sciences produced by Rhodes Scholars and Fulbright Fellows. As such, the Library features the best in scholarly accomplishment, past and present. The publisher and editors hope to maintain an intelligent and topical balance between research in the humanities and research in the social sciences as well as between older research and that most recently completed by this distinguished group of international scholars.

ACKNOWLEDGEMENTS

I am grateful to the National Endowment for the Humanities, for allowing me research and travel opportunities I might not otherwise have enjoyed; to the Fulbright Program, for the chance to teach and to conduct research for this manuscript in Poland; and to the Empire State College (SUNY) Foundation, for a grant to assist with the preparation of this manuscript. To Dr. James Hafley, who showed me rather late in my graduate career how really to enjoy literature, and to my students, past and present, in this country and abroad, with whom I was able to share my interest in Kosinski and in modern American fiction -- my appreciation. I am indebted in a deep and lasting way to my students and colleagues at the English Institute at the University of Wroclaw, Poland; they taught me -- in the days before and after the imposition of martial law -- the hidden strength of the written word (something their fellow Pole, Jerzy Kosinski, has long understood).

Finally, to my parents for their unflagging support, and to my husband, Al, for always "being there" as colleague, critic, and friend, my special thanks.

* * * * *

Portions of the Introduction, "Sacred Cow or Dead Horse? New Directions in the American Novel," first appeared in **Anglica Vratislaviensia,** the journal of the English Institute of the University of Wroclaw, Poland.

Portions of Chapter Five, "**Being There:** Hit or Myth?", first appeared in **The Polish Review** and **The New Orleans Review.**

Portions of Chapter Six, "Rooting for the American Dream: **The Devil Tree,**" first appeared in **The Polish Review.**

Portions of Chapter Seven, "The Flame Isn't Worth the Candle: **Cockpit** and **Blind Date,**" first appeared in **The Polish Review.**

TABLE OF CONTENTS

INTRODUCTION: Sacred Cow or Dead Horse?
                    New Directions in the American
                    Novel   1

CHAPTER ONE: Trying to Tell the Dancer from
                    the Dance: Kosinski and His
                    Biography   20

CHAPTER TWO: The Sheep in the Middle:
                    "Joseph Novak's" Nonfiction   53

CHAPTER THREE: The Painted Bird: Breaking
                    from the Flock   71

CHAPTER FOUR: Steps: Kosinski's Winding
                    Stair   110

CHAPTER FIVE: Being There: Hit or Myth?   141

CHAPTER SIX: Rooting for the American
                    Dream: The Devil Tree   166

CHAPTER SEVEN: The Flame Isn't Worth the
                    Candle: Cockpit and
                    Blind Date   189

CHAPTER EIGHT: Nights Errant, Knights Aberrant:
                    Passion Play and Pinball   220

CONCLUSION: Every Man's Everyman:
                    Kosinski and His Protagonists   248

AFTERWORD: A Note on The Hermit of
                    69th Street   257

BIBLIOGRAPHY   263

ABOUT THE AUTHOR   281

INTRODUCTION

Sacred Cow or Dead Horse?
New Directions in the American Novel

"Why is mathematics sane and numerology insane?
Why is astronomy sane and astrology insane?
Why is it sane to perform an autopsy and insane
to read entrails?"

Annie Dillard, **Living By Fiction**

[After God made man] Man blinked. "What is the
purpose of all this?" he asked politely.
"Everything must have a purpose?" asked God.
"Certainly," said man.
Then I leave it for you to think of one for
all this," said God. And He went away.

Kurt Vonnegut, **Cat's Cradle**

Asserting that it was a literary genre that had worn itself
out, exhausted its supply of subjects and its capacity for
technical experimentation, Ortega y Gasset and T. S. Eliot
declared the novel dead and buried it beneath the weight
of their authority.[1] Other critics, like Lionel Trilling,
rushed to the novel's rescue, but rather than resuscitating
it, they damned its recovery with faint praise: not quite
dead, it was, they agreed, ailing. Still more recent chron-
iclers -- Louis Rubin, Leslie Fiedler, Susan Sontag, and
Norman Podhoretz[2] -- have again taken up the cry of the
genre's "curious death."

Yet the novel is not dead. Like Mark Twain, who quipped
that rumors of his demise had been greatly exaggerated,
the contemporary novel speaks for itself in asserting its

vitality. In the works of Jerzy Kosinski and other important experimental writers like John Barth, Thomas Berger, Thomas Pynchon, Joseph Heller, Donald Barthelme, and John Hawkes, who ignore some of the conventions of the traditional novel, its voice is loud, sometimes controversial, often brilliant.

Why then do the rumors of the novel's untimely demise persist? Jonathan Baumbach suggests they are a "myth propagated by critics who have grown tired of reading."[3] Anais Nin proposes that "there are frequent obituaries of the novel because (like bad novelists) it is easier to kill off one's character than to diagnose him and solve his destructive impulses. So we kill off the novel because we do not like to say that it reflects our 'sick society' and that it reflects our divided selves rather than our integrations."[4] Yet fiction, as Jerome Klinkowitz observes in "The Death of the Death of the Novel," breeds its own continuity; and -- despite the critical despair -- new, substantial work continues to be produced. That work marks another division in the history of the novel, greater than the ones before because the nature of fiction itself is being challenged in a radical disruption of the genre's development.[5]

Actually, in recent years the novel in general (and the contemporary American novel in particular) has reemerged, more vital than its predecessors, from the controversy surrounding it. Yet the "new novel" is a painted bird. Like its namesake in Kosinski's fiction, it soars, "happy and free, a spot of rainbow against the backdrop of clouds, and then plunges into the waiting brown flock," where it circles from one end of the flock to the other, "vainly trying to convince its kin that it was one of them. But, dazzled by its brilliant colors, they flew around it unconvinced. The painted bird would be forced farther and farther away as it zealously tried to enter the ranks of the flock."[6]

Precisely because of its brilliance, the new experimental novel is misunderstood. Unlike earlier fictions -- from local color to realism, from jazz age to protest literature or more contemporary Southern, Jewish and Black works

-- it lacks a decisive name. It has been called by some a literature of exhaustion (John Barth), a literature of mockery (Robert Jay Lifton), a literature of anti-art and ultimacy (Susan Sontag), a literature of fabulation (Robert Scholes). Still others, many of them distinguished critics and commentators on the contemporary novel, have referred to it as existential, post-existential, absurd, post-absurd, black humor, modern, post-modern, neo-modern, post-contemporary, futuristic, and metafictional. Often lacking some of the staples of earlier successful fiction, the recent experimental novel has been perceived as overly fabular and fantastic and sometimes dismissed as inconsequential or unreal. Without the mass popular appeal of the Barbara Cartland romance, the slick intrigues of an Erle Stanley Gardner mystery, the suburban beau gestes of Erma Bombeck, or the sci-fi surrealism of Isaac Asimov's stories and novellas, the new novel is still in search not so much of an audience but of the critical acclaim it rightly deserves.

Different from conventional novels, different even from the modernist novels of Joyce, Kafka, and Faulkner, most good postwar experimental fiction seeks ways to deal with the violence, brevity, and rigidity of life and carries to great extremes the themes of combativeness, fragmentariness, coolness and meaninglessness that are the marks of modern fiction. It may originate, as Josephine Hendin suggests in her excellent essay on "Experimental Fiction," "in the modernist sense of life as problematic, but unlike the great experimental fiction of the 20s, it does not lament the brokenness of experience as a sign of the decline of Western civilization. Instead it offers an acceptance of dislocation as a major part of life and perhaps a hope that the displacement of traditional ideals might permit new ways of dealing with the human situation."[7]

The new novelist sees man differently from the way his predecessors did. The modernist hero was shaped by the humanist ethos -- political, anthropological, and psychoanalytic; the experimental hero of the postwar period (the hero typically found in Kosinski's fiction) is shaped by the concern

with the functioning and behavior that spawned and accelerated the growth of ego psychology in the late 1940s, 1950s,
and 1960s, and is characteristic of an age of increased
technical sophistication.[8]   He searches for meaning --
adaptation -- which will change his condition, yet his sense
of self is shattered and his personality is fragmented. The
stabilizing forces of memory and attachment are supplanted
by a sense of personal crisis that may be distinct to a culture
in which consolidation of economic power and estrangement
from political process throw the individual back upon
himself.[9]

The contemporary novelist, then, whose sense of futility
is more panoramic than Eliot's or Hemingway's or Kafka's,
has a difficult task indeed. Heir to the disillusionment
not only of the second world war but also of Korea, Vietnam,
and Watergate, his innocence has been repeatedly violated.[10]
The experimental novel becomes the vehicle for protest
of his absurd circumstances and for the exploration of
the shattered self. Born of "Freud, Einstein, jazz, and
science," that "swift new novel," according to Anais Nin,
can -- and must -- match "our modern life in speed, rhythms,
condensation, abstraction, miniaturization," and become
"X rays of our secrets, a subjective gauge of external
events."[11]

Many of the novelists of the late forties and fifties sought
refuge from the dislocation of contemporary life in literary
existentialism, the experience of an intensely felt need
to reclaim man in a twentieth-century world which appeared
bent on destroying him.[12] It seemed a natural direction
to take, especially since the crisis in the culture was an
existential one. Early postwar fiction, frequently focusing
its themes and plots on self-discovery, revealed the preoccupation with the self and the struggle to define and shape
a relationship between the self and the American culture.[13]
Journeying inward, novelists sought to discover psychological
reality, which lay below -- sometimes frighteningly below
-- the surface. That reality, as it rebelled against the
repression by the unconscious, held for them the keys to
madness or to affirmation of life.[14]   Affirmation   was
the result of facing the dark and then asserting the self

over the negation, as Meursault (**The Stranger**), Moses (**Herzog**), and Rojack (**An American Dream**), among others, did.

Existentialism stressed existence over essence: that order could be imposed on the universe. Existentialists from Nietzsche to Camus agreed that no god exists; consequently, man must rely upon himself in order to derive the strength necessary for survival. Nietzsche possessed such confidence in the individual potential that he could envision an Übermensch, a superman of romantic proportions. Even Sisyphus, whose unending task it was to roll a rock up a mountain only to see it fall when it reached the top, was able to surmount his absurd circumstances: Camus concluded that "One must imagine Sisyphus happy." Sartre found existentialism a kind of humanism, and Karl Jaspers urged the existentialist vis-à-vis an absurd universe to go forward as though the promise of abundance might be realized in life. Engagement in the human situation -- without illusion but with full knowledge of suffering and conflict -- was his solution.

This existential philosophy, initially European, found a peculiarly American expression in many novels. The inward-turning created a penchant for myth, which resulted in a widespread use of the mythic pattern of withdrawal and return, a variation of Joseph Campbell's "monomyth" in **The Hero with a Thousand Faces**[15] and a pattern closely connected to American tradition, according to R. W. B. Lewis in **The American Adam**.[16] Bellow's Henderson retreats from the achingly real world to the Africa of his soul and returns again with new wisdom via NewFoundLand. Styron's Cass Kinsolving returns to America from the Europe of his retreat in **Set This House On Fire**. Even Ellison's narrator in **Invisible Man** declares in the "Epilogue" that he is ready to return from his land of light bulbs, gin fizz, and holy Louis Armstrong to the arena of human responsibility.[17]

But whereas in the forties and the fifties the hero was able to journey inward and then return from his withdrawal

with a new understanding of himself and his situation --
a symbolic coming to terms, an affirmation of life -- the
contemporary hero encounters a "blurring of fact and fiction"
with its resulting confusion over the nature of reality so
intense that there is nothing very firm for him to withdraw
from or to return to. The character in contemporary literature cannot retreat to some mythic or fabulous land, as
Henderson or Kinsolving did, to find his identity; like
the nameless boy in **The Painted Bird** or Chance in **Being
There,** he exists in a fabular land already and is constantly
assaulted by the fabular nature of fact.[18]

Structurally, therefore, fewer journeys appear in recent
experimental American novels. Settings tend to be station-
ary, with static institutions like the university in **Giles
Goat-Boy,** the asylum in **One Flew Over the Cuckoo's Nest,**
or the military machine in **Catch-22** replacing the journey
as a symbol for the obstacles of human experience. When
there is movement, it is largely aimless, unproductive;
it conveys the fruitless comings and goings of modern man
as opposed to the possibilities of moral growth and spiritual
progress that are usually symbolized by the journey.[19]
The child narrator of **The Painted Bird,** for example, gains
no moral perspective from his journey; instead, forsaking
the spiritual consciousness he once possessed, he learns
to master the evil practices of his environment. Throughout
the war, he sought only a peaceful place to hide so that
he could stop his roaming; at the war's end, he despises
the thought of rejoining his family. In fact, he prefers
to keep roaming, especially at night, because "the war
continued at night."[20] Likewise, in **The Devil Tree,** Jonathan
leaves the United States and spends several months trying
to find himself -- amidst dope and mistresses -- but returns
with no clearer awareness of his identity than he had when
he left. So it is in many contemporary novels: the journeys
are not linear, beginning in symbolic darkness and ending
in light; nor do they lead from innocence to awareness.
They are merely circular patterns of flight.

The treatment of sex, a result of the continued movement away from conventional realism, further distinguishes the novels of the sixties, seventies, and eighties. Most writers of the fifties (and many of the traditional novelists of the sixties) handled sexual encounters with a reasonable amount of fidelity to detail, though few ventured into realms as explicit or as graphic as those explored by Henry Miller in his **Tropics** or his trilogy.[21] But in more recent works, sex often became fabulous and absurd,[22] presenting such situations as encounters between a man and a goat or a man and a computer (**Giles Goat-Boy**), a man advised by his homosexual lover to copulate with a saint (**Beautiful Losers**), and a woman who dresses in so many layers of clothing that it takes her lover twenty minutes to undress her -- long enough for her to take a short nap (**The Crying of Lot-49**). In **Being There,** when Chance does not know how to react to EE's advances, he explains that he would prefer "to watch." EE masturbates before him and then swears that for the first time in her life she has experienced an "open" and "honest" sexual encounter. Fabian, the horseman in **Passion Play,** finds his women in **Saddle Bride** magazine and then copulates with them in the tackroom of his stables.

Many of the characteristics of the early postwar novel (the existential novel of the forties and fifties) discussed by Ihab Hassan in **Radical Innocence** still hold true for the contemporary experimental and absurdist novels of the sixties, seventies, and eighties: absurdity ruling human actions; lack of accepted norms of feeling or conduct to which the hero may appeal; opposition between hero and environment; mixture of human motives (irony, contradiction, ambiguity); impossibility of possessing complete knowledge.[23] But an essential difference between the two visions rests in their respective concepts of resolution or reconciliation. For the existentialist, courage exists in the face of the void, and affirmation through commitment can resolve the dilemma of survival. For the absurdist, there is no comfort, no guide for coping; reconciliation with the elements of an absurd universe is almost irrelevant and certainly

impossible.[24]   The absurd hero is isolated -- from God,
from humanity, from love;[25] he endures but does not find
meaning.   He is postexistential in his response to his situation, and thus, like Fabian in **Passion Play** or Tarden in
Cockpit, his own survival is as close to affirmation as he
gets.

Another crucial difference between the novels of the forties
and fifties and those of the sixties, seventies and eighties
is the way in which their respective heroes face the obstacles
of experience. Novels used to end in institutions -- marriage
(if it was a happy novel), an insane asylum (if it was touched
by despair); but recent novels start in the institution and
aspire to go beyond. "It is," writes Raymond Olderman,
"as if Holden Caulfield's quest in **Catcher in the Rye**, ending
in an insane asylum, signaled the end of American quests
for the pure Utopia."[26]   The stories of Randle Patrick
McMurphy in Ken Kesey's **One Flew Over the Cuckoo's Nest**
(1962), Eliot Rosewater in Kurt Vonnegut's **God Bless You,
Mr. Rosewater** (1965), Billy Pilgrim in Vonnegut's **Slaughterhouse-Five** (1969), and Lancelot Andrewes Lamar in Walker
Percy's **Lancelot** (1977) -- like that of Oskar in Gunter
Grass's **The Tin Drum** (1962), a book that had a tremendous
impact on American fiction -- begin where Holden left off.
Similarly the beneficence of the Old Man provides Kosinski's
Chance with a sheltered environment and saves him from
institutionalization. But Chance is soon thrust into a world
much crazier than the one behind the asylum's doors.

An institution even more powerful and pervasive than
the asylum is the war, with its attendant physical, spiritual,
and psychological machinery. For years a metaphor for
the combativeness of the world, the struggle of modern
life, and the violence inherent to both,[27] war finds its
way into some of the most significant American experimental
fiction. And it is an apt metaphor indeed, even more so
for today's writers, who feel its nuclear fallout, than for
the writers of the twenties, who felt merely its powder
burns. Novelists like Heller and Vonnegut use the cruelty
of war to highlight the absurdity of man's condition. For

the young protagonist of **The Painted Bird**, the war is merely the prelude to many disappointments; its unimaginable horror and destruction are matched only by the brutality and absurdity of modern society. In the end, the boy -- in yet another symbolic institution, an orphanage -- swears never again to be a victim of either conflict. Like Ambrose in Barth's **Lost in the Funhouse** and later Kosinski protagonists (the narrator of **Steps,** Tarden, Levanter, and Domostroy), he learns that in order to avoid being trapped, he must construct the traps for others.

With almost every aspect of his life controlled by menacing institutions -- the government, the military, the educational system, even organized religion -- and other overwhelming forces which dehumanize him and reduce his power to choose, the contemporary protagonist often becomes passive. After all, if his efforts are useless, he cannot effect any change in his situation. He can no longer act; instead, he is acted upon. Heroes like Updike's Rabbit (**Rabbit Redux**), Bellow's Herzog **(Herzog),** Roth's Kepesh (**The Professor of Desire)** and Heller's Slocum **(Something Happened)** are unable to shape their own lives. But passivity is not always synonymous with complete resignation. In fact, passivity -- once exclusively the mark of the anti-hero's victimization -- emerges in experimental fiction as a device for coping with the status quo.[28] Before he learns to fight back, the boy in **The Painted Bird**, for example, sleeps to withdraw from painful situations. And Chance, when confronted with something he doesn't understand, changes the channel or tunes out. It is an appropriately absurd response to the absurd world.

Like passivity, fragmentation (the result of the contemporary hero's shattered self) serves an important psychological function. Josephine Hendin writes: "By disassembling the jigsaw puzzle of values, mores, and personality, a character can take refuge from the whole picture in its parts. Donald Barthelme's remark 'only trust the fragments,' and Thomas Pynchon's advocacy of the 'forcible dislocation of the self' reflect the use of fragmentation and alienation as defenses against painful confrontations. The character who can change roles at will, who has minimal memory of or attachment to his past, his nation, or others emerges in many [recent] novels not as an anti-hero but as wry 'ideal,' a shock- resistant man."[29] For example, Billy Pilgrim copes with the shock of Dresden by disconnecting from reality and travelling to Tralfamadore; Jake Horner engages in mythotherapy, a program which presumes that if man cannot fit his own role, he can fit others; and both the narrator of **Steps** and Goddard of **Pinball** undergo several metamorphoses as they attempt to define their own identities.

Anais Nin makes an interesting observation about fragmentation in **The Novel of the Future.** She argues that if the modern hero fails to achieve the wholeness of his predecessors, it is because the very notion of wholeness is an outmoded concept. Thus, concludes Nin, the new hero splits from an unreal uniformity, so his fragmentation does not prohibit ultimate integration. Like fission of the atom, fission in the psychological self results in a new dynamism, the discovery of a collective richness flowing below the consciousness.[30] Ralph Ellison expressed a similar sentiment when he wrote that "on its profoundest level American experience is of a whole. Its truth lies in its diversity and surfaces of change...."[31] It is the contemporary novelist's task to create a new synthesis to include all the newly discovered dimensions.

That new synthesis, however, is not always easy to portray in fiction. Since the contemporary hero's life lacks the logic of cause and effect, the novelist's task of conveying the breakdown in conventional reason becomes tricky indeed and has led to such experiments as Julio Cortazar's unbound novel **Hopscotch;** William Burrough's "The Cut-Up Method," which demands composition by random collages of clippings; "Frame-Tale," the opening piece in John Barth's **Lost in the Funhouse,** which consists of a Moebius strip on which is written, "Once upon a time there was a story that began ..."; the lengthy monologue of Lancelot to his friend and confessor Percival in Walker Percy's **Lancelot;** and the seemingly random vignettes punctuated by interludes of conversation between an unnamed man and woman in **Steps.**

One result of such experimentation is the deemphasis of plot. Annie Dillard has said that the contemporary writer "flattens narrative space-time by breaking it into bits; he flattens his story by fragmenting its parts and juxtaposing disparate elements on the page. He writes in sections; he interrupts himself by a hundred devices. In so doing, he keeps his readers fully conscious of the work's surface. Finally, he may wish to distance his readers so thoroughly that he dispenses with character and narration altogether."[32] Robbe-Grillet went even further: he argued that the telling of a story has become strictly impossible -- at least by traditional standards. Contemporary fiction no longer must have a distinct beginning, middle, and end. And the best works of writers like Barth, Barthelme, Vonnegut and Kosinski experiment with the very structure of narrative.

Like the novels themselves, contemporary characters are extraordinary. Concludes Annie Dillard: "Gone are the men and women of Dickens, say, or Hugo, whose exteriors are familiar to everyone, whose interiors are explored and forgiven by their authors. Also absent are characters who brood earnestly, and who seek God or the good or wisdom or love, or for that matter, money.... Gone are the trustworthy days of Trollope, the clear-headed days of Defoe, in which the author sat us down and told us a story. Now our first-person narrators are not authors: we are doing very well if they are even people. Instead they are cows, mental defectives, toddlers, dinosaurs, paranoid schizophrenics, dying cripples, breasts, axolotls, Neanderthals, or goats."[33]

Even when they are people, they are handled by their authors "at a great distance, as if with tongs,"[34] and often narratively flattened. In fact, they sometimes become so flat as to seem two-dimensional, almost like cartoon or comic book figures. Like Dillard, Eugene McNamara[35] and Leslie Fiedler[36] have commented on the "occasional obviousness and thinness of texture" of modern heroes as well as on the way in which their very names suggest comic strip ideas and attitudes. Examples abound in contemporary novels: Pynchon's Dr. Hilarius, Stanley Koteks, Oedipa Maas, Peculiar Pop, and Myrtle the Magnificent; Vonnegut's Billy Pilgrim, Dr. Vox Humana, and Amanita (a man-eater); Kosinski's Chance and Jonathan Whalen (a rich, spoiled adolescent who is always wailing and bemoaning his personal misfortune).

The use of such two-dimensional characters is not merely for campy comedy; it also allows contemporary novelists the opportunity to emphasize the artificiality of their art. As Charles Harris observes: "Their use of caricature also indicates their rejection of the assumption underlying realistic characterization that human beings can be accurately formulated. As aspects of a protean reality, human beings remain as illusive and as problematic as the absurd universe they occupy. By oversimplifying their characters in an exaggerated way, contemporary novelists of the absurd suggest the complexity of human nature by indirection."[37]

Such character presentation forces a detachment on the reader's part, a detachment which gives rise to much of the so-called "black humor." When the reader is aesthetically detached and objective, he is able to laugh at events and situations without contemplating the cruelty and violence often found behind them. "The kind of comedy that juxtaposes pain with laughter, fantastic fact with calmly inadequate reaction, and cruelty with tenderness," black humor requires a certain distance from the very despair it recognizes.[38] Bruce Jay Friedman (who first popularized the term) perhaps best captured its comic angst and its half-desperate delight in the illogical complications of life; he called it "one-foot in the asylum kind of fiction."[39] Exemplified in scenes like the relentless pursuit of Yossarian by Nately's whore, the Siamese twins' petition in Barth's story, or the "Eskimo" dialogue in **Blind Date**, black humor is compatible with the fabular tradition[40] of American absurdist writers and is perhaps the only possible logically illogical response.

The ultimate absurdity of life is suggested not only by black humor and by characters who -- although described with apparent gravity -- are often distorted, exaggerated, and caricatured, but also by a series of preposterous and ridiculous events and by language which makes use of (to use Eugene McNamara's list) "lexical distortions, meaningless puns, and insistent repetition of empty words, cliche's, exaggeration, deliberately misplaced particulars, and juxtaposed incongruous details."[41] The reason for such comic exaggeration, or burlesque, is discussed by John Barth in his article "The Literature of Exhaustion." Referring to Jorge Luis Borges' idea that as far as fictional forms are concerned, "literary history ... has pretty well exhausted the possibilities of novelty," Barth adds that "for one to attempt to add overtly to the sum of 'original' literature by even so much as a conventional short story, not to mention a novel, would be too presumptuous, too naive; literature has been done long since."[42] Only two alternatives are left to the modern writer in search of original forms: he can give up writing entirely (the direction taken by Beckett), or he can employ the "exhausted" forms of the past, revitalizing them by ironic treatment. By consciously imitating a form the possibilities of which are seemingly exhausted and employing it against itself, the writer is able to present "new human work," whose ultimate meaning is new and different,[43] thus making the "literature of exhaustion" a "literature of replenishment."[44] Through the use of such burlesque, American novelists of the absurd -- like all writers in the venerable tradition of burlesque -- are able to reject traditional forms and styles while at the same time continuing to use them.

Parody, an important vehicle for the contemporary writer, even extends to the forms he employs. Many of Kosinski's novels -- like those of other contemporary novelists -- depend for their effect, at least in part, on being recognized as parodies of earlier forms. **The Painted Bird** -- like **The**

Sot-Weed Factor -- is in part a parody of the picaresque novel. **Passion Play** -- like **Catch-22** and Purdy's **Malcolm** -- parodies the traditional American romance. **Being There** and **The Painted Bird** -- like **Malcolm** and Barthelme's **Snow White** -- parody the fairy tale. **The Devil Tree** -- like several of Vonnegut's novels, particularly **Slaughterhouse-Five** -- can be read as a parody of Utopian fantasy. And so it goes.

While burlesque and parody are hardly innovative techniques, as evidenced by such famous parodies as **Shamela** and Byron's "The Vision of Judgment," the experimental writers of the absurd give the traditional literary device a new direction. As Robert Buckeye demonstrates, burlesque is no longer directed toward the external world but often becomes "reflexive in nature.... It is an irony toward [the novelist] as author, the value of art, the possibility of language."[45] (Jack Hicks calls it more than a journey inward: "virtually a forced march now.")[46] No longer restricted to literature, burlesque branches out its ridicule toward history, religion, philosophy, and all other institutions which attempt to impose a static order on absurdist existence. In such a world, "what better way to represent reality," asks Buckeye, "than [by] parody: to present a reality that is questioned by another...."[47] By turning art back upon itself, by confronting what Barth calls "an intellectual dead end and employing it against itself," the novelist achieves a viable art form, its "newness" lying paradoxically in its "oldness."[48]

Influenced by recent social, cultural, and technological events, the American new novel is not completely nihilistic but largely cathartic. It exaggerates, dramatizes, and probes the problematic; it also offers a vision of people under pressure, of desperate measures, of sometimes horrendous solutions, of necessary attempts.[49]

How then best to characterize this experimental and absurdist literature, which is a necessary context for understanding Kosinski's novels? Annie Dillard calls it a literature which "throws out the baby and proclaims the bath."[50] It is a literature which is "equal to what is outside," to borrow a phrase from Paula Fox's Sophie Bentwood. (Bitten by a stray cat she had fed, Sophie concludes that if she is rabid, she is only "equal to what is outside.") It is the lesson of **Little Big Man** Jack Crabb, who waits over one hundred years to make sense out of his own history -- and who then dies in the middle of his own story. It is, to use an image from Italo Calvino's **Invisible Cities**, a carnival which stays put year after year while the town's banks, docks, and municipal buildings are loaded on trucks and taken on tour. It is, above all, an affirmation that the world still exists (no matter how absurd it may seem) and that literature (no matter how absurd it may seem) continues to interpret it. Or, as John Barth wrote in **Lost in the Funhouse:**

> No turning back now, we've gone too far. Everything's finished. Name eight. Story, novel, literature, art, humanism, humanity, the story itself. Wait: The story's not finished.[51]

ENDNOTES TO INTRODUCTION

1.   Chester E. Eisinger, **Fiction of the Forties** (Chicago: Phoenix Books, 1963), p. 13.

2.   See Louis Rubin, "The Curious Death of the Novel: Or, What to do About Tired Literary Critics," in **The Curious Death of the Novel: Essays in American Literature** (Baton Rouge: Louisiana State University Press, 1967); Leslie Fiedler, "Cross the Border, Close the Gap," **Playboy,** 16 (December 1969), 151+; Susan Sontag, "Against Interpretation," in **Against Interpretation** (New York: Farrar, Straus, and Giroux, 1964), pp. 3-14; Norman Podhoretz, **Doings and Undoings** (New York: Farrar, Straus, and Giroux, 1964). See also George Steiner, **Language and Silence** and Jerome Klinkowitz, **Literary Disruptions.**

3.   Jonathan Baumbach, **The Landscape of Nightmare: Studies in the Contemporary American Novel** (New York: New York University Press, 1965), p. 1.

4.   Anais Nin, **The Novel of the Future** (New York: Collier Books, 1972), pp. 165-166.

5.   Jerome Klinkowitz, **Literary Disruptions: The Making of a Post-Contemporary American Fiction** (Urbana: University of Illinois Press, 1975), pp. 1-2.

6.   Jerzy Kosinski, **The Painted Bird** (Boston: Houghton Mifflin, 1965), p. 57.

7.   Josephine Hendin, "Experimental Fiction," in **Harvard Guide to Contemporary Writing**, ed. Daniel Hoffman (Cambridge: The Belknap Press, 1979), p. 240.

8.   Ibid.

9.   Ibid., p. 243.

10.   Eisinger, p. 23, makes a similar observation about postwar novelists.

11.   Nin, p. 29.

12.   Eisinger, pp. 308-309.

13.   Ibid., p. 308.

14.   Nin, p. 43.

15.   See Joseph Campbell, **The Hero with a Thousand Faces** (Princeton: Princeton University Press, 1968). **Innocence,**

16.   See R. W. B. Lewis, **The American Adam: Innocence Tragedy, and Tradition in the Nineteenth Century** (Chicago: The University of Chicago Press/Phoenix Books, 1967).

17.   Raymond Olderman, **Beyond the Waste Land: A Study of the American Novel in the Nineteen Sixties** (New Haven: Yale University Press, 1977), pp. 17-18.

18. Ibid., p. 18.

19. Ibid., p. 15.

20. Kosinski, **The Painted Bird**, p. 265.

21. Olderman, p. 20.

22. Ibid.

23. Ihab Hassan, **Radical Innocence** (Princeton: Princeton University Press, 1961). See also Olderman, op. cit.

24. Olderman, p. 7.

25. Dick Penner, ed. **Fiction of the Absurd: Pratfalls in the Void: A Critical Anthology** (New York: Mentor Books/ New American Library, 1980), p. 6.

26. Olderman, p. 33.

27. Hendin, p. 245.

28. Ibid., pp. 257-62, 273.

29. Ibid., p. 241.

30. Nin, pp. 193-194.

31. Donald M. Kartiganer and Malcolm A. Griffith, **Theories of American Literature** (New York: Macmillan, 1972), p. 431.

32. Annie Dillard, **Living by Fiction** (New York: Harper Colophon Books, 1982), pp. 47-48.

33. Ibid., pp. 36-37.

34. Ibid., p. 37.

35. Eugene McNamara, "The Absurd Style in Contemporary American Literature," **Humanities Association Bulletin,** (Spring 1968). Also cited in Charles Harris, **Contemporary American Novelists of the Absurd** (New Haven: College and University Press, 1971), p. 22.

36. Leslie Fiedler, **The Return of the Vanishing American** (New York: Stein and Day, 1968), p. 184.

37. Harris, p. 27.

38. Olderman, p. 26.

39. Robert F. Kiernan, **American Writing Since 1945: A Critical Survey** (New York: Frederick Ungar, 1983), p. 38.

40. In **The Fabulators** (New York: Oxford University Press, 1967), p. 11, Robert Scholes writes that "the emergence of fabulation in recent fiction is not only an exciting development in itself; it also provides one answer to the great question of where fiction could go after the realistic novel."

41. McNamara, pp. 44-45; also cited in Harris, p. 22.

42. John Barth, "The Literature of Exhaustion," **Atlantic,** 220 (August 1967), p. 33. Reprinted in Barth's **The Friday Book** (New York: G. P. Putnam's Sons, 1984).

43. Harris, p. 23.

44. See John Barth's "The Literature of Exhaustion" and "The Literature of Replenishment" in **The Friday Book,** op. cit.

45. Robert Buckeye, "The Anatomy of the Psychic Novel," **Critique,** 9, No. 2 (1967), 37.

46. Jack Hicks, **In the Singer's Temple: Prose Fictions of Barthelme, Gaines, Brautigan, Piercy, Kesey, and Kosinski** (Chapel Hill: The University of North Carolina Press, 1981), p. 8.

47.   Buckeye, p. 37.

48.   Harris, p. 23.

49.   Hendin, p. 243.

50.   Dillard, p. 63.

51.   John Barth, **Lost in the Funhouse** (Garden City: Doubleday, 1968), pp. 107-108.

CHAPTER ONE

TRYING TO TELL THE DANCER FROM THE DANCE:
KOSINSKI AND HIS BIOGRAPHY

"What we remember lacks the hard edge of
fact. To help us along we create little fictions,
highly subtle and individual scenarios which
clarify and shape our experience. The remembered event becomes a fiction, a structure to accommodate certain feelings."

"[In a totalitarian state] Instead of writing fiction,
I imagined myself as a fictional character."

Jerzy Kosinski, **Paris Review**

Victim of the Holocaust, European émigré, international
jetsetter, prize-winning novelist, avid sportsman, critically
acclaimed author: Jerzy Kosinski has led a life as rich
and as exciting as his fiction -- a fiction often based on
his own experiences.

But perhaps more than any other writer in recent years,
Kosinski so closely intertwines life and art that the task
of accurately documenting his biography is difficult.
Jack Hicks, in **In the Singer's Temple**, writes that Kosinski's
"public persona is fully documented and more thoroughly
crafted than that of any [recent] serious literary figure";
this public persona, "'a new wall' from 'the stones' of his
past," is "finally a literal pseudolife, a mythic carapace
first hardened on the pseudonymous Joseph Novak," a historical self created "by the dissimulation of materials selected
from his past [which] mirrors the process of self-creation
and invokes the same themes and preoccupations undertaken
by the protagonists of his fiction."[1]   John Corry puts it

more simply: "Critics say that his works are autobiographical; he says they are novels. Declare that his works are
pure fiction, however, and he will say that everything in
them is true."[2] His friend Barbara Gelb admits, "He is
secretive about many things, and often he contradicts himself, possibly by design -- another form of trick or test,
to catch you out, part of his social experimenting."[3] Less
generous commentators, including **The Village Voice** writers
Geoffrey Stokes and Eliot Fremont-Smith (who in 1982
initiated a highly publicized controversy over the question
of authorship of Kosinski's novels), suggest that Kosinski's
best fiction is in fact his own life story and that he frequently
embellishes it with carefully orchestrated and well rehearsed
anecdotes.

Jerzy Nikodem Kosinski was born on June 14, 1933, in Lodz,
Poland, the only child of well-to-do Jewish parents. His
father, Mieczyslaw, was a philologist and a teacher. "He
was born in Russia," Kosinski has said. "He saw the Revolu-
tion of 1905, then he escaped from Russia during the Bolshi-
vik [sic] Revolution, and then he lived through the Second
World War. So if anyone had reason to be fed up, he had.
And he withdrew from the twentieth century altogether.
He studied Ancient Greece, and the origins of European
languages. It was his escape device."[4] His mother, Elzbieta
(Liniecka) Kosinski, was a pianist trained at the Moscow
Conservatory. When the Nazis invaded Poland in 1939,
Jerzy ("Jurek") was six years old; fearing that he would
not survive the war, his parents sent him away from the
city in order to save his life. Unfortunately, like so many
other children in that time of terror, he was abandoned
and became a wanderer, forced to beg for food and shelter
among the most backward, brutish peasant communities
of the inaccessible countryside[5] -- experiences on which
he bases **The Painted Bird**, his first novel. Kosinski recalls:

> I once counted on the map the villages and
> settlements I went through between 1939 and
> 1945. I came out with over seventy "addresses."
> These were not exactly my foster "homes,"

but rather "pit stops." I might add that I was
one of many wandering people and children.
By comparison with the urban destruction, and
tight occupation of the cities by the Nazis,
the faraway villages offered relative safety.[6]

Still, he claims, he moved from place to place "because
no peasant would keep me for long. Many guessed I was
either a Jew or Gypsy, and they were justly afraid of harboring either one."[7] These peasants, Kosinski now contends,
had no hate for Jews but were merely terrified by the Germans, by the Nazi propaganda.[8] Though he was constantly
"afraid of pain, of being molested, raped, drowned, starved,
killed by a German bullet, or taken to a gas chamber,"[9]
Kosinski survived the war, but not without wounds. Whether
in fact, as one of Kosinski's friends asserts, he suffered
physical wounds -- one arm longer than the other, the result
of being hung "by the arms from a beam for several hours
every day for 18 months," and permanent damage to his
intestinal tract[10] -- is not clear. That he suffered psychic
wounds is certain.

An accident at the age of nine left him mute for several
years. That accident -- one of the bases for the controversy
initiated by **The Village Voice** -- occurred "In a church,
on Corpus Christi in June 1942." Kosinski says:

> while serving in a Mass as one of the altar boys,
> I was supposed to transfer the Bible from one
> side of the altar to another but fell with it.
> Since moments before it happened I knew I
> was going to fall -- both physically and, I thought,
> forever in the eyes of the church -- I am con-
> vinced that I lost my speech from the tension
> before the actual fall.[11]

(In **The Painted Bird**, the actual muteness occurs shortly
afterwards, when angered peasants who already suspected
the boy of being a Gypsy or Jew carried him out of the

church and flung him into a pool of human ordure, which closed over his head.)[12]

In 1945, his parents found him -- still mute -- in an orphanage in Lodz. For some reason -- either as "therapy" after spending two years at school for the handicapped,[13] for "his health,"[14] or as a result of his vagrancy and "my brushes with the law five months after my parents found me"[15] (the various explanations are a small example of the problem of accurately chronicling Kosinski's biography) -- the Kosinski family moved to the Karkonosze mountains, where Jerzy learned to ski under the tutelage of a deaf-mute ski instructor. After a skiing accident in 1948, the boy suddenly regained his speech.

> I was skiing downhill toward my ski instructor, himself a deaf-mute, a warm, older man who lived in the mountains all his life. There was a precipice on the way, and sliding toward it I was gripped by the fear that something unavoidable and horrible was about to take place.... This fear, I think, snapped my muteness, moments before I actually fell into the precipice and fractured my skull. My speech emerged a few weeks later.[16]

(In **The Painted Bird,** the protagonist, recovering from a similar skiing accident, is lying in his hospital room; the phone rings, he picks up the receiver and utters the first sounds he has spoken in years.)[17]

Kosinski quickly worked his way through high school and then went on to the University of Lodz, where he completed magister (master's) degrees in political science and history. His dissertations were published as monographs. The first, **Dokumenty walki o Czlowieka: Wspomnienia Proletariat-czykow** (Documents Concerning the Struggle of Man: Reminiscences of the Members of "The Proletariat"/1954; published by Lodzkie Towarzystwo Naukowe, Lodz, 1955), contrasts the social revolution with the prevailing nineteenth-century

"Bourgeois philosophies, for which the most important dogma was individualism, the cult of the individual" (which Kosinski covertly favored).[18] With the rhetoric required by the Stalinists, Kosinski nevertheless expressed his faith in the power of the self: "The true apotheosis of man, the fight for humanity and the respect for human rights, was not created in the fervor of academic and philosophical discussions, the subject of which was the abstract analysis of Nirvana, phenomenalism, voluntaristic metaphysics of Schopenhauer, the classics of pessimism, or the inductive-naturalistic method of Hartmann. It was born in the places of execution, in the prison cells, in the dungeons and casements, in the torture chambers, and amidst the ice of Siberia."[19] The czarist prisons tried foremost to destroy the self; but even if only by suicide, the self protested and finally triumphed. The second monograph was **Program Rewolucji Ludowej Jakoba Jaworskiego** (The Program of the People's Revolution of Jakob Jaworski/1954; published by Lodzkie Towarzystwo Naukowe, Lodz, 1955).[20]

"As a sociologist, as a social scientist," Kosinski has said, "I assumed that I was already operating on a high level of abstraction. Indeed, equal to that of fiction; after all, a sociologist abstracts certain social forms into meaningful formulas which could be perceived by others in an act of self recognition." But during the Stalinization of Poland, Kosinski perceived that his art was being corrupted, "that the 'plot' of my 'fiction' was given to me by the very forces which I resented and abhorred and was terrified by -- the Communist Party, and its totalitarian system."[21] He continued to study and conduct research at the Institute of the History of Culture in Warsaw and at Lomonosov University in Russia. (While at Lomonosov University, he started documenting his conversations with Russians and his own observations on Russian life. These conversations became the basis for his two nonfiction works, **The Future is Ours, Comrade** [1960] and **No Third Path** [1962], both published by Doubleday.)

Around this time, he also began to develop a new interest which would satisfy his creative needs in a totalitarian state. He turned not to writing ("It's not even a matter for speculation. I would never have written in Polish. I never saw myself as a man expressing his opinion in a totalitarian State"),[22] but to photography ("Within the limits of photography, I could point out certain aspects of human behavior as contrasted with collective behavior").[23] Forced to live the life of an "inner émigré" until he left for America, he sought solace in his photography -- through which he felt he could make "a sort of political statement" -- and the darkroom emerged as the perfect metaphor for his life. Kosinski says: "It was the one place I could lock myself in (rather than being locked in) and legally not admit anyone else.... Inside, I would develop my own private images; instead of writing fiction I imagined myself as a fictional character."[24] Sometimes behind the locked door he even read forbidden literary works. (The darkroom is still of importance to Kosinski. He says, "I have always kept a photographic darkroom in my apartment. The darkroom remains even today my device for escaping from the ideologies of political terror."[25] Recently, learning that his eyesight was in danger, he feared the darkroom would become the metaphor for his American existence as well and he has started to practice dictating to a tape recorder -- in the darkroom.)

As an art, photography "was less ambiguous than fiction and more open to general scrutiny,"[26] and his photographs eventually proved troublesome. When he produced "some nudes of rather attractive, non-socialist female forms," he was "accused of being a cosmopolitan who sees the flesh, but not the social being."[27]

Such totalitarian oppression became increasingly intolerable for him, but escape from the Communist-run society seemed even more difficult than escape from the Nazis had been. Kosinski says, "By the time I was 16, I started to think about getting out of Poland. At the age of 17, I had officially applied to the Ministry of Internal Affairs for permission to emigrate -- alone -- to Israel. I was turned down with dreadful consequences for my family -- and for me."[28] By the mid-fifties, the moment was more auspicious. Using "the creaking bureaucracy and the confusion of the aftermath of the Hungarian revolution, and Khrushchev's bent for liberalism, to obtain a passport,"[29] Kosinski says that he invented academicians who would endorse and sponsor his research study. With letters written on official-looking stationery which he himself had printed, he was determined to get out of Poland, one way or another. Choosing to protect his parents by not telling them about his plans and carrying -- he claims -- a capsule of cyanide in the event his fraud was exposed, he was finally able to secure the passport and plane ticket which would allow him to embark on his fictitious "Chase Manhattan Bank Fellowship." (Others have disputed Kosinski's version; fellow Pole and scholar Zdzislaw Najder   told Jerome Klinkowitz that Kosinski "left late in 1957.... That was during a six-month thaw in relations with the West: you can look up the announcements from the Party Congresses here and in Moscow. Visas were very easy to get; going West was encouraged. Kosinski would have had nothing to worry about -- a cyanide capsule under his tongue, indeed!")[30]

With a "bit of French and Latin and Esperanto," Kosinski had initially intended to defect to a Romance-language-speaking country. He claims that, starting at the beginning of the alphabet, he applied to Argentina and Bolivia. Both turned him down because of his Marxist background. Then, he says, he went to the other end of the alphabet, applied to the United States, and was granted entrance as a "highly skilled alien."[31]

On December 20, 1957, Jerzy Kosinski arrived in the U.S. He was twenty-four years old, had no friends, little knowledge of English, and only $2.80 in his pocket. He began working at a succession of odd jobs -- doing scab labor, scraping paint, cleaning bars, driving cars and trucks, working as a parking lot attendant -- and quickly honed his English skills. He had also apparently made a decision which would affect his future. A believer in "portable skills" which would leave him "mobile, free to exit," Kosinski stated: "When I reached the United States, I said to myself that since photography, unfortunately, requires such expensive equipment, my exit would have to be language itself, writing prose."[32] He soon acquired fluency in English (within four months, asserts one critic/biographer)[33] and secured an actual grant -- from the Ford Foundation -- to pursue doctoral studies at Columbia University in New York. (Kosinski's friend, Barbara Gelb, insists in her profile of him in **The New York Times** that he "obtain[ed] his American Ph.D.,"[34] but Columbia's records do not verify Gelb's claim.)

In one of his classes, Kosinski made a presentation on Soviet collectivization; a classmate urged him to write a book about his Russian experiences. (Even on this point there is some confusion. Critic Norman Lavers contends that the classmate, Roger Shaw, was a junior editor at Doubleday.[35] **The Village Voice** checked Doubleday's records, which did not list Shaw as an employee at the time; **Voice** writers Stokes and Fremont-Smith used this evidence in part to charge Kosinski with dishonesty and obfuscation. But records from Columbia University's Russian Institute show that Shaw <u>was</u> a student and classmate, as Kosinski claimed.)[31] However the book found its way to the publisher, **The Future is Ours, Comrade** was printed by Doubleday in 1960, under the pseudonym Joseph Novak. A bestseller serialized by **The Saturday Evening Post** and condensed in **Reader's Digest**, it earned Kosinski $150,000.[37]

It also earned Kosinski a following -- including the admiration of Mary Hayward Weir, the attractive widow of steel magnate Ernest Weir, a man almost 50 years her senior. Weir had left Mary a huge trust for her lifetime. She also had a Park Avenue apartment; houses in Hobe Sound and Southampton; a permanently reserved floor at the Ritz in Paris; a large suite at the Connaught in London; a villa in Florence; the use of a corporate plane, a yacht, four automobiles; and a huge staff.[38]

In Paris after returning from a trip to Russia, Mary read the serialization of **The Future Is Ours, Comrade** and wrote Kosinski a fan letter. They corresponded and arranged to meet in New York. Kosinski envisioned her as a frail, elderly widow, and she, aware of his error, impersonated her own secretary during their first meeting. (The scene is described in **Blind Date**.) "A woman who could play a trick like that," writes Gelb, "was, of course, a woman Kosinski couldn't resist."[39] Two years later they married. That same year-- 1962 --Kosinski published his second book, **No Third Path,** a sociological study of Russian life which elaborated on some of the observations in **The Future Is Ours, Comrade.**

Kosinski's earnings, by no means inconsiderable, were converted into pocket money for their travels -- money for tips to staff on ships and in hotels -- and were rapidly exhausted. Nevertheless, his life was the stuff of fiction: Palm Beach, polo, prominence in society. Says Kosinski, "I had lived the American nightmare, now I was living the American dream."[40]

His first novel, **The Painted Bird** (1965), was written as a way of preserving the nightmarish memory of his childhood and of explaining his past to Mary and her friends. Even in those moments of loneliness and unhappiness in his early years, Kosinski says he always felt alive enough to ponder his own awareness of self.

> That state of awareness has always been, to me, less a possession than a mortgage, easily terminable. Perhaps that's why, in the 60s, in the midst of the affluent existence my marriage had provided, so much removed from the misery I'd once known, living in secluded villages, flying in private planes, floating on custom-built boats that turned the world into one's playground, I sat down to write **The Painted Bird,** a novel of an abandoned boy in a war-

ravaged, small pocket of rural Europe, which
I remember so intimately.[41]

Dedicated "To Mary Hayward Weir, without whom even
the past would lose its meaning," **The Painted Bird** was
shocking and brilliant, a masterpiece of modern Holocaust
literature which won the Prix du Meilleur Livre Etranger
in 1966.

Mary soon became ill with cancer of the brain and her
health deteriorated rapidly. Kosinski was divorced from
Mary in 1966; she died in 1968. (Kosinski says that with
all of her money in trust, Mary left him nothing after her
death.) That same year Kosinski's second novel, **Steps,**
appeared to generally wide critical acclaim. An innovative
and experimental work, **Steps** won the National Book Award,
the highest literary prize of the United States, the following
year. Kosinski was the first foreign-born author to win
the coveted prize.

Other awards and honors followed, most notably the Award
in Literature by the National Institute of Arts and Letters
and the American Academy of Arts and Letters, for creative
achievement in furthering literature and the fine arts (1970);
the Brith Sholom Humanitarian Freedom Award for distinguished contribution to the advancement of humanity
(1974); election in 1973 as President of the American Center
of P.E.N., the international association of poets, essayists,
novelists, and playwrights, a position in which Kosinski
served the maximum two terms and for which he was honored
for his contributions by a P.E.N. Resolution (1975); the
American Civil Liberties Union Award, for demonstrating
the vitality of the First Amendment's right of free expression
in a long and distinguished career in the creative arts (1978);
and -- for the screenplay for the movie **Being There** --
the Writers Guild of America Best Screenplay Award (1979)
and the British Academy of Film and Television Arts Best
Screenplay of the Year Award (1980).

Numerous novels followed as well: **Being There** (1971); **The Devil Tree** (1973; revised edition, 1981); **Cockpit** (1975); **Blind Date** (1977); **Passion Play** (1979); **Pinball** (1982); and **The Hermit of 69th Street** (1988).

But writing was not Kosinski's only occupation. From 1968 to 1973, Kosinski held several academic positions -- in 1968-1969, as Fellow at the Center for Advanced Studies at Wesleyan University; from 1969-70, as Senior Fellow, Council of Humanities, at Princeton University; and from 1970 until 1973, the year he decided to give up teaching, as Visiting Professor of English Prose at the School of Drama and Resident Fellow of Davenport College at Yale University. (He has since returned to Yale as a Fellow of Timothy Dwight College.) Commenting on "the great gray educational machine" and "the devaluation and disparaging of the imagination,"[42] Kosinski criticized American students for being benumbed, manipulated and unthinking. They are "dead souls on campus ... isolated by a collective medium which permits each of them to escape direct contact with others. Deafening sound effectively rules out every interchange. No one ever questions the intruding voice, for unlike an individual character, the collective identity requires no explanation or justification."[43]

Despite his criticisms of American education, he was a provocative instructor. **Current Biography** recounts one anecdote involving his teaching technique:

> The first day of his seminar on "Death and the American Imagination" at Yale stands out. No more than twenty students were expected -- or wanted -- but 2,000 showed up. Kosinski whittled the crowd down to twelve by explaining, in the course of his introductory lecture, that the seminar would confront the experience of death as directly as possible, through visits to hospitals, morgues, and mortuaries. "Regrettably," he solemnly added, "in order for the experience of death to be complete, it will

be necessary for one member of the seminar to die." There was a mad, mass rush for the exits.[44]

A former student, Adrienne Kennedy, shared another story in her letter to **The New York Times**:

> When I lived in New Haven, I audited a course at Yale given by Jerzy Kosinski. He lectured in creativity and reality. His lectures were unorthodox and popular. One week he announced that, at the next class, teachers from a professional dance studio in New Haven would come and teach us all to tap dance, and that, when it was over, he would have a point to make.
>
> The following week the dance teachers came and gave us lessons in basic tap steps. We practiced for more than an hour. When the lesson was over, Mr. Kosinski told us we had just had a lesson in reality. He pointed out that, as inept as the teachers had been, because he had told us they were dance teachers, none of us, not one, had even questioned it.
>
> The dance teachers were, in fact, undergraduate students at Yale. It had all been staged.[45]

In and out of the classroom, Kosinski was always a born actor. In 1980, he even tried his hand at acting in a movie directed by and starring his friend Warren Beatty. Claiming initially to have declined the role of Zinoviev in **Reds,** Kosinski said that -- as a novelist -- he could not afford to miss the opportunity of such an experience. But his prime motivation was moral and political. "[Beatty] said that, after my having been imprisoned for twenty-four years by totalitarian philosophy, I now had a chance as Grigori Zinoviev to show millions of Americans what a committed Communist is really like -- both ideologically motivated, bureaucratic, and detached from concrete experience at the same time. Warren said I could show such a bureaucrat in confrontation with John Reed, who was a writer very much like I am today, a man defending his moral right to write what he, not the party, perceives to be truth."[46] As Zinoviev, Kosinski could speak for the philosophy that long oppressed him.

He claims that Beatty used a clever ploy to throw him back into his past. The extras surrounding Zinoviev were actually Soviet bureaucrats who had recently left the Soviet Union; they spoke only Russian, forcing Kosinski to respond in that language. Realizing who Kosinski was, they made him feel profoundly uncomfortable. Kosinski recalls, "I was in a state of emotional seige and ... emotionally I became Zinoviev."[47]

When asked if he was satisfied with his performance, Kosinski responded merely, "No, I was not. I would rather have played John Reed, and be handsome and glamorous, and kiss Diane Keaton."[48] Acting helped Kosinski realize that no artist is as free as the novelist; nevertheless, his reviews for the role were almost as impressive as the reviews of his novels -- and in some cases even more so. **Time** magazine wrote that "Novelist Jerzy Kosinski acquits himself hand-somely -- a tundra of Russian ice"; **Newsweek** noted, "The surprise is novelist Jerzy Kosinski's delightfully abrasive performance; he's like an officious terrier gnawing on the bone of the Marxist-Leninist dogma"; and **The Times'** Vincent Canby, who was "astonished" to learn that Zinoviev was played by the novelist whose works he had read, said Kosinski's performance is "one of the reasons 'Reds' works so well."[49]

His acting in **Reds**, like his appearances on late-night tele-vision, has brought Kosinski a tremendous visibility. Yet Kosinski insists that his motto is still Larvatus Prodeo (I go forth disguised).[50] He explains what seems to be the paradox:

Since the end of World War II, when I was twelve,
I have structured my life to be both private
and public. I like to openly participate in the
life of the community. I am committed to
certain ideas and I want to be able to fight
for them. Nothing interests me more than
people. In the States, I felt safe enough to
go public both as a writer and as a social activist
in the field of human rights. Once you are
public, the public looks for what it has already
seen. At one time, everyone tried to trace
Salinger, to find Pynchon. No one tries to find
Kosinski. In a sense, my visibility is my ultimate
camouflage: nothing hides one better from
the public than appearing on the Johnny Carson
show, because everyone thinks they know what
one is doing and what one is all about -- and
yet there are 364 other days in the year, when
they don't.[51]

Nevertheless, there are times when Kosinski does go out
in disguise -- though "not too often and only for the sake
of privacy."[52] It is a habit he acquired many years ago,
when, as a mute adolescent, he tried to readjust to life
with his family in postwar, totalitarian Poland. "In a country
where one out of four people was either gassed or murdered
some other way," says Kosinski, "losing my speech was
hardly something one would pay attention to. Surrounded
by boys and girls without legs, without tongues, without
eyes -- no one, neither my parents nor I, myself, was likely
to pay much attention to me as a victim."[53] To survive
among the peasants during the war, he learned to fight
back. Himself betrayed and abused, he discovered a talent
for duplicity, for concealment, for disguise.[54] Today he
continues to wear disguises occasionally -- to museums,
industrial exhibits, and cinemas; the disguises, he insists,
give him a sense of feeling abandoned, as if an outer censorship has been lifted.[55]

One of his most frequent methods of disguise and concealment is through his night wanderings, which also date back
to his postwar experiences. After his parents traced him
to the orphanage in Lodz and brought him back to their home,
Kosinski found that he had a new brother, a baby his parents
had adopted. Even more than he hated the memory of
the war, he despised the baby who had usurped his place
with his parents. "And so," he says,

> I began to go out at night and seek the attention,
> respect, and love of strangers, even though
> the authorities warned my parents I was a poten-
> tial runaway. Imagine! I survived the war by
> running away from one village to the next in
> the rather harsh region of Eastern Europe and
> when the war ended, the authorities warned
> my parents I might run away![56]

Yet Kosinski claims he was not running away but merely
running. He needed to be out at night, when fewer people
would notice his muteness and where he could test his freedom to hide. Kosinski was -- as he described the protagonist
of his novel **Passion Play** -- "a displaced person in an uncharted landscape," and the camouflage of night offered
a certain protection and security. Today, as he told one
interviewer, a custom-made trenchcoat with thirty-two
concealed pockets can hold his false identity cards; his
vintage Buick remains stocked with food and weapons in
the event of his need for a quick getaway.[57]

News reporter Mike Wallace fears that "Jerzy is going
to get himself killed one of these nights." Kosinski retorts,
"I worry about Mike. I can hide in the night, far better,
from my enemies than he can hide from his. Has he got
a machete in the trunk of his car?" He adds that the danger
for him at night is less than the risk involved in skiing or
polo.[58]

Sometimes, especially while in disguise, he enjoys little
pranks. One night, for example, he and some friends met

a Yale graduate who was once Kosinski's student; they began discussing Kosinski as an instructor -- his teaching methods, their opinion of him personally. Disguised, Kosinski did not participate but merely observed and listened -- and enjoyed the insight into his own past. Another time, in the Dominican Republic, he hid under a desk. His accomplices in the trick spoke to a visiting diplomat about the interesting environment of the area, which was known for its tarantulas, while Kosinski tickled the diplomat's ankle. (The diplomat responded, not surprisingly, by leaping into the air.)[59] Once, during a reception for Abba Eban at the home of a U.S. Government official, Kosinski placed himself, full-length, across the back of the couch. He covered himself with pillows and waited. Soon Eban sat down, as did film director Louis Malle. Kosinski began pushing and kicking against the pillows, but everyone refused to acknowledge the presence of something unusual behind their backs. When Kosinski finally raised his head from behind the pillows, they all jumped up in terror.[60] On yet another occasion, he arranged dates for four macho polo players; late in the evening, the players discovered their beautiful companions were transsexuals in progress. And on a visit to France, Kosinski grew impatient standing in a queue at the post, so he imitated a spastic. (The other customers moved him immediately to the head of the line.) Kosinski acknowledged the "charge" he gets from these "experiments with social structure"[61] and sometimes even goes to sex clubs in disguise -- though he admits little need for disguise there, since most of the club people "aren't into recognizing others. Usually they are there to seek inner recognition."[62] Similar scenes appear in his fiction.

Even in his own apartment, Kosinski has hiding places. Afraid that some oppressive societal force will come after him and penetrate even his inner life, he recently told an interviewer, "I have hiding places everywhere. If I were alone in your apartment for half an hour, I'd find a hiding place there."[63] Critic Cleveland Amory can attest to Kosinski's skill. At the conclusion of an interview, Kosinski dared Amory to find him in his small Manhattan apartment.

Kosinski hid; Amory searched. He finally gave up without finding Kosinski.[64] Even the drafts of Kosinski's manuscripts are well hidden, in bank vaults larger than his apartment.

In interviews and television appearances, Kosinski has himself publicized (some would say exploited) his penchant for secrecy and concealment. It is therefore not surprising that his consciously eccentric behavior has on occasion had some negative repercussions. For instance, Jerome Klinkowitz, one of the first important literary critics to treat Kosinski's work in a substantive way, recently wrote that he "felt obliged to sort out my own experiences with the man and with his writing" because of "the conflicting stories that Jerzy himself had been telling me" and the conflicting stories he had heard about Kosinski, both in the U.S. and in Poland. In an article entitled 'Betrayed by Jerzy Kosinski," Klinkowitz says he now regrets having endorsed Kosinski's "unverifiable [biographical] material as scholarly fact."[65] Even more significantly, **The Village Voice**, in a front-page article, claimed that Kosinski's "disguises" are evidence of his chronic prevarication -- which they allege extends to his novels. In fact, in "Jerzy Kosinski's Tainted Words," Geoffrey Stokes and Eliot Fremont-Smith launched an attack on both the writer and his fiction which initiated one of the hottest literary controversies ever.

Among Stokes' and Fremont-Smith's claims were the following: that Kosinski hired editorial assistance so substantial as to amount to co-authorship of at least three novels in the last decade; that the two early nonfiction sociological narratives Kosinski published under the pseudonym Joseph Novak were actually ghostwritten and financed by the Central Intelligence Agency; that **The Painted Bird** -- critically hailed as a small masterpiece and a linguistic tour de force for any foreign-born author to have written in English -- was first written in Polish and then rendered into English by an unnamed translator; that Kosinski has manipulated the facts of his biography and gives conflicting accounts of his childhood, his escape from Nazi-dominated Poland, and the beginnings of his U.S. career as a writer;

and that, because of these manipulated "facts," it is impossible to accept the validity of <u>any</u> of his statements. They claim, "Almost <u>nothing</u> he says can be relied on."[66]

The story, which stated explicitly that Kosinski was a liar, was picked up and commented on by newspapers around the world. According to an article in **The New York Times** which appeared shortly afterwards:

> In Hamburg, for example, one of Mr. Kosinski's publishers said it would be unwise for him to visit Germany now because "the press would pay more attention to the articles" than it would to his last novel. In Paris, a story in the periodical Les Nouvelles Littéraires asked Mr. Kosinski, apparently seriously: "Why do you always carry arms? Why the dozens of false identities? Why the tear gas bomb in your car? Whom are you afraid of, Jerzy Kosinski?"
>
> And in Warsaw, newspapers cited the story in the American weekly as confirmation of what they had been saying all along: that Mr. Kosinski, an enemy of all things Polish, was a fraud....[67]

Friends and supporters rallied to Kosinski's defense. They agreed that the Stokes-Fremont-Smith claims were inaccurate and unsubstantiated and that such shoddy reporting would no doubt lead to a follow-up story "proving" that Kosinski did not do his own acting in **Reds.** William Safire, in his essay "Suppressing Fire" in **The New York Times,** called the attack on Kosinski "the destruction of the reputation of a writer who refuses to conform to the prevailing leftist maundering of much of the literary set" by the propagandist who "merely scatters his seeds and waits. Then dupes rush in where agitprop knows better than to tread." Safire concluded that Kosinski is a "complex and kooky genius. Because I am barely acquainted with him, I feel

especially free to embrace him for the fierce iconoclasm
of his vision and for the enemies he has made."[68]

Kosinski, naturally disturbed by the rumors which discredit
both his life and his works, remarked soon after the **Voice**
article was published that "I must now prove that I even
exist."[69] Arguing his staunch support of First Amendment
rights in general and of the **Voice** writers' First Amendment
rights to publish their conclusions in particular, he says
he refused to sue. He did, though, reiterate the falsity
of the claims: "Nothing, absolutely nothing in the Village
Voice article is true. Only my name."[70] Realizing his
very celebrity and self-promotion may have won him the
onerous attention, Kosinski feared the damage could not
easily be undone -- if it could be undone at all: "I'm an
easy target, I know. There are a lot of people who probably
don't like me -- who don't like my politics, the way I write
about sex, who don't like what is perceived as my lifestyle...
But to do this! To say I don't write my own books...! And
this claim that I am connected with the CIA. Absolutely
untrue. What I am afraid of is that my European publishers
will just drop me. In Europe, the suggestion of a CIA connection is even worse than here. But what can I do? The
charges have been made."[71]

The hype aside, there appears to have been little substance
to Stokes' and Fremont-Smith's claims about the authorship
of Kosinski's novels. Within six weeks of the publication
of "Tainted Words," John Hackett, Barbara Mackay (spelled
Mackey in the **Voice**), Frank Gibney, and others -- in fact,
all but one of the people cited as collaborators to Kosinski's
career and/or books -- had disavowed the article. According
to follow-up reports and interviews, Mr. Hackett, allegedly
one of Kosinski's ghostwriters, said "he is 'very disturbed'
by the article in The Village Voice" and explained that
he had worked on the manuscript of **Cockpit,** but only in a
strictly editorial way.[72] In a letter to the **Voice** (August
10, 1982), Ms. Mackay, another alleged ghostwriter, affirmed
she "did nothing but editing"; anxious to correct what she
termed the **Voice's** "inaccuracy," she complained that she

was asked "leading questions" by Stokes and that her quotes -- used without her permission -- gave a "skewed vision" of her role. Frank Gibney, whom Stokes and Fremont-Smith claim was in the CIA's employ and thus instrumental in an agency-funded "book development" program which subsidized authors and publishers, was reached by phone from Japan. Furious at the article, he said of Stokes and Fremont-Smith that "They're cheap mudslingers. I guess they think if they throw enough mud some of it will stick."[73] (Stokes and Fremont-Smith countered that the sources, like Kosinski himself, lack credibility -- an amusing Catch-22 which undermines their original argument.)

Only one of the original "co-authors," Richard Hayes (who appears to have his own axe to grind with Kosinski) still stood by the **Voice's** account of his "exceedingly visible presence" in **Passion Play.** Allegedly sitting with Kiki in the living room one day, he recalls Kosinski's "coming out with a rather exotic passage and jauntily dropping it in front of me. 'Here,' he said, 'Poeticize this sex.'" He contends that "The initial manuscripts were so raw that they could have led in many directions. All one can say for certain is that [**Passion Play**] would have been very, very different" without his contribution.[74] Yet, as Stokes and Fremont-Smith concede in their original article, Hayes, like Kosinski's other assistants, was paid by checks drawn on Kosinski's corporation -- a curious fact, if Kosinski were really trying to hide his collaborators, and one which considerably weakens their case.

Though it made for hot copy, "Tainted Words" was generally seen as a hatchet job on a popular and important -- if largely self-promoting -- writer. Austin Olney, Editor-in-Chief of Houghton Mifflin, publisher of three of Kosinski's novels, asserted that the **Voice** attack was "misleading and unfair." In his letter to **The Village Voice** (July 6, 1982), he wrote that "It is clear that Kosinski, whatever his distractions with the world of celebrity, is a writer of great talent, and I'm sorry to see his literary reputation impugned on such flimsy evidence." In the same "Letters" column, past

Editor-in-Chief of **The Village Voice** Thomas B. Morgan commented similarly that "nothing in this tissue-thin, self-righteous confusion of the Stokes-Fremont-Smith article, 'Jerzy Kosinski's Tainted Words,' comes close to justifying a front-page article (or any page article) in any publication, let alone **The Village Voice.**" He added, "I don't believe that any argument in the 'Tainted Words' article has sufficient credibility to prove that Kosinski's reputation is 'in jeopardy'.... Indeed, nothing about the Stokes-Fremont-Smith effort smells right. Talk about reputations in jeopardy. Did Geoffrey Stokes and Eliot Fremont-Smith really write 'Jerzy Kosinski's Tainted Words?' I can't believe that either."

What then was the purpose of the virulent attack? John Corry, in his "case history" for **The New York Times** entitled "17 Years of Ideological Attack on a Cultural Target," offered one explanation: that Jerzy Kosinski is and has been the subject of a longtime campaign to discredit not only his life, but also his art. That campaign reaches back to the publication of **The Painted Bird**, his first and still most celebrated novel; continues with various accusations (including Kosinski's rejection of Judaism, his financially and propagandistically lucrative marriage to Mary Weir, his "gigolo extravaganzas, his blackmail, and his cheats," and his literary plagiarism); and finds fresh voice in his criticism of the Polish government and his support of Solidarity in the early 1980s. Kosinski, Corry concludes, is the victim of a continuing attempt to discredit him, both as a man and as a writer, and the **Voice** article is merely the latest manifestation of such attacks.[75]

But Jerome Klinkowitz offers another explanation, one that merits attention -- that Kosinski himself is responsible for many of the conflicting and frequently misleading stories about himself; in fact, "Inventing his own life of fiction is Jerzy Kosinski's most natural act." In "Betrayed by Jerzy Kosinski," Klinkowitz demonstrates how Kosinski regularly creates the details of his autobiography, often timing the revelation of the "new facts" to coincide with his most recent novel. Though at times harmless, "the problem is that Jerzy Kosinski's life of fiction goes on night and day, on and off the page, influencing lives other than his own. Stories about him rebound as reactions to the sometimes cock-and-bull narratives that he's created about himself or perhaps to rumors whose seeds he has planted to spice up the plot." Klinkowitz proposes that Kosinski may feel he needs a "myth" to surround his novels, and he has been careful to keep that mythology consistent with the changes in the American political sensibility, from Cold War hostility through detente and back again to rambunctious anti-Communism.[76]

In the end, it is Kosinski's fiction which holds the answer to the controversy initiated by the **Voice**, and a study of the plots, characters, and images in the fiction demonstrates that the novels are part of a cycle. As Austin Olney wrote the **Voice** (July 6, 1982), "The remarkable consistency of tone in all his novels seems to me sufficient evidence that they all come from his hand alone." And even Jerome Klinkowitz, while raising suspicions about Kosinski's autobiography, reports "happily ... [that] his texts survive intact."[77]

Several months after the appearance of "Tainted Words," **New York** magazine (Febuary 28, 1983) published an exclusive account of the controversy, "Revealed: The Real Authors of Jerzy Kosinski's Books." Obviously done with Kosinski's assistance and consent, the story was a humorous attempt to dismiss the **Voice's** allegation by exposing -- with exclusive photographs and biographical data -- the "real authors" of Kosinski's fiction. The nine authors -- all of whom, according to **New York,** "share an uncanny ability to write in the style the world has long recognized as Kosinski's -- are actually Kosinski in nine different poses and disguises, playing on some facet of his biography and cleverly retaliating against his accusers. In the first photograph, Kosinski appears as Patrick Domostroy (also the name of his protagonist in **Pinball**), a burnt-out composer of East European origin and a CIA collaborator who met Kosinski at Columbia and wrote the two nonfiction books; in the second, he is George (English for Jerzy) Lewinkopf, a Polish

Jew from Lodz and former assistant professor of sociology in Poland, who wrote **The Painted Bird** in English,"though retaining his Polish accent in an obvious imitation of Joseph Conrad." Nikodem (Kosinski's middle name) Niskisko (an anagram for Kosinski), a writer-photographer known on the New York scene as the "existential cowboy," won the Guggenheim for his research on the benefits of sleeping twice a day (which Kosinski is known to do) and later wrote **Steps,** while Jurek (a nickname for Jerzy) Sulkin is a professor of English at Yale who plagiarized **Being There** from several European novels and "turned the character [of Chance] into a saintly American vidiot, unwittingly creating an entirely original work and film by the same name." Vladimir Boris, a shoe repair man, acknowledges that **The Devil Tree** was his novel "from heel to toe" but begged not to be quoted; Arthur Duffy, another freelance editor who also appears as a minor character in Kosinski's fiction, wrote **Cockpit** (off the record) to force the CIA's hand; and Jerry (the only name, according to his wife Kiki, that Kosinski truly despises) Levanter, devotee of Monod and author of **Blind Date,** refused to use his own name on the novel. (But "Kosinski chanced it.") Richard Costeiro, a gay Argentinian drama critic, wrote **Passion Play** in a typically Polish Latinate style while "on drugs." Finally, Marcello Schwartz, a rock musician and waiter, wrote **Pinball** after serving Kosinski his favorite drink, Cuba Libre, and spotting an invisible ink tattoo on his hand. That tattoo -- "I am the boy/That can enjoy/Invisibility" -- is a comment on the invisibility lost to Kosinski as a result of the **Voice** exposé. In fact, the whole **New York** article -- on the one hand, a very successful parody -- is a reminder of the lingering damage to Kosinski's reputation as a writer.

If the **Voice** article attacked Kosinski's credibility, another attack, Kosinski contends, almost claimed his life. One evening, in August, 1969, Kosinski was due at the home of friends in California. An airline misdirected his luggage from Paris to New York, so his trip west was delayed by one day -- one very crucial day. The friends he was to visit were Sharon Tate, the pregnant wife of fellow Pole, Roman Polanski; coffee heiress Abigail Folger; hair stylist Jay Sebring; and Woytek Frykowski, a longtime acquaintance from Poland. Charles Manson and his gang surprised the guests at the Polanski home and stabbed, slashed, or shot all of him. Had no airport mix-up occurred, Kosinski says, he would have been among the slain, a victim of the violence which seems as much a part of his life as of his fiction. (Roman Polanski, in his autobiography, **Roman**, remembers the sad events differently: "Scores of people later claimed to have been invited to the house that night.... But no one was expected that night, not even Jerzy Kosinski who later said that had it not been for a piece of luggage going astray at the airport, he would also have been among the victims.")[78]

After the Manson murders, Kosinski scored the press for their coverage. He criticized not merely the content of the news stories but also the philosophical attitude underlying the content, especially the suggestion that "A decent man dies in nature's time and the one who is butchered deserved it in some way." The actual coverage, he claimed, utilized every "single stereotype of the fourth-rate criminal porno-graphic novel" as a potential fact and played on "the prejudice against the rich, the ethnic prejudice because some of the victims were Polish, and a 'special' prejudice because one of the victims was a male hairdresser."[79] (In a perverse twist noted by Polanski in his authobiography, someone had suggested that Kosinski -- because of the patterns of his fiction -- matched the profile of the killer.)[80]

Today, as one of America's most successful writers, Kosinski spends his time writing and taking other kinds of risks -- playing polo, skiing -- and enjoying sunny beaches. Described by friend Barbara Gelb as a "lithe man with the grace of an athlete, a little under six feet tall," emphatically foreign looking, with thick dark hair, a beaked nose, a crisply enun-ciated and accented English and a gentle, polite and courtly manner,[81] he commutes between homes on several continents and fights for causes for which he has special concern.

Known for his humanitarian efforts worldwide, he takes a particular interest in the plight of a number of writers and artists. (Some of his actual involvements appear in his fiction: his friendship with Jerzy Pawlowski is chronicled in **Blind Date**, for example, and his acquaintance with Jack Abbott is referred to in **Pinball**.)

His constant companion is Katherina von Frauenhofer, to whom he has been dedicating his books since 1970. "Kiki" acts as his business manager, secretary-typist, proofreader, housekeeper, travelling companion, fellow polo player and skier.[82] When she first met Kosinski in 1966, she was an account executive at an advertising agency; they began seeing each other regularly after his first wife Mary's death. Kiki was attracted by "what he seemed to bring out in me -- a memory of myself that I'd hidden, that I'd covered with other people. Suddenly I found myself being totally myself. Because that's what Jerzy demands of people -- that they be themselves."[83] Although she quit her job in 1973 when Kosinski gave up teaching, she continues to do some freelance market research in cosmetics. By all reports, Kiki and Kosinski make a striking couple. Gelb says they "are an exotic, attractive pair and they are pleasurably conscious of the effect they create together. They could be characters in a Maugham short story. They will probably never marry."[84] (Contrary to Gelb's prediction, they did marry, early in 1987.)

Aside from Kiki, Kosinski appears to have few attachments. By his own definition a portable man with portable skills, he enjoys his freedoms, both personal and literary. He writes only in his adopted language English because of the special freedom it offers him. "It was," he says, "a great surprise to me ... that when I began speaking English, I felt freer to express myself, not just my views but my personal history, my quite private drives, all the thoughts that I would have found difficult to express in my mother tongue. It seemed that the languages of my childhood and adolescence -- Polish and Russian -- carried a sort of mental suppression. By the time I was 25, in America, my infancy in English had ended and I discovered that English, my stepmother tongue, offered me a sense of revelation, of fulfillment, of abandonment -- everything contrary to the anxiety my mother tongue evoked."[85] He adds that "I have talked with some of my compatriots, writers, film-makers, and other artists who in midlife emigrated from eastern Europe and have been forced to embrace English, or French, or German as their second language. Like me, most of them profess to be creatively freer in the adopted language."[86] Because "English helped me to sever myself from my childhood, my adolescence,"[87] it provides Kosinski "one more curtain" to separate him "from spontaneous expression"[88] -- just as his fiction provides one more way to recreate his experiences.

As many critics and commentators have observed, Kosinski's protagonists indeed resemble their author. Anonymous wanderers, familiar with death and violence, outsiders (often of Eastern European origin), "most of them," according to Kosinski, "are desperate to find out who they are. And if this requires freeing oneself from an outer oppression, then some of them have trained themselves to fend off the threat of society using complex bureaucratic means as well as camouflage, escapes, and so forth." Yet, empha-sizes Kosinski, "my protagonists do not isolate themselves. They are adventurers but also self-appointed reformers of an unjust world: they interfere on behalf of the weak and the fallen and the disfigured. I see this as an important part of the philosophy of the self: you cannot be faithful to your own sense of drama in your life if you disregard the drama in the life of others."[89]

Kosinski's protagonists are also all picaros of a sort. The picaro, whom Kosinski called "the last champion of selfhood," is a character constantly in a state of becoming, a character like Odysseus, Don Quixote, Tom Jones, Moll Flanders, Felix Krull, "the freelancers, the freebooters who played out their whims and caprices and lived their lives rather than considering their condition."[90] Detached and often dispassionate, the heroes of Kosinski's fiction live on the edge of life and of society. Separated by time, space, or language from their past, they have no enduring ties in the present either. Relentless, industrious and inventive survivors -- like Kosinski himself -- they are all "Horatio Algers of the nightmare, the first and the last frontier."[91]

Sometimes called a political writer, Kosinski denies that he proposes any political solutions. In his fiction, social environment is important only in terms of its impact "on the psyche, in terms of its drama, its role in one man's life."[92] And in his novels, Kosinski tries to jolt the reader into a recognition, a judgment, a new attitude -- "to turn a commonplace of daily routine into a dramatic arena, to transform mere experience into adventure. If I succeed, my novel will detonate a fragment of reality which had lost for us its detonating power. The explosive force is still there; a reader can see himself as a protagonist of his own story, a hero in charge of his own life and his soul."[93]

In his life as in his literature, Kosinski has created drama from the commonplace, transformed experiences into adventures, and championed the self -- always with explosive force. But, especially since Kosinski's life and art appear to be so utterly intertwined,[94] it is often difficult to separate the real Kosinski from the product of his imagination -- as difficult as Yeats found it to separate the dancer from the dance.

ENDNOTES TO CHAPTER ONE

1.   Jack Hicks, **In the Singer's Temple** (Chapel Hill: University of North Carolina Press, 1981), pp. 184; 181-182.

2.   John Corry, "17 Years of Ideological Attack on a Cultural Target," **The New York Times,** 7 November 1982, Section 2, p. 1.

3.   Barbara Gelb, "Being Jerzy Kosinski," **The New York Times Magazine,** 21 February 1982, p. 46.

4. Cleveland Amory, "Trade Winds," **Saturday Review,** 17 April 1971, pp. 16-17.

5. Gelb, p. 42.

6. Martin L. Gross, "Conversation with an Author: Jerzy Kosinski," **Book Digest,** November 1980, p. 20.

7. Ibid.

8. Ibid., p. 22.

9. Barbara Leaming, "Penthouse Interview: Jerzy Kosinski," **Penthouse,** July 1982, p. 170.

10. Gelb, p. 45.

11. Leaming, p. 170.

12. Jerzy Kosinski, **The Painted Bird** (Boston: Houghton Mifflin Company, 1965), pp. 155-61.

13. Norman Lavers, **Jerzy Kosinski** (Boston: Twayne Publishers, 1982), pp. 3-4.

14. Gelb, p. 52.

15. Leaming, p. 168.

16. Ibid., p. 170.

17. Kosinski, **The Painted Bird,** pp. 267-69.

18. Jerome Klinkowitz, **Literary Disruptions** (Urbana: University of Illinois Press, 1975), p. 85.

19. Ibid.

20. Ibid., p. 83.

21. Jerome Klinkowitz, "Jerzy Kosinski: An Interview," **Fiction International**, 1 (Fall 1973), 3, reprinted in **Literary Disruptions**, p. 83.

22. George Plimpton and Rocco Landesman, "The Art of Fiction: Jerzy Kosinski," **Paris Review**, 54 (Summer 1972), 184.

23. Ibid., p. 185.

24. Ibid., p. 186.

25. Ibid., p. 194.

26. Gail Sheehy, "The Psychological Novelist as Portable Man," **Psychology Today**, December 1977, p. 56.

27. Plimpton and Landesman, p. 185.

28. Gross, p. 24.

29. Lavers, p. 5.

30. Jerome Klinkowitz, **Literary Subversions** (Carbondale: Southern Illinois University Press, 1985), p. 145.

31. Wayne Warga, "Jerzy Kosinski Reaches Down into Life and Writes," **Los Angeles Times**, 22 April 1973, p. 1, cited in Lavers, p. 5. Kosinski relates the same incident in his **Paris Review** interview.

32. Plimpton and Landesman, p. 192.

33. Lavers, p. 6.

34. Gelb, p. 42.

35. Lavers, p. 6.

36. Corry, p. 29.

37. Lavers, p. 6.

38. Gelb, p. 54.

39. Ibid.

40. Lavers, p. 6.

41. Sheehy, p. 128.

42. Hicks, p. 188.

43. Jerzy Kosinski, "Dead Souls on Campus," **The New York Times,** 13 October 1970, p. 20.

44. Hicks, pp. 182-183. The scene appears in **Passion Play.**

45. Adrienne Kennedy, Letters Column, **The New York Times Sunday Magazine,** 28 March 1982, p. 110.

46. Leaming, p. 170.

47. Ibid.

48. Ibid., p. 171.

49. Gelb, p. 53.

50. Lavers, p. 2.

51. Leaming, p. 167.

52. Ibid.

53. Gelb, p. 45.

54. Ibid.

55. Leaming, p. 167.

56. Ibid., p. 168.

57. Gelb, p. 46.

58. Ibid.

59. Ibid.,p. 45.

60. Ibid.,pp. 45-46.

61. Ibid., p. 46.

62. Leaming, p. 167.

63. Gelb, p. 46.

64. Amory, p. 17.

65. Klinkowitz, **Literary Subversions**, pp. 126-127.

66. Dave Smith, "Kosinski Whodunit: Who Ghost There if Not Jerzy," **Los Angeles Times**, 1 August 1982, p. 3. Also Dave Smith, "One Interpretation of Novelist's Words," **Kansas City Star**, 15 August 1982, p. 1-I. End quotation taken directly from Geoffrey Stokes and Eliot Fremont-Smith, "Jerzy Kosinski's Tainted Words," **The Village Voice**, 22 June 1982, p. 41.

67. Corry, p. 1.

68. William Safire, "Suppressing Fire," **The New York Times**, 18 November 1982, p. 27.

69. Corry, p. 1.

70. Jan Herman, "Did He or Didn't He?" **Chicago Sun-Times Book Week,** 25 June 1982, p. 24.

71. Smith, **LA Times,** p. 5.

72. Corry, p. 29.

73. Smith, **LA Times,** p. 4.

74. Stokes and Fremont-Smith, p. 42.

75. Corry, p. 1+.

76. Klinkowitz, **Literary Subversions,** p. 132.

77. Ibid., p. 128.

78. Roman Polanski, **Roman** (New York: William Morrow and Company, 1984), p. 313.

79. Martin Koppell, "Novelist Attacks American Press for Tate Murder Coverage." The lack of factual coverage of the Tate killings by the press was discussed by Kosinski in numerous interviews, including "Butchered Reputations Live On After Death," by Dick Kleiner, Newspaper Enterprise Association, 18 December 1969, and "Hippies Hit and Press Criticized," Kimmis Hendrick, **The Christian Science Monitor,** 2 January 1970.

80. Polanski, p. 319.

81. Gelb, p. 42.

82. Ibid., p. 54.

83. Ibid., p. 58.

84. Ibid.

85.   Sheehy, p. 56.

86.   Ibid.

87.   Plimpton and Landesman, p. 193.

88.   Klinkowitz, **Literary Disruptions,** p. 85.

89.   Sheehy, p. 55.

90.   Geoffrey Movius, "An Interview with Jerzy Kosinski," **New Boston Review,** 1, No. 3 (Winter 1975), 4.

91.   Elizabeth Stone, "Horatio Algers of the Nightmare," **Psychology Today,** December 1977, pp. 59-60.

92.   Movius, p. 4.

93.   Ibid.

94.   Michele Slung, "The Wounding of Jerzy Kosinski," **Washington Post Book World,** 11 July 1982, p. 15.

CHAPTER TWO

THE SHEEP IN THE MIDDLE:
"JOSEPH NOVAK'S" NONFICTION

"Have you ever seen a large flock of sheep
in motion? Which ones are the safest, which
ones are not bitten by dogs, nor lacerate their
flanks against the trees, nor are reached by
a shepherd's whip? Those in the middle, in
the very middle."

Joseph Novak/Jerzy Kosinski, **No Third Path**

When Jerzy Kosinski emigrated to the United States in
1957, he brought with him some of the notes he made while
studying and conducting research in the Soviet Union. His
first two nonfiction works, **The Future is Ours, Comrade**
(1960) and **No Third Path** (1962), are based on those notes.
Published under the pseudonym Joseph Novak, the books
examine collective behavior. While not as historically
or sociologically relevant today as when they were written
during the Cold War, their importance now is primarily
literary. Both works anticipate many of the methods and
techniques of Kosinski's fiction: the episodic structures;
the stripped prose; the seemingly noncommittal reporting;
the very characters, episodes, and metaphors of his later
novels.[1] And both introduce the philosophy so essential
to Kosinski and to a proper understanding of his fiction:
the struggle of the self for definition against collective
forces which threaten to restrict its freedom.

The Future is Ours, Comrade is a record of Kosinski's
"Conversations with the Russians" (the subtitle of the book).
As a "minor bureaucrat from one of the satellite countries,"
Kosinski was invited to Russia for a protracted stay, and,

as he says, "allowed to manage my Soviet life according to my own wishes, without being hampered or limited by anyone."[2] Yet his interest was not so much in the political or economic system but in the daily life of the Soviet citizen -- his pleasures, his troubles, his thoughts, his image of himself in relation to the system and to the world. It is those impressions, those individual recollections and reflections, both of the Soviets and his own, which he attempts to document.

Kosinski begins **The Future Is Ours, Comrade** with an examination of the private lives -- or more accurately the nonprivate lives -- of Russian citizens. In a section entitled "This Is My Home," he relates the virtual impossibility of maintaining independence and individuality in a collective environment. He notes that the living conditions, which compel several unrelated families and individuals to live together in a limited space, had "created a new cooperative pattern in life, in which each person had to accommodate himself to his fellow tenants" (p. 18). In fact, the communal living arrangement comprises the most basic collective of Soviet life. New and better Soviet housing is constantly relegated to a low priority; other needs must first be served -- and lofty explanations are offered. "Socialism had more important tasks in its first stage than the ending of holes in roofs. Then came the war ... [and now] we still have more important goals" (pp. 17-18), claims a newspaperman.

The enforced cooperative existence of the Soviets also necessitates their deemphasizing personal privacy ("There are no secrets in the group" [p. 27]) and redefining the basic family structure to ensure communal peace. Children are encouraged to participate in activities outside the home; youth groups, school groups, summer camps (indoctrination into collective behavior begins early); while the elderly, especially those who are incapacitated, are sent off by their own children to different types of collectives: Homes for the Old and Incurable. An old or sick person interferes by his very presence with the

established order of cooperative living since he either
requires special care at home or uses the common facilities,
particularly the bathroom, disproportionately. In a wry
anecdote worthy of inclusion in one of his novels, Kosinski
recalls visiting a family and being greeted enthusiastically
by a young boy. The youngster told happily about all of
his toys and concluded, "And we have a new TV set. Come
and see how big it is. It stands where Grandpa used to
sleep. Oh, and Grandpa is gone... " (pp. 30-31).

The communal living arrangements have also created a
special relationship between the street and the citizen;
the citizen finds that his only privacy exists away from
both home and work. Paradoxically, his most private
moments are his most public ones.

The street has its own special symbolism: with its multitude
of museums, universities, and public monuments, it is a
testament to socialism and itself a symbol for the forces
of collectivism. Even the motorcars, so prized and envied
by most Soviets, symbolize a cooperation with the system,
as do the "people's" monuments, like the mausoleum of
Lenin and Stalin, where the embalmed and waxen bodies
of the Soviet heroes suggest to Kosinski the waxen
inflexibility of a totalitarian system which embalms its
living as well as its dead.

Living with such restrictions, the Soviet citizen is indeed
"in a cage": even marriage, which should help his spirits
soar, only grounds him in the Soviet reality. Marriage
is strategic. The main motivation is "to stabilize the kind
of life which existed before marriage and which was
considered desirable" (p. 53). The approach is realistic,
not romantic; marriage must be based on intellectual
compatibility and not physical attraction. (Physical
attraction, claims Kosinski, is a somewhat alien notion
to Soviet man, since Communism emphasizes social conformity and not individual beauty. In fact, Kosinski recalls,
when a well-executed painting of a nude was exhibited
at a gallery, even the art critics did not know how to assess

it. "How can a nude serve socialism?" asked one, adding that "a nude painting is a clear transfer of the center of interest from social man to physical man" [p. 57].)

While in Russia, Kosinski was attracted to a young woman named Agniya. He remembers that she wore a pony-tail and a tight-fitting blouse, like those of Western movie actresses. But the Komsomol City Committee accused her of imitation of bourgeois attire, morality alien to the Soviet nation, and improper behavior. She was advised to apply to join a transport of young Komsomol volunteers who had pledged themselves to the patriotic task of spending four months harvesting in a remote part of the U.S.S.R.

Like the protagonists in his later novels, Kosinski, ever the detached observer, decided not to prolong his stay in that town and to take a train due to leave almost immediately. Agniya and he both knew they were seeing each other for the last time:

> For a few moments Agniya walked alongside the window, then it pulled away from her. A minute later she was just a tiny spot pasted against the gray of the disappearing station. The train picked up speed. I drew the curtains closed across the compartment window and began to complete my notes. (p. 67)

The description of Agniya here is similar to that of the painted bird, which appears as "a spot of rainbow against the backdrop of clouds" in Kosinski's first novel; and she is among the first of many characters in Kosinski's fiction who, like the painted bird, are persecuted for their lack of conformity.

In their work as in their personal lives, the Soviet citizens are defined primarily in terms of the group and not of the self. "We are in life what we are in work," says a young economist (p. 68). And the Soviet at work is engaged in an organized chaos, like an ant on an anthill, with many levels of political activity occurring simultaneously. Urged to stick "with the crowd" and "follow the majority" (p. 88), he can distinguish himself only when working for and with the system, particularly by pledging to increase his quota. Kosinski recalls visiting a factory and noticing a board on which were posted pictures of shock workers who had accepted the challenge of competing to increase productivity:

> I went closer and studied the faces of shock workers looking at me from large photographs. They were the normal faces of normal people. They stood very stiff in carefully pressed suits.... They looked somewhat ludicrous, but the high figures representing the percentage of norms performed that were printed under the photographs filled me with respect: 175 percent, 160 percent, 202 percent, 138 percent.... It started to rain.... Thick drops splattered the bulletin board with the competition lists. The water found its way under the glass pane protecting the photographs of the shock workers. A stream of purple ink ran down from the caption, "Through Socialist competition, on to victory at the front of socialist work, on to socialism." It ran down the inside of the glass distorting the faces of the shock workers and washing away the big-bellied figures representing norms exceeded.
>
> I, too, performed a heroic deed. As fast as I could, I ran through the courtyard and burst like a bomb into the gatekeeper's office.
>
> The gatekeeper turned to me and asked half seriously, half jokingly, "And what are you running away from, comrade? What from?" (p. 99)

Although rain can wash away the shock workers' names, nothing can dilute the power of the Soviet authorities.

Whether in the socialist army or in the hospital, that authority is enforced and a military attitude prevails. Patients
in Soviet hospitals must cope with the same kind of militar-
ism which soldiers in the army face: neither questions a
supervisor or is allowed any alternatives.

The university student in this "Republic of Scholars" is also
subject to various forms of authority, which approve books
("We learned from it [the text] that almost all of the fundamental inventions were made by Russians ... the radio, the
telephone, the electric light, the airplane, the internal-
combustion motor, the steam engine, the pneumatic hammer"
[p. 155]) and monitor daily activities ("A group of three
students is in control of our whole life. They have been
appointed to check on our state of preparedness, on the
list of books we read, the way we make our notes in the
lectures, our proficiency in seminars and discussions" [pp.
164-165]). Students learn to monitor each other to enforce
conformity and reinforce socialistic attitudes. When Mishka,
a fellow student, stated that he has the right to arrange
his private life as he pleases, he is told sharply: "That is
not true, comrade, not true at all. Your private life does
not take place on a desert island, not even in a bourgeois,
capitalistic island.   Your private life takes place in a socialistic
society and by grace of this society. That's   why   your   private
life is subordinated to the life of this society" (p. 163).

While the "University is a factory producing scholars" (p.
169) to be used by the State, the factories produce more
tangible goods -- but never enough to equal the demand
by the people. (The government deliberately maintains
this policy of a "producer's market.") To acquire the goods
he needs and which he cannot purchase easily, the Soviet
citizen has to engage in the practice of "good will," or
bribes. Fairly common, the "good will" usually involves
a tip to a salesclerk or department store manager, who
"reserves" an item under the counter or schedules a "delivery"
for the precise moment the giver of that good will arrives
-- by prearrangement -- at the store. Generally, the Soviet
citizen, used to the producer's market, learns to content

himself with far less than his counterpart in the Western world; this is one reason Kosinski calls him the "hero of gray daily life" (p. 284).

The final chapters of **The Future Is Ours, Comrade** examine more closely these heroes -- and also their enemies. The heroes are typified by Comrade Dymitrij, the son of laborers, who rose through the Soviet hierarchy. Dymitrij obeyed all orders that he received:

> During vacations I harvested to "help the nation." I reported the hostile attitude of one of my school teachers who was dismissed as a consequence, "on behalf of the working class." I frequently criticized myself "for my own good" ... [During the war] I volunteered for an auxiliary unit and since I was physically well-built and developed and since my record in the Komsomol and school was excellent, I was accepted. After a period of digging trenches and transportation work, I was transferred to a regular unit.... I discovered the same social mechanism in my regiment: a collective, meetings, debates. It did not take me long to become an activist in my regiment, a sought-after speaker, agitator-communist, the right hand of the commander and of the political commissar.
>
> Towards the end of the war I made up my mind to seek a Party-political career. (pp. 210-11)

Dymitrij realized that to be successful "you can't live outside the organized group" (p. 213) and that "a man is only what others think he is, nothing more" (p. 220). (Kosinski, like his later protagonists, finds Dymitrij's attitude untenable because it is destructive of the self. As "Joseph Novak," he sums up his philosophy quite simply: "I would like to depend on nobody. You know, to tailor my life to my own yardstick, and not to rifle around in ready-made-clothes stores...."[3])

Among those forced to live· outside the group are Russia's Jews, ironically referred to as "The Chosen People" because they are, in fact, chosen -- for a particular kind of persecution within the Soviet state. Their accomplishments and thus their identities have been taken away by the State. As Z--baum tells Kosinski: "We have been erased from the Soviet reality for which we must work" (p. 227). Though there were about thirty thousand Jewish scientific workers, mostly in mathematics, physics, chemistry, and statistics -- many of them old professors, the original organizers of scientific institutions, inventors, research workers -- in the U.S.S.R. at the time, their names were not mentioned anywhere. The results of their work were published anonymously, or under the name of a non-Jewish scientist. During the war, Z--baum says, of the eleven thousand soldiers and officers in the Soviet Army who received the title of Hero of the Soviet Union, about 530 were Jews. But they too have been forgotten, and though publications about Heroes of the Soviet Union list various nationalities, they never mention the Jews.

An assistant professor of Russian literature, F--man, adds (in images developed more graphically in **The Painted Bird**):

> A great number [of the Jews of the White Russian Republic] were murdered by the Germans and by the Ukrainian-Tatar Mercenaries serving in the German Army. They were shot like animals. They were hung up by their hands and feet. Their tongues were torn out. They were burnt alive in barns set on fire. Soldiers raped wives before the eyes of their husbands, and daughters before the eyes of their parents. Driven by fear of the German troops, some of them managed to escape. However, everywhere they were looked on as aliens, everywhere spat at, beaten, humiliated. They wandered through strange republics, woods, steppes, tundras, and mountains. When the war ended they

slowly began to return to their former homes and were greeted by rubble and graves. (p. 229)

An "alien element" in the Soviet nation and in the national ideology of the Communist Party, the Jews are considered "agents of imperialism" who try to hinder Russia in its attempt to liberate the colonial and dependent peoples, especially the Arabs, from under imperialistic oppression.

Having described the daily life and activities of the Soviet citizen, Kosinski concludes his first study of collective behavior with a last look at the common man -- stooped, dressed in a gray suit of shoddy material, his collar covered with dandruff, his complexion equally gray as the result of vitamin deficiencies.

> Today, just as in the past forty years, the newspaper brings him news in the same spirit, interpreted in the same way. The small man believes that this news is true and lives up to the title of the paper, **Pravda** (Truth). He believes the paper he holds in his hands. He trusts it blindly. He lives by it, because what else can he do? (p. 284).

But Kosinski tells us that he, like his later fictional protagonists, is a seeker of truths not given to blind trust. Unable any longer to "walk in a mask" ("larvatus prodes" [p. 267]), he leaves Russia (and ultimately Europe). As he writes in "Words Instead of an Epilogue," the day came to leave the U.S.S.R. Boarding a plane, his pockets full of baggage checks, he concludes that "There are some who will say that in an era of mass conflict endangering the existence of the whole of mankind, a small man with his individual experiences and his one-sided appraisal of them ceases to count. My answer is that these great mass conflicts count only so far as they affect the life, the thoughts, and the fate of the small man, the hero of gray everydayness" (p. 286). And, in a scene reminiscent of the protagonist's departure in **Steps** and of a symbolism natural to his fiction, his plane climbs and "Joseph Novak" soars -- like a painted bird -- above the grayness of totalitarianism and towards the white-blue of sky and freedom.

No Third Path (1962), whose author is still the pseudonymous Joseph Novak, is a more elaborate development of the ideas in **The Future Is Ours, Comrade.** A long sociological essay on collective behavior which, writes Joseph G. Harrison of **The Christian Science Monitor** in the introduction, concentrates "on the overriding question: why has Moscow been able to persuade so vast and diverse a population that a system of totalitarianism, denying many fundamental human rights, deriding religion, and openly employing cruelty and ruthlessness, was to their advantage and was worthy of support" (p. 14), it is actually a philosophical treatise on the nature of the self which derives its title from Lenin's assurance to the Soviets that only two kinds of power are possible ("Either total power to the working class or total power to the bourgeoisie: there is nothing in the middle, there is no third path!").

In **No Third Path,** Kosinski examines not only the system of self-policing, the degrading practice of public self-criticism, and the stifling of individual doubt through the intellect-benumbing repetition of dogmas, slogans and clichés, but also the very real ways in which individuals try to survive spiritually and psychologically by resisting the encroachments of that totalitarian regime and by preserving some sense of internal freedom.

Beginning with a quotation from Khrushchev -- "It is not for you to teach us. Sooner or later you gentlemen of the United States will be obliged to learn how a government should be set up, so that in that government there will be respect for the rights of every human being. This is possible only under Communism; this is possible only in the socialist countries" (p. 17) -- Kosinski explains in the Foreword the purpose of the current study: to show Soviet people living and acting in concrete groups in the U.S.S.R. today and "to present an analysis of only such patterns of Soviet everyday life and thinking as are considered by the representatives of various Soviet groups to be typical and proper of these groups and of everyday life." Though about "the attitude of what is individual toward what is collective and historical in the Soviet reality," it is "not a scientific treatise" but "a book about living people" (pp. 20-21). Like **The Future Is Ours, Comrade,** Kosinski's **No Third Path** is based on conversations because, as he claims, "It is a fact that during intimate conversation a man can express the philosophy of his own life, the quintessence of his actions, the synthesis of his motives" (p. 19).

An epigraph from Stalin opens the book: "There neither is nor should be an irreconcilable contrast between ... the interests of the individual personality and those of the collective" (p. 23). The conversations which follow reveal, however, that an irreconcilable contrast does exist. Fedor M., an ambitious young physician and scientist, hopes to win a research scholarship to advance his own career, but "friends" testify that he is "detached from the labors of the collective." Not merely does he lose the scholarship; he is ruined. Evgeny V., who works at 235% above quota, does not want to join a worker's brigade in which outstanding workers elevate poorer ones. Rather than being rewarded for his diligent labor, he is transferred to a remote place for his offense to collective behavior. K., a bookkeeper in a Moscow bank and a "very cautious man" who nevertheless considers himself as "free as a bird" (p. 52), shares with Kosinski his formula for survival:

> Have you ever seen a large flock of sheep in motion? Which ones are the safest, which ones are not bitten by dogs, nor lacerate their flanks against the trees, nor are reached by a shepherd's whip? Those in the middle, in the very middle. (p. 53)

To achieve "the <u>essence</u> of solitude" (p. 54) and privacy, he retreats to a restroom in the Moscow bank where he is employed, a measure he recommends highly to Kosinski and advice which a character in **Steps** (nicknamed "The Philosopher") heeds.

So prevalent is the collective impulse that Soviet citizens are discouraged from spending time alone in reflection or reading; rather than contemplation, which leads to analysis and questioning, they are encouraged to pursue group activities, with other students or workers. There seems to be little escape from the group. A French journalist quoted by Kosinski remarks that in the U.S.S.R. even the cemeteries, which bury only desirables, house "a chosen and politically pure Collective of the Dead" (p. 61).

But like Kosinski's other protagonists, "Joseph Novak" resists the encroachments of the collective on the self and prefers to view himself "in his own terms" rather than being evaluated "by the eyes of the others" (p. 27). Such an attitude is met with suspicion and disdain. A young woman, Zina F., calls him "a little egoist, wrapped up in yourself":

> Your own nose, which you consider too long, your naturalistic remembrances of childhood and the war, your hatred of village life and primitive conditions, your "exercise of intimacy" -- all this causes the world of today to reach you in a distorted image. You reflect it, as it were, in a prism. That more human and humanist institution which is the Soviet collective and our meetings, you consider as contrary to the nature of the "free man!" But what is a free man if not just one of us, one of the people armed in Marxism-Leninism, people freer than anyone else because they realize that liberty means the recognition of necessity? (pp. 58-59).

She accuses Kosinski, "the poor painted bourgeois," of failing to recognize any necessity but his own egotism, of being "the man on the fence," the worst phenomenon of the co-existence of two social systems, and asks "Where will your 'philosophy of the distorted image' lead you?" (pp. 59-60). It is an intriguing question. In fact, Kosinski might argue that his entire literary career has been aimed at answering Zina's passionate searching question.[4] His novels have been devoted to defining and pursuing freedom and "the fullness of life" (the quest for the elusive self)[5], and his protagonists, instead of sitting on the fence, have aggressively resisted the collective force in its various manifestations (e.g., television and big business).

Moreover, through Novak's conversations, Kosinski demonstrates that in fact it is the Soviet who has a distorted image because of the conflict inherent to the collective philosophy. Peter G., for example, is a musician. Receiving state support and publicly proclaiming himself the most fortunate of artists, Peter plays only approved music; but among his papers is a "Drawer IV - Experimental," where he keeps magnificent lyrical work so modernist and Western that it must be suppressed. He plays the experimental pieces infrequently and privately -- but passionately, not mechanically. To Kosinski's political mentor and second father Gavrila (who also appears in **The Painted Bird**), the musician is an example of one of "the positive heroes of the U.S.S.R." (p. 80), whose versatile talents can only truly be developed in and through the collective. Yet Kosinski disregards Gavrila's warning that "the Soviet world is not for people of dual faces and consciences" (p. 103), thus one must "follow the group" (p. 104); he sees instead the inherent hypocrisy, the duplicity in which Peter G. must engage in order to survive professionally and personally. A similar duplicity is evident in the powerful speeches of Maxim J., another of Gavrila's positive heroes. Maxim speaks to the people in a calculatedly primitive, ungrammatical way; his posture and clothing are deliberately poor, yet his message is spellbinding. He is clever enough to realize that "Today's Soviet speaker, agitator, propagandist -- is one of the masses.... He is one of the proletariat, a worker's speaker, and as simple as a worker's life" (pp. 72-73). The fact that Krylov's fairy tales lay on his desk next to the works of Marx and Lenin and issues of **Pravda** is no accident; Maxim's proletarian appearance and demeanor, Kosinski suggests, are a construct, a fabrication, a fairy tale for the masses. (It is interesting to observe that Maxim, like the protagonist Chance, becomes for the people what they want him to be. It is equally interesting to note that Kosinski refers again to Krylov's fables -- also as a fabular construct, this time for the metamorphosed Chauncey Gardiner -- in **Being There.**)

While Western ideas are deplored within the Soviet system, a few stilyagi, or local foreigners with Western tastes in clothing and hairstyles, exist. The stilyagi are marginal nonconformists, in outward appearance alone. Not really rebels, they are tolerated by the authorities because they provide an example to be scorned and demonstrate that a price, possibly several years of detention at a corrective labor colony, must be paid by those who try to separate themselves from the masses. Their Western tastes are symbols for degeneration, alienation from society, and inevitable downfall. An East European scientist explained: "A society which holds conformity as the basic principle of coexistence between people, while simultaneously practicing blind obedience to one central authority, has as much natural need for nonconformists, who constitute an example of the negative man and citizen, as it has for the positive type of socialist man ... the man in the street must know what is nonconformity, before he can begin condemning it" (pp. 136-37).

Like the musician, Peter G., or the bathroom-bounding bookkeeper, the stilyagi also symbolize an alternative, however suppressed or marginal. (Their precarious position in society may have paralleled Kosinski's own in a totalitarian state; it reflects as well that of the Kosinski protagonist as an outsider or marginal participant in his society, a man threatening and sometimes threatened because of the different values he espouses.) The nonconformity of the stilyagi appeals, at least in theory, to people like the student, Victor D. While looking at the map which charts destinations by a tiny colored lightbulb in the Sverdlov subway station, Victor utters a familiar sentiment: "I have no intention of following such a route, chosen by others, to any of my 'life's destinations'" (pp. 110-11).

The price nonconformists pay is to become the painted birds of their societies, persecuted for being different. His friend Varvara tells "Novak":

> I remember how once a group of kids caught a sparrow in a trap. He struggled with all his might -- tiny heart thumping desperately -- but I held on tight. We then painted him purple and I must admit he actually looked much better -- more proud and unusual. After the paint had dried we let him go to rejoin his flock. We thought he would be admired for his beautiful and unusual coloring, become a model to all the gray sparrows in the vicinity, and they would make him their king. He rose high and was quickly surrounded by his companions. For a few moments their chirping grew much louder and then -- a small object began plummeting earthward. We ran to the place where it fell. In a mud puddle lay our purple sparrow -- dead. His blood mingled with the paint.... The water was rapidly turning a brownish-red. He had been killed by the other sparrows, by their hate for color and their instinct of belonging to a gray flock. Then, for the first time, I understood. (p. 107)

This episode is attributed to Lekh in **The Painted Bird,** and the image of the colored sparrow becomes the controlling metaphor in Kosinski's first novel.

No Third Path concludes with Gavrila's vision of what lies ahead for Soviet Communism; like the omniscient narrator of a novel, Gavrila ties together many of **No Third Path's** thematic threads.

> Don't be disappointed ... if you don't find here,
> among us, such Communists as you read about
> in the Soviet literature on the epic of the Revolu-
> tion and the Civil War period. Each era requires
> its own characters, creates, as Marxism teaches,
> a distinctive kind of <u>demand</u> for heroes, for
> leaders, for organizers.... At present many
> types of Communists exist in the world. The
> Soviet Communist is no longer a man with a
> rifle who is ready to give his life for the Cause
> on the field of battle; now he is a man with
> a map in his hand, a calculator, tactician, and
> strategist, gazing into the future with a calm,
> trained eye" (p. 311).

Kosinski wryly observes that the Soviet Communist is also
a man who increasingly subscribes to the "cult of ownership,"
the drive to acquire both necessary and luxury-type consumer
goods (a consumerism Kosinski lampoons later in his novels,
especially in **Being There** and **The Devil Tree**). With typical
Orwellian doublespeak, his comrades retort that possession
of goods merely validates the Communist goal of upgrading
the standard of living -- and that now people, to maintain
that standard, will work harder with and for the collective.
(Kosinski's pride in the fact that he is a portable man with
portable skills -- a characteristic most of his protagonists
share -- is, as he has contended in numerous interviews,
rooted in his refusal to be possessed by any system, communist or capitalist.)

Gavrila's "new hero" is best illustrated by Yuri Gagarin,
the first Russian as well as the first ever cosmonaut, the
man of the future. A symbol of the global victory of socialism, Gagarin's accomplishments in opening up the newest
frontier proves, for Gavrila, that an average Soviet man
can become a hero "solely with the support of the collective,
and solely through the recognition awarded by that collective" (p. 354).

Yet Kosinski, an "outsider" who had reached "such a degree of cohesion and identification with his new environment" that he attained an understanding of it and became "able to view himself according to the criteria" of that environment, was unable to accept the "vision of himself" which he had to maintain in order to live and coexist with others. Somewhere "in the well of his soul" lay, still alive, writes Kosinski, a

> desire for something other than could be supplied to him by that collectivized new world. His subconscious came into conflict with his conscious self, his former self rebelled against his new self. He began to view his surroundings with a suspicious eye -- and perceive suspicion in the eyes of his friends. He attempted intensively to "separate himself from his own ego" and to work out a method of becoming a "detached observer of himself," of observing himself in the most objective and critical manner, in the same manner in which he observed those whom he distrusted. As a consequence he ceased to live in harmony with himself, and this in turn made it more difficult for him to retain his self-control and self-possession in his relations with others. (p. 357)

Unable to act out convincingly his role of good citizen and creative member of the socialist community, fearful of his raison d'etre disappearing, and feeling unmasked, Kosinski rejected totalitarianism and its demands. "This was no longer merely the personal revolt of an individual who could not find a place for himself in the collective snare but also an intellectual-moral revolt, external and superior to personal considerations" (p. 358). So, in 1957, the same year Gagarin made his successful space flight, Kosinski left the oppression of Eastern Europe behind him to take up a residence -- and a new identity -- in the United States.

This notion of identity -- the concept of self which must be preserved against the collective societal forces which demand conformity -- is a familiar one; it underlies all of Kosinski's works, from his master's theses to his latest novel, and is essential to the nonfiction, **The Future Is Ours, Comrade** and **No Third Path.** Joseph Novak, the persona of both volumes, is thus the first real Kosinski protagonist, the first quester for moral values. Able to travel without the usual restrictions (physical and metaphysical), he is "a lone agent on no one's side, the observer from outside, the individual where individuality is forbidden, privileged with freedom, yet because of his freedom, condemned to be alone."[6] Like Levanter, the small investor of **Blind Date;** Tarden, the double agent of **Cockpit;** Fabian of **Passion Play;** or the unnamed narrator of **Steps,** Joseph Novak/Jerzy Kosinski is an agent for his own freedom, a man who needs to control himself and his environment -- a painted bird perhaps, but never the sheep in the middle.

ENDNOTES TO CHAPTER TWO

1.   Norman Lavers, **Jerzy Kosinski** (Boston: Twayne, 1982), p. 16.

2.   Joseph Novak (pseudonym for Jerzy Kosinski), **The Future is Ours, Comrade** (Garden City, New York: Doubleday, 1960), p. 15. All subsequent references will be to this edition and will be cited by page number in the text.

3.   Joseph Novak (pseudonym for Jerzy Kosinski), **No Third Path** (Garden City, New York: Doubleday, 1962), p. 53. All subsequent references will be to this edition and will be cited by page number in the text.

4.   Lavers, p. 26.

5.   See Samuel Coale, "The Quest for the Elusive Self: The Fiction of Jerzy Kosinski," **Critique,** 14, No. 3 (1973), 25-37.

6.   Lavers, p. 19.

CHAPTER THREE

THE PAINTED BIRD:
BREAKING FROM THE FLOCK

Man carries in himself his own private war,
which he has to wage, win or lose, himself --
his own justice, which is his alone to administer.

Jerzy Kosinski, **The Painted Bird**

Jerzy Kosinski's first novel, **The Painted Bird**, published
in 1965, is a "trip into the world of nightmare and anxiety"
which "surpasses most of the books in which experience
of terror and physical cruelty are told."[1] The story of
a young boy's wanderings through occupied Eastern Europe,
it is an odyssey from innocence to maturity in a hostile
world.[2]

As a novel based on the horrors of World War II, **The Painted
Bird** has few rivals; possibly only Vonnegut's **Slaughterhouse-
Five,** Heller's **Catch-22,** and Mailer's **The Naked and the
Dead** come close to matching its brilliance and intensity.
But, writes Jack Hicks, **The Painted Bird** is denied their
healing black laughter and is thus more disturbing:
"Kosinski's hero is no Frederick Henry, disillusioned by
life and war. Nor can Kosinski accept man's way with
a weary Vonnegut 'so it goes.'"[3] James Sloan, in comparing
The Painted Bird ("probably the finest novel to emerge
from World War II") with **The Naked and the Dead** ("that
incisive piece of novelistic sociology"), observes that in
his novel "Kosinski omits a few small details: the war,
the adversaries, the reasons, the soldiers. He doesn't bother
to place his characters in a precise sociological context."
Yet, he concludes, "Mailer, with all of his stacks of corpses,

never caused me to miss a meal. The eyeball plucked by a fork in **The Painted Bird** succeeded in stealing my appetite for a dinner of prime ribs."[4]

Though **The Painted Bird** is based on the author's adult reminiscences of that harrowing time in his own childhood, the years 1939 through 1945 in Poland, Kosinski's purpose is not to characterize the impact of the war on a particular culture or generation. In fact, as he restored an editorially corrupted first edition (in 1966) and prepared a revised edition (in 1970), he made a point of blurring or omitting places and dates, of purging the limiting modern details of the boy's journey.[5] In the prologue to the 1965 first edition, for example, the protagonist is described as "a six-year-old boy from a large city in central Poland." But the 1966 and 1970 editions change "central Poland" to "Eastern Europe." A similar change concerns the narrator's acquaintance in the Soviet Army who is killed by a mob of drunken peasants. The first edition gives his name as "Wanka," a Polish spelling; the later editions transliterate this diminutive to the more usual (and more Russian-sounding) "Vanka." At the orphanage school, the boy refuses to learn to read and write "in Polish"; this is altered in later editions to "my mother tongue." Such revisions are probably an attempt both to play down the resemblances between author and narrator and to universalize the experience of the young boy.[6] (In his **Notes of the Author**, Kosinski goes so far as to suggest -- somewhat disingenuously -- that "the names used in **The Painted Bird** are fictional and cannot with any justification whatsoever be ascribed to any particular national group. The area is only vaguely defined, since the border regions, continually torn by strife, had no unity of nationality or faith. Thus no ethnic or religious group has cause to believe itself to be represented.")[7]

Once cited in the introductory paragraphs, the war is not mentioned again until a quarter of the way through the novel, and then it intrudes almost by accident,[8] as the boy stumbles across a "military bunker with massive reinforced-concrete walls"[9] while he makes his way through the countryside. But in many ways the world war is merely a backdrop, a reflection of the narrator's own struggles. "Man carries in himself his own private war," writes Kosinski in **The Painted Bird,** "which is his alone to administer" (pp. 186-187). The boy's "private war" is (as was Joseph Novak's before him) one of survival of the self against the collective forces which threaten it and try to deny its very existence.

Perhaps most disturbing in **The Painted Bird** (and what resonates in the American consciousness shaped by Vietnam) is the fact that clear-cut borders of morality, especially in war, no longer exist. Absolute heroism and villainy, good and evil, and the rightful triumph of one group or ideology over another are dissolved.[10] Cruelty and amorality become the norm. As Arthur Miller recognized in a letter to Kosinski: "To me the Nazi experience is the key one of this century -- they merely carried to the final extreme what otherwise lies within so-called normal social existence and normal man. You have made the normality of it all apparent, and this is a very important and difficult thing to have done."[11]

Similarly, even the peasants, whose exercises of power at times seem as brutal and sadistic as the practices of the Nazis, are merely acting out the primitive fears which all of us possess. Reacting to their fear of punishment at the hands of the Germans for harboring gypsies or Jews, the peasants -- like the boy -- are victims of the war. "These peasants became part of the great holocaust of violence, murder, lawlessness and destruction which the war had been preparing for them. They understood this terror, because it occurred within the elementary categories of brutality." Thus, "their cruelty is extremely defensive, elemental, sanctioned by traditions, by faith and superstition, by centuries of poverty, exploitation, disease, and by the ceaseless depredations of stronger neighbors" (NA, pp. 22-23). Moreover, according to David Richter, "we sense for the first time, perhaps, that the repulsive peasantry have had their emotional sensitivities blunted by years of pain and suffering just as ours have been by Kosinski's pages, that we and they are essentially one."[12] This helps to explain why, in the primitive and chaotic world Kosinski describes -- a world in which the center no longer holds, a world in which young boys are hung by their arms and thrown into manure pits, while less fortunate boys are burned alive in ovens -- the bestial and the sensational become the ordinary.

But the world Kosinski recreates is not strictly the medieval terrain of Hieronymous Bosch, whose "Last Judgment" glares ominously from the first paperback edition of **The Painted Bird.** It is also a world which "exists beyond time in a rich alchemical cauldron of fire, water, earth, and air, of warring demons and contrary spirits, of real and symbolic humors and ethers -- all the elements that have nourished folk literature and literary transformations from Ovid, through Grimm, to the present day."[13] If Kosinski's intention in **The Painted Bird** is indeed "to peel the gloss off the world," to strip "reality down to natural terms," there is perhaps no better way than to return, as he does, to "the black roots of the fairy tale" (NA, p. 19).

Kosinski is hardly the first or the only contemporary American writer to use the mythic or fabulous as a mode for his fiction. Raymond Olderman demonstrated in **Beyond the Waste Land** that the grail motif has inspired some of the best recent novels, including Ken Kesey's **One Flew Over the Cuckoo's Nest,** Joseph Heller's **Catch-22,** Peter Beagle's **The Last Unicorn,** Thomas Pynchon's **V.** and **The Crying of Lot-49,** and Kurt Vonnegut's **The Sirens of Titan, Mother Night, Cat's Cradle,** and **God Bless You, Mr. Rosewater.** John Barth, "mythically refreshed since his exhausted start,"[14] also turned naturally to sophisticated mythic compressions and recyclings in novels from **Giles Goat-Boy** and **Chimera** to **Lost in the Funhouse** (published in the same years as **Steps),** while John Steinbeck (**The Acts of King Arthur and His Noble Knights),** Thomas Berger (**Arthur Rex),** and Walker Percy (**Lancelot),** through their retellings and interpretations, stimulated new interest in the Arthurian tales. Donald Barthelme, in his portrait of a newly liberated woman cohabiting with her seven beer-guzzling lovers and waiting for a prince to help her come, created a Snow White much different from the virginal heroine of Disney's film, just as John Updike gave her witchy nemesis a new complexion. (Updike's witches in **Witches of Eastwick** are attractive, Connecticut divorcées who exercise in hot tubs and exorcise their libidinous desires.)

Yet Kosinski, using the conventional fairy tale as a basis, brings to it a new dimension. His is no simple story in which the principals all live happily ever after; in fact, explains Kosinski in his **Notes, The Painted Bird** "can be considered as fairy tales experienced by a child, rather than told to him" (NA, p. 19). Drawing on Jung's statement that "The primitive mentality does not invent myths, it experiences them"[15] and on his concept of the "Collective Unconscious," Kosinski finds in his protagonist's wartime wanderings an analogue to the developing self, "since only in the growth of the child can we observe an approximation of the mind's evolutionary processes" (NA, p. 16).

Dr. Bruno Bettelheim, in his excellent study on **The Uses of Enchantment: The Meaning and Importance of Fairy Tales,** argues that fairy tales aid in this evolution. Because a child's life is often bewildering to him, he needs the chance to understand himself in the complex world with which he must learn to cope. But to do this, he must be helped to make coherent sense out of the turmoil of his experiences; specifically, the child needs -- "and this hardly requires emphasis at this moment in our history" -- a moral education which subtly, and by implication only, conveys to him the advantages of moral behavior, not through abstract ethical concepts but through that which seems tangibly right and therefore meaningful to him: the kind of meaning found in fairy tales.[16]

J. R. R. Tolkien, himself a fabulist, describes the elements of a good fairy tale: fantasy, recovery, escape, consolation, and a happy ending, which all complete tales must possess.

(The happy ending is "a sudden joyous 'turn'.... However fantastic or terrible the adventure, it can give to child or man that hears it a catch of breath, a beat and lifting of the heart, near to tears.")[17] Bettelheim adds one more: an element of threat to the hero's physical or moral existence, which the hero often accepts without question. "Snow White," he writes, "does not wonder why the queen pursues her with such deadly jealousy, nor do the dwarfs, although they warn Snow White to avoid the queen. No question is raised as to why the enchantress in Rapunzel wants to take her away from her parents -- it just happens to poor Rapunzel."[18]

As the fairy tale story begins, the hero is usually secure, with hardly a worry in the world; but in an instant he finds that everything changes. His friendly world becomes a nightmare of dangers and horrors. The "threat" often takes the form of separation anxiety -- a parent dying, a subsequent fear of desertion or of being left all alone. Seeking ultimate consolation (happiness and fulfillment), the hero attempts recovery and searches for the integration which will transcend his separation anxiety. He undergoes an initiation process or other rites de passage, such as the metaphoric death of an old, inadequate self, in order to be reborn on a higher plane of existence. Finally, confident that (despite all the tribulations he has to suffer) he can succeed, he achieves peace of mind and is restored. Jack outsmarts the giant; Hansel and Gretel dispose of the witch; Snow White, Sleeping Beauty, and Rapunzel marry their princes -- and all live happily ever after because they can run their own kingdoms and control their lives.[19]

These patterns are all present in **The Painted Bird.** But whereas typically the fairy tale provides the child with a means for confronting existential anxieties and offers solutions that the child can grasp on his level of understanding,[20] **The Painted Bird** reverses the process and forces the adult to become a child again and thus to confront (on a level of immediacy and one-dimensionality) memory as well as fact. "The result of the slow unfreezing of a mind long gripped by fear, of isolated facts that have become interwoven into a tapestry," **The Painted Bird** allows Kosinski not simply to draw up "an adult's catalogue of tidy facts" but also to spill out "the involved, pain-wracked, fear-heightened memories, impressions, and feelings of the child" (NA, pp. 14-15). Yet the objective recounting of war casualties is not what creates the novel's horror. The facts (e.g., the atrocities of the concentration camps, the deaths of four million at Auschwitz alone), after all, are familiar to us -- almost too familiar -- and do not register as strongly as they should on our psyches. Instead, it is the subjective impression -- the effect of the war on one young victim and survivor -- that gives the novel its potency. We fear, with him, the raven's approaching to peck out his eyes; we sense the stench of excrement into which he is thrown; we marvel as the plowboy's eyes, still observing, roll in front of him. These vivid scenes make the boy's experiences unforgettable.

The unnamed protagonist (who, lacking a proper name, suggests other generic fairy-tale heroes and heroines), like the "child" in all child myths according to Jung, "'is on the one hand delivered helpless into the power of terrible enemies and is in continual danger of extinction, while on the other he possesses powers far exceeding those of ordinary humanity.'" The boy survives "because he cannot do otherwise, because he is a total incarnation of the urge for self-realization and self-preservation. He possesses no ability to limit himself, or to prevent the full force of his potential from developing." Equipped only with those powers of nature and instinct which further his ability to survive, his conscious mind is halted as he endures test after test. The fact that the narrative is written in the first-person, concludes Kosinski, "implies certainty that he will" (NA, p. 16).

The Painted Bird begins with the separation of the child from his parents, when, like thousands of other children in the first weeks of World War II, he was sent to the shelter of a distant village. (Families of a certain social and financial stratum in Poland, who for political or other reasons were forced into hiding, often paid atrociously high prices to save their offspring from the imminent perils of war.) But in the confusion of war and occupation, especially with the continuous transfers of population to forced labor or concentration camps, life for the new foster families became increasingly difficult: many became ill; some, like the boy's original foster mother, died; others simply abandoned the wards entrusted to their care. The boy, and others like him, were left to survive by their own instincts and to wander among peasants who were ignorant and brutal ("though not by choice," claims Kosinski).[21] The very area the peasants inhabit is a physical -- and spiritual -- wasteland: "The soil was poor and the climate severe. The rivers, largely emptied of fish, frequently flooded the pastures and fields, turning them into swamps. Vast marshlands and bogs cut into the region, while dense forests traditionally sheltered bands of rebels and outlaws" (p. 2). It is into this territory that the narrator is thrust, and in the forests that he is forced to seek shelter.

In the traditional fairy tale, the forest is an ambivalent archetype -- a dappled glade by day and a dense, foreboding wood by night, with accompanying suggestions of life and death; it is also a place where heroes and heroines, traversing the worlds of light and dark in a full circle, can achieve self-realization and become transformed.[22] But for the boy in **The Painted Bird**, the forest at first offers no respite or restoration, merely a grim shelter between his flights. Gradually, though, he comes to know and to welcome the wood, especially since it provides a more hospitable environ than do the peasant villages, where he is passed from master to master, each progressively meaner and more sadistic. With the acquisition of his fiery "comet," a can with holes and full of burning matter which can be used not only for warmth and cooking but also as a kind of natural weapon, he is even able to pass entire winters there. The forest, in fact, becomes the only earth mother the boy knows, and the most important discovery which he makes about his own life -- Mitka's lesson of revenge -- occurs in its bosom.

The abandonment of the child, according to Jung, is compensated by "Mother Nature herself," who takes the child under her wing where it is nourished or protected by animals until it reaches a higher stage of self-realization (which in nature is the world of instincts). Thus, the separation, while traumatic, is actually the beginning of the child's evolution toward independence, which cannot be achieved without detachment from its origins; and the abandonment is "therefore a necessary condition, not just a concomitant symptom."[23]

The animals in **The Painted Bird** rarely nourish or protect; they do, however, reflect the bestial horrors of the modern world and even define its parameters. But unlike the beasts in traditional fairy tales, who speak to and instruct the characters, in **The Painted Bird** it is the characters who speak to and mate with their creatures and themselves become "mammals of a different breed," as the bitter opening epigraph from Mayakovsky suggests.[24] Kosinski offers the parallels between men and animals in the novel as a deliberate textual device, a "natural subplot" in which "human action is either first enacted or subsequently repeated in animal images" (NA, p. 17).

A forceful example of this natural subplot, according to Kosinski, is the dinner scene at the miller's, when the two cats are used to evoke the heightened air of sexual tension (NA, p. 17). The instinctive mating ritual between the inflamed tabby and the pouncing tom mirrors the not-so-secret attraction between the plowboy and the miller's plump and lusty wife. The would-be lovers are compelled to acknowledge their feelings for each other and to accept the brutal wrath of Jealous.

The device is employed again "when the coital seizure of dogs provides an expanded parallel to the situation of Rainbow and the Jewish girl" (NA, p. 17). After Rainbow "rescues" a young woman who had been thrown from or who had escaped from a passing train en route to a concentration camp, he takes her home with him, rapes her, and then finds himself caught in her embrace, like a mating dog. It is almost as if the girl, in her outrage over her violation, gains her revenge by attempting to destroy them both. But an old woman from the village cuts them apart, killing the girl and releasing Rainbow, who speaks afterward of having been "sucked in" by the Jewess. The "locking" simply reinforces everything the peasants believed about Jews, their desire to destroy the Gentile and the Christ in him, even at the expense of their own lives.[25]

Throughout the novel, each character's most real image is an animal -- Marta and the snake, Garbos and the dog, the plowboy and the tomcat -- but "the continual identification with the animal as the outsider" points "toward the dominant image of the Boy" (NA, p. 18). For instance, in the chickenhouse at Marta's farmyard, the chickens run from a lonely pigeon as he tries to court their favor. One day, while the pigeon is trying as usual to consort with the hens, a hawk swoops down on the helpless bird who -- outside of his element -- has no place to hide. He is pinned and then impaled on the hawk's beak. From the pigeon's anguish, the boy, himself a bird of a different type and plumage, learns that despite his efforts to assimilate himself into the new group into which chance has thrust him, he will always be rejected. Just as the undomesticated pigeon is unwelcome in the coop, the boy is an uneasy intruder on the peasant's turf and -- without escapes and contingencies of his own -- an easy victim.

In another episode, the friendless boy finds comfort in a squirrel who "visited me daily, sitting on my shoulder, kissing my ears, neck, and cheek, teasing my hair with its light touch" (p. 5). But one day some village boys trap the squirrel before it can reach the safety of the forest, pour flammable liquid over its body, and gleefully watch it burst in flames. (What makes the scene even more gruesome is the realization that not very far away bigger "boys" are committing greater horrors -- not with gas cans, but with Zyklon-B, a more efficient instrument of death.) To escape the squirrel's fate -- and the Jews' -- the boy learns that he must strike back, sometimes with methods almost as horrible as those of his persecutors.

Later, when the boy is living with Lekh, he witnesses an example of the birdcatcher's wrath. Angered by the disappearance of his girlfriend, Ludmila (who, because of her addled brain and earthy, unrestrained sexuality, is also a painted bird much different from the gray flock of peasant women, who are jealous of the attraction she holds for their men),[26] Lekh paints a bird and releases him into the thick of the forest. The bird flies nervously and attempts to draw the attention of the flock, who soon turn on and kill their more colorful brother: "It would soar, happy and free, a spot of rainbow against the backdrop of clouds, and then plunge into the waiting brown flock. For an instant the birds were confounded. The painted bird circled from one end of the flock to the other, vainly trying to convince its kin that it was one of them. But, dazzled by its brilliant colors, they flew around it unconvinced. The painted bird would be forced farther and farther away as it zealously tried to enter the ranks of the flock. We saw soon afterwards how one bird after another would peel off in a fierce attack. Shortly the many-hued shape lost its place in the sky and dropped to the ground" (p. 44). The ritual killings occur until Lekh empties all of his cages.

Like the painted bird, the boy never shares in the comfort or the safety of the flock (at first because he is made into an outsider; later because he chooses to reject the collective), but already he learns to draw his circle of flight tighter and tighter and to gird himself for a variety of attacks which threaten him with extinction. The episode of the painted bird, which appeared originally in **No Third Path** and was described to Joseph Novak by his friend, Varvara, is not simply the central image of novel; the "continued statement of image, its prolonged use throughout the narrative, [culminates] in its metamorphosis into a symbol" (NA, pp. 17-18), much like the boy's metamorphosis from object to subject, victim to victimizer, shattered identity to newly emergent self by the novel's end.

Another time, after being freed by a partisan soldier, the boy escapes again into the woods, and this time he discovers an injured horse which faithfully follows him back to town. But the next morning, rather than being healed, the horse is strangulated and beaten. The boy, fearing that he will be the farmer's next victim, is forced to skin the hide and cut up the carcass. Again, the boy's fate is linked to the animal's. This episode, and many others like it, are not simply random acts of cruelty, but important lessons which help to teach the boy what he must do in order to survive. The brutalized animals guide the brutalized boy toward the instinctive knowledge which will keep him alive.[27]

But the boy must also pass other tests on his journey, almost all of which are linked in some way to primitive nature, especially to the "palpable natural symbols" and the "natural images and motifs ... [that] we have learned to associate with fairy tales" (NA, pp. 16, 19). Fire, as an element that lies at the very border of life and death, is particularly significant.[28] In **The Painted Bird**, fire can be healing, like the boy's comet, "a constant source of heat" (p. 24) and light and thus a promise of life. Or it can be destructive. Marta's hut is burned to the ground -- with Marta still in it -- as a result of the kerosene the narrator spills. The carpenter suspects the boy's hair to be a conductor of lightning; during a storm, he locks the boy in the barn -- and, in a self-fulfilling prophecy, lightning strikes his farm. Soaps, another bitter legacy of the war (and one of the few weapons the boy possesses), explode and cause injuries. And, of course, the ever present locomotives puff smoke and billow fire as they stretch to Auschwitz and other camps, where millions burn. There are also fires of passion -- the broken heart of Labina, mourning for her Laba; the boy's infatuation for Ewka and her gentle lovemaking -- and the fires of hatred -- of the women toward Ludmila, of the miller toward the plowboy, of the frenzied, drunken Kalmuks toward the villages they attack.

There are images, too, of water, which mostly harms rather than heals. The boy is thrown by peasants into a river atop a giant fish bladder ("agonized at the thought that I would have to spend all night in this manner," knowing "that if the bladder should burst, I would immediately drown. I could not swim" [p. 23]). Later, while sailing across the ice to escape the boys who are pursuing him, the narrator is thrown through a hole in the surface ("The icy water shut over me" [p. 143]) and almost drowns again.

Several times he is buried alive (and revived metamorphosed), once when Olga plants him in the ground overnight to relieve him of his demonic fever and again when he drops the missal on the feast of Corpus Christi and angry peasants heave him into a pit of ordure. He is forced into the wilderness of the peasants' terrain and later into an urban postwar wasteland of night people, who alone can understand his need to roam like Byron's Cain,[29] where he dreams of transformation, of snakes shedding their skins and of transcendent birds, and is himself transformed from "the Evil One" to a penitent into an evil one again, from an outsider into a mute observer and finally into a purveyor of words.

Words -- language -- are of great concern both to Kosinski and to his protagonists. And since "the child perceives through and learns from the same symbols as did the prehistoric tribes -- for example, animal imagery and instinctual association with the natural ... the preoccupation with speech and the lack of it is interesting" (NA, p. 16). At first, when forced into the peasant villages, the boy is unable to speak in the dialect of the region. His inability to communicate is considered by those around him to be a cause for laughter and derision or a sign of his legion with the devil. When he is finally beginning to understand and use the dialect, he is deprived of the power of speech entirely. Kosinski writes that he "purposely" prevented the boy "from having the advantage of normal communication" and that "this imposed silence fulfills several functions":

> When the means of speech is lost to him the Boy is consequently thrown back into motivated action. Whereas speech may be a substitute for action, or an oblique method of suggesting it, action speaks for itself.

> The modern literary use of language is contrapuntal, employed to lay bare the significant area which exists between language and action, and to highlight the gulf between them. This gulf also seems to be the focal point of modern art. But in **The Painted Bird** the situation is taken further; in the attempt to recall the primitive, the symbols are sought more pertinently and immediately than through the superficial process of speech and dialogue. In addition, the sense of alienation is heightened by depriving the characters of the ability to communicate freely. Observation is a silent process; without the means of participation, the silent one must observe. Perhaps this silence is also a metaphor for dissociation from the community and from something greater. This feeling of alienation floats on the surface of the work and manifests the author's awareness, perhaps unconscious, of his break with the wholeness of self. (NA, pp. 16-17)

In the traditional fairy tale, the hero or heroine is sometimes injured; in the Grimm's tale, "Our Lady's Child," a young girl who has disobeyed the Virgin even loses her speech, undergoing severe ordeals before she confesses her misdeed and regains her voice. The injury is usually reversed when the "test" is completed.

Yet in **The Painted Bird**, the boy's muteness occurs not at the hands of some evil force (a witch or wicked queen);

it happens during mass -- the antithesis of pagan magic -- in a church, a place which ironically should provide divine protection from harmful spells and curses. The muteness is partly or largely self-willed, the result of the boy's extreme alienation. Unable to escape totally from his oppressive society, the boy begins to withdraw. Though surrounded by witches like Marta and Olga, he possesses no magical instrument like Oskar's in Gunter Grass's **The Tin Drum** upon which to drum away reality, so he withdraws in several stages, ranging from sleepiness to muteness. Though everyone has to sleep, Kosinski is careful to show the desensitized boy sleeping only in withdrawal situations. The narrator sleeps to escape from reality ("I heard the distant voices of people and the crash of falling walls, and then I fell asleep"); to restore equilibrium (he "slept and woke by turns" after seeing Ludmila killed); to substitute for physical flight (when being carried in a sack he "sat hunched as though in a stupor" and when tied to a cart he "dozed off into sleep"); and to return to the womb ("there was my warm, secure bed where I could safely sleep and forget about everything").[30]

His loss of speech occurs significantly after a long period of sleeplessness: "at night I was so terrified of Judas that I could not sleep." His former mode of withdrawal no longer proves a satisfactory retreat from reality, for "even when I finally dozed off, my sleep was disturbed by dreams of dogs" (pp. 107-108).[31] The strain from this final atrocity, combined with the past experiences in which his accent belied his "strangeness" to the peasants, creates a mentally -induced muteness in the boy which is not so much deliberate as merely hysterical and reactionary. It is only months later, when he is in a securer environment and able to escape at least some of his feelings of estrangement, that he speaks again. (The restoration of speech, however, also follows an accident -- this time a skiing mishap in which he is soaring like a bird down a slope of icy snow with a speed that takes his breath away. His brush with death in natural surroundings enables him to come full circle and to regain something once lost under somewhat similar conditions.)[32] Revived by the April sunshine which fills his hospital room, he answers a ringing telephone and begins to speak again, "enraptured by the sounds that were heavy with meaning, as wet snow is heavy with water" (p. 213).

Like Oskar in **The Tin Drum**, who evades his parents' desire to put him eventually behind their grocery counter by not growing up, Bruce Jay Friedman's Stern, who develops an ulcer because he is unable to avenge the "kike-haters'" insults, and Billy Pilgrim in **Slaughterhouse-Five**, who, after his war experiences, is "unstuck" in time, the boy in **The Painted Bird** becomes mute as a defense mechanism. But the muteness is also the result of "the complete exhaustion of the language of childhood."[33] When religion proves as false a panacea as black magic had, the boy is left with nothing -- at least until the skiing accident, when his convalescence seems to provide him with the opportunity for recovering or renewing his powers of moral assertion. Though in Kosinski's world language is never the adequate tool for formulating the nature of human experience, in its many varieties it constitutes the only means for establishing a perspective on any experience; therefore language represents the necessary and thus inescapable limit that no man, not even Kosinski's protagonists, can exceed.[34] Yet the language which the narrator regains when he recovers his speech is no longer the language of a victimized boy; it is the mature language of one who controls -- or withholds -- it, as the narrator of **Steps** and later protagonists do.

In **The Painted Bird**, the return of the boy's speech also constitutes the full circle, the "happy ending" which Tolkien suggests is required of all good fairy tales. But it is not the reunion with his parents which restores the boy's security or even his voice; the boy's family situation, especially the intrusion of a baby brother, causes him consternation, not joy. He is reluctant to leave his surrogate fathers, Gavrila and Mitka; his metaphysical twin, the Silent One; even the orphanage, which symbolizes his displacement from normal society. (The names of the orphans -- Saber, Cannon, Tank, Grenade, Torpedo, Partisan, Sniper, Flame-

THE PAINTED BIRD 87

thrower, Airplane -- suggest that the war is far from over.)[35] Only in his separation from -- and then his reintegration at the novel's end with -- language, with "that speech [which] was now mine" (p. 213), is the boy able to make himself whole. And only through his appreciation of language's power to define and control (a lesson Joseph Novak learned in the collective climate of **The Future is Ours, Comrade** and **No Third Path)** can he finally master his own experiences, the very episodes which almost shattered his psyche as they shattered his faith. Perhaps that is why, in the midst of the affluence of his American-dream marriage to Mary Hayward Weir, to whom **The Painted Bird** is dedicated, Kosinski undertook the writing of this first novel of European nightmare. Perhaps also only in the naming of the horrors he observed and in which he participated could he begin to exorcise them.

The boy's muteness and the community's severe action which provoked it occur in a churchyard on Corpus Christi Day; Kosinski calls this one "use of the natural ... in the juxtaposition of life and death" (NA, p. 18). There are numerous other uses: a murder is committed during a wedding feast, which is then turned into a funeral gathering. The peasants ghoulishly loot the bodies of dead Jews and carry the souvenirs home in great triumph -- a photograph of a murdered Jew hangs next to a religious picture. (The life after death afforded the Jews is their image in the hands of the peasants. Writes Frederick Karl: "Ironically, everything that was dear to them in life and family is reified and blasphemed. They become the possession of the peasants, and even in death they cannot rest in peace. The use of one's most personal items after death destroys their sanctity, but such usage, in this curious dance of death, also ensures that one is not forgotten, no matter how abysmal the perpetuation. The peasants are, incongruously, receivers of the Jewish legacy; the Germans, agents of the gift.")[36] Even more ironically, the extermination camp trains   run past the villages most frequently during the fecund days of the mushroom harvest (NA, p. 18).

Likewise, familiar fictive structures are employed and totally inverted. Just as indifference replaces joy during the boy's reconciliation scene with his parents, so do the wanderings of the Silent One and the boy comprise an idyll of childhood, completely blackened by the tragedy of their situation. Similarly, Lekh and Ludmila, "one mad, the other demented," are the inamorati of a story in which hatred, not love, is dominant (NA, p. 18). In fact, the whole novel, with its fairy tale structure, is actually in many ways a bitter anti-fairy tale.[37]

Nevertheless, whether read as a fairy tale or as its inversion, **The Painted Bird**, with its protagonist's wanderings, is prototypical of the journey into an alien environment which figures prominently in recent absurdist literature. By the mid-sixties, when **The Painted Bird** was first published, the abstraction of society had proceeded so far that the fictional hero did not need to travel to foreign lands to find himself surrounded by indifferent or hostile people or to feel unable to communicate with anyone or uncertain even about who he was.[38] Like Humbert Humbert, who discovers more than continental America in his cross-country trip in Nabokov's **Lolita**, or Stern, who takes a terrifying nightly walk from the bus stop after moving from the ghetto security of the city to the suburbs, or Les and Little Jimmie, who travel from Harlem to Broadway in Charles Wright's **The Wig**, Kosinski's unnamed boy has only to venture among people of his own nationality and homeland to experience alienation.

The journey motif further dramatizes the identify crisis of the narrator, who feels bereft even of a sense of his own authenticity. When the SS officer surveys him sharply in Chapter 10, approximately the middle of the novel, the boy feels like a squashed caterpillar or some other loathsome creature in the presence of a resplendent, uniformed being: "I gazed at the ornate clasp of his officer's belt that was exactly at the level of my eyes, and awaited his wise decision ... I knew my fate was being decided in some manner, but it was a matter of indifference to me. I placed infinite confidence in the decision of the man facing me. I knew that he possessed powers unattainable for ordinary people" (pp. 100-101). The boy considers himself no more than an object to be judged; he so loses all sense of himself that he exists only in the other's eyes. This is the ultimate in passivity, the boy's negation of himself because he has ceased to function as a subject.[39] Just as Stern, a Jewish American, and Lester Jackson, a Black American, are reduced to pseudo-existence in their own country, so the boy, a Pole (at least in the first edition; later simply an East European), must "half-live" among other Poles. Like Stern and Les, whose sense of identity depends in part on their relationship to the conventional age groups of their society, he is trapped in an impersonal round of homogenized activities (the peasant collective villages and later the Soviet collective). Like Joseph Novak in the nonfiction works, he is both physically a part of and mentally apart from the collective community; he lives in it but he does not belong to it. He is a non-person, vividly dramatized by his lack of real involvement with the people around him.[40]

Yet, unlike Kosinski's later protagonists, most of whom choose to be outsiders, the boy in **The Painted Bird** is made into an outsider. The ignorant and brutish villagers, along with the purveyors of a modern ideology that appeals to the peasant's basest instincts, are out to destroy him simply because he is different.[41] Still, he survives, perhaps because, like the birds Lekh selects for his experiments, he is the strongest -- or perhaps because, as Kosinski has already suggested, he cannot do otherwise. Either way, however, he survives by metamorphosing; he undergoes a series of significant changes and as he does so, "beneath the Gothic tales of human evil a quiet Bildungsroman unfolds."[42] (Though, as Norman Lavers points out, almost any novel which has as its protagonist a young boy who grows older during the course of it is "an education novel," for "young boys are voracious of experience, and almost everything that happens to them happens for the first time, and teaches them something new about their world.")[43] At first, the boy is utterly naive and ignorant about life and death. He watches calmly as Marta burns in her hut, sure that she will be transformed and that her magic incantations will prevent any real harm from befalling her. Later, when Jealous the miller plucks out the plowboy's eyes, the boy is still not aware of the permanence of the situation: "Something like a glimmer of hope crossed my mind that the gouged eyes could be put back where they belong." But while kicking his cats the miller squashes the eyeballs under his heavy boots, and instead of "marvelous mirror[s], which could reflect the whole world ... there remained on the floor only a crushed bit of jelly. I felt a horrible sense of loss" (pp. 33-34). He vows at that point to become an observer -- to remember everything that he sees, so that if anyone should ever pluck out his eyes, he would retain the memory of all he has observed for as long as he lived.

As he is exposed to ever-greater acts of appalling and numbing violence, the boy becomes aware of an invisible order of evil.[44] Since he is already assumed to be "the Evil One," he decides to join forces with the damned. He counts his persecutors' teeth, collects insects and hairs, and memorizes chants and incantations. Reasoning that the devil alone gives him a chance against Chance,[45] he figures that "the more harm, misery, injury and bitterness a man could inflict on those around him, the more help he could expect" (p. 135).

But when he gazes into his persecutors' eyes and they don't die or even fall ill, he senses the failure of witchcraft. Soon he turns to religion for both spiritual and physical deliverance. Learning from a village priest that "the greater the number of prayers offered, the better one would live, and the smaller the number, the more troubles and pain one would have to endure," the boy feels the ruling pattern of the world revealed to him with beautiful clarity (p. 111). Just as he had earlier counted teeth, now he begins to count days of indulgences. Just as he had earlier memorized spells, he now memorizes prayers. He devotes every spare minute to prayers; he prays from dawn until dusk and some-

times through the night. He prays even as Garbos hangs
him inches from Judas' gaping teeth. Yet, as his store
of indulgences accumulates, his condition seems to worsen.
He is beaten and tortured more than usual by Garbos, and
finally -- despite all his praying -- he is carried out of the
church and into a pit of human excrement. The pit is adja-
cent to an outhouse whose small windows are cut into the
shape of the cross -- "the subject of special pride to the
priest" (p. 123). He emerges from the sucking maw of
ordure shocked by his cruel betrayal. The sweet promise
of indulgences as foul as the muck which envelops him,
he is unable to pray -- or to speak -- any more.

Having rejected the spiritual (both the black magic of superstition and the white magic of Christianity), he embraces
yet another panacea: Communism. Mesmerized earlier
by the striking death's head uniform of the SS officer who
ironically spared his life and delivered him to the village
priest who in turn gave him to Garbos, the boy now becomes
infatuated with the Soviet officers, Gavrila and Mitka (both
of whom first appear in **No Third Path**). But unlike the
SS officer, who reduces him to an object by negating his
identity, his new friends help him to recover what he has
lost and even provide him with a uniform -- an identity
-- of his own. Gavrila, a regimental officer rumored to
have lost his entire family in the first days of the Nazi
invasion, teaches him to read and write and shares with
him his governing philosophy, "that the order of the world
had nothing to do with God, and that God ... did not exist."
The only realistic way of promoting goodness was as part
of the Communist Party; only through the group, which
was called "the collective," could man be useful and leave
his mark (pp. 168, 172).

On the other hand, Mitka, a sharpshooting instructor and
a Hero of the Soviet Union, shows the boy compassion and
introduces him to less serious things than the role of the
Party: poetry, songs, cinema, engine mechanics. After
Mitka's friends are killed by jealous and drunken peasants,
Mitka takes the boy with him into the forest, where he

scopes out several villagers and picks them off with his
deadly accurate aim. "Regardless of the opinions of others,
risking his position in the regiment, and his title of Hero
of the Soviet Union," he takes revenge, because "Of what
value was the rank of Hero, respected and worshiped by
tens of millions of citizens, if he no longer deserved it
in his own eyes?" So, from Mitka, the boys learns a lesson
different from Gavrila's: "A man, no matter now popular
and admired, lives mainly with himself. If he is not at peace
with himself, if he is harassed by something he did not
do but should have done to preserve his own image of himself,
he is like the 'unhappy Demon, spirit of exile, gliding high
above the sinful world'" (p. 187). Like all of Kosinski's
later protagonists, the boy recognizes the importance of
choosing to act.   While chance still rules, he realizes that,
by striking back, he need not always be its helpless victim.[46]

Each of the would-be panaceas -- witchcraft, Christianity,
Nazism, and ultimately even Communism (which collectively
parallel the grim road travelled by Western man) -- ends
in disappointment because the crude flaws of humanity crop
up inevitably under any system. Therefore, the boy learns
that there is no escaping evil except in complete, self-
centered independence[47] and illusion-free self-reliance.
In a world devoid of values, he must create his own. Explains
Kosinski: "It is only by employing [the world's] lessons of
hate and revenge that he is able to part himself from it.
This hate allows him to see with some clarity why and
what he hates. Paradoxically this process causes his desires
for revenge to cease being directed at any single person
or group; now they become attitudes, deeply ingrained,
the wellspring of the purpose of his life, the basis for his
behavior in all situations." It is the act of revenge that
counts -- "the act above all" -- as the boy carries with him
his own brand of justice and metes out punishment to others
according to his own reckoning (NA, pp. 26-27).

When all children have to be delivered to orphanages at
the end of the war, Gavrila and Mitka give the boy money
and small gifts, in addition to the Red Army uniform which

they had the regimental tailor cut to scale for him. The boy wears the uniform proudly, the way a mythic hero bears his name. After the orphanage principal forces him to remove it, he puts into practice the other badge of his new identity (the only badge which no one can take from him): Mitka's lesson of revenge. He runs out into the street and signs to four Soviet soldiers that his uniform has been stolen from him by landlords and that -- because of his Soviet affiliation -- he has been victimized. He successfully uses the system against itself: the soldiers respond by systematically smashing flowerpots in the principal's office and by chasing and slapping the nurses, and afterwards the staff leaves him alone.

Later, when he accidentally overturns some produce at the market, a farmer beats and kicks him. He recalls Mitka's teaching that "a man should never let himself be mistreated, for he would then lose his self-respect and his life would become meaningless. What would preserve his self-respect and determine his worth was his ability to take revenge on those who wronged him" (p. 194). Two weeks later, he and the Silent One derail the train heading to the market. The crash kills many people, but the dairyman who had humiliated him is not among the victims. Although the Silent One cries in frustration, the boy does not because he appreciates the chance involved in the situation. Like Mitka, who avenged his colleagues' death by the random shooting of villagers, it is satisfaction enough for the boy that he has acted -- and that he has acted specifically upon a train, one agent of destruction. (Trains, Kosinski contends, play a vital role in **The Painted Bird.** Not only do they bear Jews to their deaths in the concentration camps; they also provide the boy, a potential victim of the camp trains, with an additional challenge: "the nerve-wracking, danger-fraught sport of lying between the tracks while the trains speed over him. He exposes himself to and survives the danger that the trains present" [NA, p. 26].) With the derailment of the market-bound train, "the oppressed become the oppressors. Those who might have been borne away to the camps by the trains, are now destroying the peasants who stood by as the trains roared past. It is those who were so nearly victims who now stand by the tracks and silently rejoice" (NA, p. 26).

As the metamorphosed painted bird, more brilliant in his flights than either his peasant captors or his own chaotic, collective postwar society, the boy is a kind of picaro.[48] A number of critics have already commented at some length on the picaresque qualities of The Painted Bird: Norman Lavers, for example, traces the genre back to its beginnings and compares Kosinski's narrator with the protagonist of Lazarillo de Tormes, a sixteenth-century Spanish work and the prototypical novel in the picaresque tradition.[49] But it is Kosinski who has the last -- and best -- word on his own character. Acknowledging that all of his protagonists, from The Painted Bird on, are picaros, he explains that the picaro, a character constantly in a state of becoming, "is the last champion of selfhood," a notion which he notes with regret is "on the way out."[50] The boy, for Kosinski, is thus a champion of the self -- not simply a painted bird but also a phoenix, rising out of the ashes of the Holocaust to testify to his own survival.

Readers and critics have responded in curious ways to Kosinski's unique method of transforming fact into fiction in The Painted Bird. Some, like Alfred Kazin, have downplayed Kosinski's role as author by seeing him simply as an accurate observer of historical circumstance: "We say about a book like Jerzy Kosinski's The Painted Bird ... 'What a writer!' And to ourselves we add, 'With experiences like that, how can you miss?'"[51] (Kosinski considers this the "give a boy a war and you give him a novel" philosophy.) Others suggest the opposite: that the actual narrative formula of The Painted Bird -- like that of almost all of Kosinski's novels -- is flimsy. According to John Updike, for example, Kosinski's fictional world "rests on a realistic basis less substantial than sand."[52]

But The Painted Bird succeeds precisely because of Kosinski's ability to transform real experiences into a creative --

and fictive -- remembrance, laden with symbolic and mythic overtones. Though the wandering child is both the ideal image for the alienated, estranged, disenfranchised postwar man and Jung's archetype for the unconscious, the fact is that there were all too many children like Kosinski's protagonist during the war who were forced to undertake macabre journeys and suffer terrifying ordeals. Henryk Grynberg's **Child of the Shadows,** published in the same year as the **The Painted Bird,** recounts the story of one such odyssey:

> There was a boy I knew about who, when all his family had been killed and he had been left completely alone, went to the countryside to mind cows. No one knew him, and he knew nobody there. He said that he did not remember where he came from, or what his name was. And the people did not ask him any more questions. He was given a corner to sleep and a bowl for his food, and spent all his time with the cows. Summer and winter. And there no other man was as fortunate in those days as he was. For in the end he really forgot where he had come from and what his name was.
>
> Others, who were just as lucky, went away later, for they could still remember who they were, or there was someone who remembered them. But that boy stayed put. Perhaps he is there to this day.[53]

Similarly, while Kosinski's peasants are symbols of the evils inherent in any collective system, detailed accounts of peasant life abound in Polish literature -- accounts by no means flattering -- which corroborate Kosinski's recollections. In Eliza Orzeszkowa's novel **Dziurdziowie,** for example,

> We are given a grim picture of the frightening ignorance of the peasants and their belief in

the real existence of witches, who with
Beelzebub's assistance cause cattle to die, the
soil to be barren, men to meet with sudden
death, etc. In this medieval atmospherc of
superstition, a young, kind and pretty woman,
destined by nature for a better sort of life,
is accused of "magic" and perishes.[54]

Stanislaw Wyspianski's masterpiece, **Klatwa** (Curse), whose
village scenes share the grotesque atmosphere of **The Painted
Bird** as well as part of **Steps**, depicts a similar atrocity
in a remote Polish village. The hamlet's inhabitants are
poor, ignorant and superstitious; they are disarmed by the
presence of the local parish priest's animalistically sensual
mistress. When a dry hot summer occurs and kills all of
their crops, they interpret the drought as God's warning,
brought on by the illicit love affair. The mob, feeling that
such amorality and sinfulness require punishment, burns
the young girl alive and awaits the rain. Karol Hubert
Rostworowski, in his peasant tragedy **Niespodzianka** (Surprise), based on an actual police chronicle, describes an
elderly peasant couple who kill a kindly stranger who has
enlisted their hospitality for one night. They murder him
for money, and while ransacking his belongings they learn
that they have assassinated their own son, who after an
absence of many years has come back to them.

Even Wladyslaw Reymont, whose Nobel-Prize-winning four-
volume epic **Chlopi** (The Peasants) paints, for the most
part, a rather pastoral portrait of Polish village life, is
unable to camouflage completely the sadism of the peasants.
Though his chlopi are less ignorant than their counterparts
in Prus, Wyspianski and Rostworowski, they are almost
as hard and as full of passion and hatred. In a scene from
Volume Four, "Summer," on the punishment of Yagna:

A hundred hands shot out to seize her in their
greedy clutches, ravenous with hatred; she
was whirled away like a bush torn by the roots,
and she was dragged out into the enclosure....

By the roadside stood a cart prepared for her, filled to the very top with hogs' dung, to which cart a couple of black cows had been yoked. Into the dung they tossed her, bound fast and unresisting; and then, in the midst of a deafening uproar -- laughter, foul invectives, imprecations -- the procession set out.... Thus did Yagna, bound, on a bed of dung, the blood oozing from her beaten limbs, disgraced for all her life, unutterably degraded, and supreme in wretchedness, lie neither hearing nor feeling anything around her; but the tears streamed down her bruised cheeks ... there rained upon her clods and stones and handfuls of earth, while she lay motionless looking up into the trees that waved over her.[55]

This punishment scene recalls another gruesome and sadistic description -- the death of Ludmila in **The Painted Bird**:

The women held Stupid Ludmila down flat against the grass. They sat on her hands and legs and began beating her with the rakes, ripping her skin with their fingernails, tearing out her hair, spitting into her face ... Stupid Ludmila lay bleeding. Blue bruises appeared on her tormented body. She groaned loudly, arched her back, trembled, trying vainly to free herself. One of the women now approached, holding a corked bottle of brownish-black manure. To the accompaniment of raucous laughter and loud encouragements from the others, she kneeled between Ludmila's legs and rammed the entire bottle inside her abused, assaulted slit, while she began to moan and howl like a beast. The other women looked on calmly. Suddenly with all her strength one of them kicked the bottom of the bottle sticking out of Stupid Ludmila's groin. There was the muffled noise of glass shattering inside. Now all the women began to kick Ludmila; the blood spurted round their boots and calves. When the last woman had finished kicking, Ludmila was dead. (pp. 47-48)

The almost medieval practices of torture by the Eastern European peasants also have precedents in Slavic literature, as a comparison between passages from Kosinski and Nobel Prize winner Henryk Sienkiewicz demonstrates:

From **The Painted Bird:**
Apparently this man had treacherously killed the son of an influential farmer and the farmer had decided to punish the murderer in the old-fashioned manner. Together with his two cousins the man brought the culprit to the forest. There they prepared a twelve-foot stake, sharpened at one end to a fine point like a gigantic pencil. They laid it on the ground, wedging the blunt end against a tree trunk. Then a strong horse was hitched to each of the victim's feet, while his crotch was leveled with the waiting point. The horses, gently nudged, pulled the man against the spiked beam, which gradually sank into the tensed flesh. When the point was deep into the entrails of the victim, the men lifted the stake, together with the impaled man upon it and planted it in a previously dug hole. They left him there to die slowly. (pp. 16-17)

From Sienkiewicz's **Pan Wolodyjowski,** a description of the execution of a traitor and kidnapper:

The horses started to move forward; stretched ropes dragged Azya's legs. His body rolled for a while through the soil, then hit a jagged prick. The edge began to plunge into him. Something frightful happened, something contrary to nature and human feeling. The poor wretch's bones snapped apart, the flesh tore in half; the pain became so unbelievable, so sharp, that

it penetrated him like an atrocious orgasm.
The stake went farther and farther. Tuhay
Bey's son locked his teeth and his throat vomited
a scream -- "Aaaaa!" -- like a raven's croak....
They quickly unharnessed the horses and raised
the stake, planting its broader end into the
soil ... this macabre punishment was made even
more horrible by the fact that the victims on
the stake lived sometimes up to three days.[56]

Peasants' brutality was often based on superstitious fear.
A typical scene of the consequences of superstitious belief
can be found in **Dziurdziowie,** written in 1885. Ignorant
neighbors believe the blacksmith's young wife to be a
witch responsible for bringing death to the village and
harm to their cattle. One evening, the men of the Dziurdzio
family, drunk and blinded by the snow storm, are unable
even to find their way home. At the edge of the forest,
they recognize the woman, who is returning to her house:

> In the radiant white darkness, their faces were
> not visible, but from the loud panting, gloomy
> murmurs and drunken outcries arose a swelling
> volcano of fiercest passions -- of fright and
> vengeance. A minute went by. In the snowy
> fog, a few feet away from where the three
> sleighs stood parked together, grew the shadow
> of a group, struggling. Dreadful screams and
> moans erupted, but they were silenced by the
> roaring wind that carried them whistling away
> over the wide stormy fields.
>
> Another five minutes went by, and a huge wave
> of wind momentarily cut through the fog to
> show the track leading straight ahead, and on
> the track, three sleighs with four peasants.
> They had destroyed the devil's power and found
> their way out. Now, whipping the horses, calling
> to them with long shouts, they sailed rapidly

through the smooth surface and then disappeared
in the thickening haze of snow.

They left behind Petrusia, the wife of the blacksmith Michal. She lay motionless, a dark stain
on a white soil. They had broken her breast
and ribs with bludgeons; they had bloodstained
her baby face, and left her on an empty field,
a wide field, for the snow to fall on her, for
the crows and jackdaws to feed upon her.[57]

It is not surprising, therefore, that the narrator of **The
Painted Bird**, a victim because he too is suspected of being
"in league with the Devil," undergoes similar horrors:

She called me the Black One. From her I learned
for the first time that I was possessed by an
evil spirit, which crouched in me like a mole
in a deep burrow, and of whose presence I was
unaware. Such a person as I, possessed of this
evil spirit, could be recognized by his bewitched
black eyes which did not blink when they gazed
at bright clear eyes. Hence, Olga declared,
I could stare at other people and unknowingly
cast a spell over them.... When bewitched eyes
look at a healthy child, he will immediately
begin to waste away; when at a calf, it will
drop dead of a sudden disease; when at grass,
the hay will rot after the harvest.

... Yet when the eagerly awaited warmer weather
came at last, it brought along a plague .... [Olga
buried me up to my neck in a pit of earth.]
Thus planted in the cold earth, my body cooled
completely in a few minutes, like the root of
a wilting weed. I lost all awareness. Like an
abandoned head of cabbage, I became part of
the great field.... Noises woke me.... A flock
of ravens circled over my head.... In terror
I watched their shining black-feathered tails

and darting eyes. They stalked around me, nearer and nearer, flicking their heads toward me, uncertain whether I was dead or alive. (pp. 16-17, 18-21).

In fact, to give more validity to the peasant superstitions and practices in **The Painted Bird**, Kosinski turned to the works of the Polish anthropologist, sociologist and expert on Eastern European folklore, Henryk Biegeleisen, whose studies document superstitions relating to eyes, hair, teeth, vampires, changelings, and other demonism rampant among peasants for centuries. (Kosinski himself acknowledged his familiarity with Biegeleisen in **Der Spiegel**; answering charges that the events described were far-fetched and sensational, he wrote a letter to the German journal in which he suggested that critics refer to Biegeleisen's works for corroboration of the numerous peasant superstitions which he documented in **The Painted Bird**. Ironically, he was later harangued by several Polish journalists, who felt that he was too cognizant of folk life as a literary source. In "Fun and Games of the Polish People During the Second World War," Hanna Wydzga and Jan Zaborowski accused him of various crimes against Poland and concluded that the folk matrix of **The Painted Bird** is stolen whole from a 400-page work by Professor Biegeleisen, published in 1929, under the title **The Healing Practices of the Polish Peasantry.**[58] Wydzga and Zaborowski's allegations, among others, were later used by Geoffrey Stokes and Eliot Fremont-Smith in their attack on Kosinski's integrity as an author, discussed more fully in Chapter One.)

Yet the peasants are not the only ones in the novel to commit sadistic violations. Their cruelty, especially in the first half of the book, is counterbalanced by that of the occupation armies -- the perversity of the Nazis' final solution; the madness of the murderous Kalmuks; the suppression of free thought and expression in the nightmarish collective of the Stalinist Soviets (already chronicled by Joseph Novak in the nonfiction). After all, writes Kosinski, the peasants merely "symbolize and personify the level to which the

so-called European Civilization was forced down by World
War II ... and became part of the great holocaust of violence,
murder, lawlessness and destruction which the war had
been preparing for them" (NA, p. 22).

While **The Painted Bird** makes reference to actual traditions,
attitudes, philosophies, and historical events, there are
also some obvious parallels between the boy's story and
Kosinski's own biography. Kosinski, born in 1933, was six
years old when the war broke out; he was separated from
his parents, spent many months in peasant villages, and
was often victimized because he looked different -- like
a gypsy or a Jew; he became mute, was sent to an orphanage
in Lodz, and was eventually reunited with his parents, who
had adopted another child; he got into a number of scrapes
with the authorities; and eventually he recovered his speech
after a skiing accident. But Kosinski is quick to point out,
both in his **Notes of the Author** and in interviews he has
given subsequent to **The Painted Bird's** 1965 publication,
that while the novel is based on fact, it is not wholly factual
(as a history or an autobiography, for example, would be).
The Painted Bird, then, "could be the author's vision of
himself as a child, a vision, not an examination, or a revisita-
tion of childhood" (NA, p. 13) -- a kind of "fictive reality"
which lacks "the hard edge of fact" (NA, p. 11). Kosinski
believes that we all unwittingly create patterns to help
along our thinking and identifying, and "we fit experiences
into molds which simplify, shape, and give them an acceptable emotional clarity. The remembered event becomes
a fiction, a structure made to accommodate certain feelings.
If there were not these structures, art would be too personal
for the artist to create, much less for the audience to grasp.
There is no art which is reality; rather, art is the using
of symbols by which an otherwise unstateable subjective
reality is made manifest" (NA, p. 11).

So, while based on reminiscences through which the author
-- in his archetypal wanderings (physical and/or mental)
-- can confront his past, **The Painted Bird** is a work of
fiction, just like **Slaughterhouse-Five** or **The Naked and**

the Dead (both based, like Kosinski's novel, on their authors' actual wartime experiences). Moreover, as successful fiction, **The Painted Bird** relates the symbolic journey by which a young boy -- a contemporary Everyman -- moves from innocence to experience, from childhood to adolescence, from group responses to individual action,[59] and thus provides an archetype for existence which people from all cultures and of all ages can understand and appreciate.

Stylistically, **The Painted Bird** is fragmentary and highly episodic in nature[60] -- or, in Kosinski's words, organized "in little dramas, in spurts of experience, with the links largely omitted, as is the case with memory" (NA, p. 12). Though frequently compared to senior émigrés Conrad and Nabokov, Kosinski is colder and more detached. His vocabulary is deliberately more limited, his syntax more simplified, and his language more direct. Jack Hicks writes that "his strength is in conveying disquieting scenes with absolute lucidity, and his language, to that end, must be transparent as water."[61] "It is the opposite, for instance, of what Nabokov does," notes Kosinski. "His language is made visible ... like a veil or a transparent curtain with a beautiful design. You cannot help seeing the curtain as you peek into the intimate room behind. My aim, though, is to remove the veil."[62] Furthermore, since he was writing in an adopted language, Kosinski claims he was never certain whether his prose was sufficiently clear, and so he counted words "the way Western Union does." His prose "was like a night letter. Every word was there for a reason, and if not, I would cross it out." His language had to be as unobtrusive as possible, so the reader "is drawn right away into each dramatic incident."[63]

Perhaps the uniqueness of both Kosinski's style and his vision accounted for the initial problems in publishing **The Painted Bird**. Kosinski says that after he completed the manuscript, he showed it to four of his friends, all editors in large, respectable publishing houses in New York. All four had an interest in Kosinski's work because of his non-fiction, yet all four told him "in very plain language" that the novel was not publishable in America because it treated "a reality which is alien to Americans, set in an environment that Americans cannot comprehend, and dealing with situations, particularly the cruelty to animals, that Americans cannot bear. No fiction could possibly alter this, they said, and certainly not **The Painted Bird.** Their verdict was: Go back to writing nonfiction. I asked them who, in their view, would be the least likely publisher for this book. They said short of Vatican City, I should try Houghton Mifflin in Boston. I sent the manuscript to Houghton Mifflin, and a few weeks later they cabled that they wanted to publish it."[64] Since translated into at least thirty-four languages, **The Painted Bird** won the Prix du Meilleur Livre Etranger in France and is recognized today as a masterpiece of modern literature.

While living on the edge of nightmare, the boy in Kosinski's first novel dreams of transformation. His dreams become real -- in later novels, when his adventures take him to a new world, to the pinnacle of American celebrity, to the apex of the American dream. As a "painted bird" much different from the brown flock around him, he soars to great heights -- above devil trees, beyond cockpits, on blind dates, into passion plays. But, if **The Painted Bird** is any indication, his flights -- though transcendent -- will never be smooth.

ENDNOTES TO CHAPTER THREE

1.   Attributed to Luis Bunuel and Anais Nin on the dustjacket and front flyleaf of the Bantam paperback edition of **The Painted Bird** (1972).

2.   Dorothy Seidman Bilik, in **Immigrant Survivors: Post-Holocaust Consciousness in Recent Jewish American Fiction** (Middletown, Connecticut: Wesleyan University Press, 1981), calls this type of novel "a Jewish Huck Finn."

3.   Jack Hicks, **In the Singer's Temple** (Chapel Hill: University of North Carolina Press, 1981), p. 195.

4.   James Sloan, "On Kosinski," **University Review,** No. 18 (Summer 1971), 1.

5.   Hicks, p. 196.

6.   David H. Richter, "The Three Denouements of Jerzy Kosinski's **The Painted Bird,**" **Contemporary Literature,** 15 (Summer 1974), 378.

7.   Jerzy Kosinski, **Notes of the Author** (New York: Scientia-Factum, Inc., 1965; 3rd ed., 1967), p. 14. Hereafter referred to as NA, with page number, in the text.

8.   Hicks, p. 196.

9.   Jerzy Kosinski, **The Painted Bird** (New York: Pocket Books, 1966), p. 52. All subsequent references will be made by page number in the text. This is the first trade paperback edition of **The Painted Bird** and in some ways the true first edition, since it restores the textual omissions made by the publisher of the clothbound edition (Boston: Houghton Mifflin, 1965). A later edition of **The Painted Bird** (New York: Modern Library, 1970) also incorporates "changes ... made by the author" which did not appear in the Houghton Mifflin edition.

10.   Hicks, p. 196.

11.   Arthur Miller, in a private letter to Jerzy Kosinski, cited on the front flyleaf of the Bantam paperback edition (1972) of **The Painted Bird** and in **Notes of the Author.**

12.   Richter, p. 373.

13.   Hicks, p. 197.

14.   Ibid.

15.   Carl G. Jung, "The Psychology of the Child Archetype," in Carl G. Jung and C. Kerenyi, **Essays on a Science of Mythology** (New York: Harper Torchbooks, 1963), transl. R. F. C. Hull, p. 73.

16.   Bruno Bettelheim, **The Uses of Enchantment: The Meaning and Importance of Fairy Tales** (Middlesex: Penguin Books, 1985), p. 5.

17.   J. R. R. Tolkien, **Tree and Leaf** (Boston: Houghton Mifflin, 1965), as cited in Bettelheim, p. 143.

18.   Bettelheim, pp. 144-145.

19.   Ibid., pp. 35, 146-147.

20.   Ibid., p. 10.

21.   **The Painted Bird**, p. 2, and also in **Notes of the Author**, pp. 21-25.

22.   Hicks, p. 200.

23.   Jung, p. 87.

24.   Hicks, p. 200.

25.   Frederick R. Karl, **American Fictions: 1940-1980** (New York: Harper and Row/Colophon Books, 1985), p. 154.

26.   Norman Lavers, **Jerzy Kosinski** (Boston: Twayne, 1982), p. 37.

27.   Possibly with reference to the bestial world of **The Painted Bird**, Kosinski used "The Jungle Book" as the code name and working title of his first novel. Kosinski mentioned

his use of the code name in an interview with George A. Plimpton and Rocco Landesman, published as "The Art of Fiction," **Paris Review,** 54 (Summer 1972), 200.

28.   Karl, p. 152.

29.   Ibid., p. 151.

30.   Meta Lale and John Williams, "The Narrator of **The Painted Bird:** A Case Study," **Renascence,** 24, No. 4 (Summer 1972), 199-200.

31.   Ibid., p. 200.

32.   Karl, p. 154.

33.   Paul Bruss, **Victims: Textual Strategies in Recent American Fiction** (Lewisburg: Bucknell University Press, 1981), p. 170.

34.   Ibid., p. 171.

35.   Hicks, p. 222.

36.   Karl, p. 154.

37.   Anne Halley, "Poor Boy Spreads His Wings," **Nation,** 29 November 1965, p. 425, argues persuasively for **The Painted Bird** as "anti-fairy-tale."

38.   Max F. Schulz, **Black Humor Fiction of the Sixties** (Athens: Ohio State University Press, 1973), p. 97.

39.   Karl, p. 154.

40.   Schulz, pp. 97, 112.

41.   Ivan Sanders, "The Gifts of Strangeness: Alienation and Creation in Jerzy Kosinski's Fiction," **The Polish Review,** 19, Nos. 3-4 (Autumn-Winter 1974), 173.

42.   Ibid.

43.   Lavers, p. 48.

44.   Sanders, p. 173.

45.   Karl, p. 151.

46.   Ibid.

47.   Sanders, p. 174.

48.   By definition, a picaresque novel is a chronicle, usually autobiographical, presenting the life story of a rascal who makes his living through his wits rather than industry. Episodic in nature, the picaresque novel is, in the usual sense of the term, structureless. The picaro, or central figure, through the nature of his various pranks and predicaments and by virtue of his associations with people of varying degree, affords the author an opportunity for satire on the social classes. Romantic in the sense of being an adventure story, the picaresque novel nevertheless is strongly marked by realistic methods in its faithfulness to petty details, its utter frankness of expression, and its drawing of incidents from low life (C. Hugh Holman, **A Handbook to Literature**, 3rd. ed. [Indianapolis: The Odyssey Press, 1972), pp. 391-392).

49.   Lavers, pp. 33-36.

50.   Geoffrey Movius, "An Interview with Jerzy Kosinski," **New Boston Review**, 1, No. 3 (Winter 1975), 4.

51.   Alfred Kazin, **Bright Book of Life: American Novelists and Storytellers from Hemingway to Mailer** (Boston: Little, Brown and Co., 1973), p. 235, as cited in Sanders, p. 187.

52.   John Updike, Review of **Being There, The New Yorker**, 25 Sept. 1971, p. 131, as cited in Sanders, p. 187.

53. Henryk Grynberg, **Child of the Shadows** (London: Vallentine, Mitchell, 1969), translated by Celina Wieniewska, p. 116.

54. Manfred Kridl, **A Survey of Polish Literature and Culture** (New York: Columbia Slavic Studies, 1956), p. 375.

55. Wladyslaw Reymont, **The Peasants** (New York: Alfred A. Knopf, 1942), transl. M. H. Dziewicki, pp. 281-282.

56. Henryk Sienkiewicz, **Pan Wolodyjowski** (Warsaw: Panstwowy Instytut Wydawniczy, 1955), p. 575. My translation.

57. Eliza Orzeszkowa, **Dziurdziowie** (Warsaw: Ksiazka i Wiedza, 1952), p. 370. My translation.

58. Jerome Klinkowitz, **Literary Disruptions** (Urbana: University of Illinois Press, 1975), p. 101. Also mentioned in Hicks, p. 198.

59. Hicks, p. 195.

60. Sanders, p. 182.

61. Hicks, p. 192.

62. Plimpton and Landesman, p. 196.

63. Ibid.

64. Ibid., p. 203.

CHAPTER FOUR

STEPS: KOSINSKI'S WINDING STAIR

> I see the purpose of any imaginative enterprise
> from poetry to photography, from fiction to
> drama and film, to hint at the various possibilities
> of change: emotional, physical, political, spiritual
> ... an awareness of the power of the individual,
> personal will to change one's life. And I think
> the instructive power of the destructive protagon-
> ist in fiction might be greater than that of
> a romantic "Fiddler-on-the Roof" type of charac-
> ter.

Jerzy Kosinski, **New Boston Review**

> Revenge can be a positive force -- the victim's
> final dignity.

Jerzy Kosinski, **Penthouse**

Jerzy Kosinski's second novel, **Steps,** published in 1968,
is a brilliant and experimental work which won the distinguished National Book Award and much critical acclaim.
An "essentially cinematic novel in the New Wave fashion,
a book composed of fragments of experience or splinters
of consciousness, having to do with a young man's odyssey
through yet another Grand Guignol world in which, all standards being dead, violence and perversity register on the
mind as unjudgable increments of the given -- mere data
in the mechanical procedure of being," it created, according
to John Aldridge, "not merely new but exceedingly bold
effects in a form in which the possibilities for adventure
have for many years seemed reduced, and recent experimental efforts have often resulted in a purely technical clever-

ness or the haphazard production of a mere grotesquerie."[1]
As an experimental work, it followed partly upon the "tradition of the new" that has dominated Western writing for
the past century; but it also deviated sharply in tone and
technique from that tradition. "A work highly problematic
in aesthetic strategy and moral implications," wrote Irving
Howe, "**Steps** is the kind of fiction a critic finds easy to evoke
but difficult to describe."[2]

An almost surrealistic study of absurdity and morality,
at once subtle and structurally sophisticated,[3] **Steps** recounts,
in a simple and deliberately unembellished style and in
the first-person, a narrative of young manhood. After all,
if **The Painted Bird** tells of the outrageous cruelties visited
upon a young boy attempting to survive the atrocities of
World War Two, then **Steps** follows somewhat logically
as a chronicle of the changes, perversions, and deformations
in character of that survivor.[4] The boy in **The Painted
Bird** is a contemporary Everyman who attempts to remain
whole despite the fragmentation of his identity and the
disintegration of his society. The narrator of **Steps** faces
a task just as compelling but even more difficult: he must
find "the most meaningful and fulfilling gesture" aimed
against the collective, against "those formerly protective
agencies like society and religion" which prevent the self
from functioning freely and move "towards the solitude
within which the self can display its reality."[5] But, in
The Painted Bird, the brutality of Eastern Europe was directly attributable to ignorance and poverty; in **Steps**, America's
social inhumanity, the casual barbarity of an impersonal,
technological civilization, is more gratuitous, more gamelike, more deliberate -- and therefore far more disquieting,[6]
like the narrator himself.

The episodes of **Steps** would seem to offer little solace
or solitude; they comprise a series of sexual aberrations
and acts -- including defloration, adultery, rape, incest,
brutality, gang bangs, homosexuality, prostitution -- which
blend into a kind of erotic symphony[7] and are counterbalanced by the violence of murder, suicide, and genocide.

Yet it is through this miasma of modern madness that the
narrator must venture in his search for the self, for the
peace and control described in the epigraph from the
Bhagavadgita. The epigraph ("For the uncontrolled there
is no wisdom, nor for the uncontrolled is there the power
of concentration; and for him without concentration there
is no peace. And for the unpeaceful, how can there be
happiness?"), like the dedication ("To my father, a mild
man"), serves as a counterpoint to what the narrator sees
and discovers, step by step.[8] He ultimately achieves a
degree of peace and control -- though he does so through
some unpeaceful and often chaotic means. Complete control,
however, eludes him (in the last scenes he is again the
victim of revolution, this time forced to slit the throats
of men he does not know); but, like the boy of **The Painted
Bird,** he learns that he must master the practices of his
environment if he is to survive and to persist in his quest
for the self.

According to Norman Lavers, Kosinski had planned **Steps**
to be his first novel.[9] But he decided that he was too close
to some of the events he wanted to portray in it, and so
in 1961 he began work on **The Painted Bird,** "his more
remote past."[10] Though **Steps** seems quite innovative in
its loose, almost structureless form, it is in many respects
similar to the nonfiction works, **The Future Is Ours, Comrade**
and **No Third Path** -- a series of episodes linked by a freely
moving first-person narrator who in each episode finds
himself in a different place, a different situation, interacting
with different people -- and to **The Painted Bird.** In fact,
suggests Lavers, "some of the episodes in **Steps** might actually have been episodes originally written for the nonfiction
books or **The Painted Bird** and later left out."[11]

The narrative method Kosinski chose for **Steps** is one which
immerses both author and reader "in the heart of the trauma
itself" (AS, pp. 35-36). Hence, writes Jerome Klinkowitz:

> many scenes from **The Painted Bird** -- copulation
> with beasts, castration, the cool revenge of

after passage of absolute stylistic control. But
Steps, like its predecessor, tells its own story,
too. Through forty apparently disconnected
episodes (structured in the manner of Vonnegut's
Tralfamadorian novel) Kosinski describes a
hero exploring his own reality and ability to
relate to others. Unity is ultimately derived
from the same source as **The Future Is Ours,
Comrade** and **No Third Path:** a young man, "at
the university," who journeys out to villages,
other cities, and finally to the United States,
relentlessly investigating the substance of human
behavior. He gives lessons in the power of
credit cards and learns the vulnerability of
poverty. He suffers under cruel masters and
becomes a master himself. Power and powerless-
ness, notions derived from the two worlds of
The Painted Bird and **No Third Path,** are the
tensions which create **Steps.**[12]

The vagrant boy who was everybody's victim[13] in **The Painted
Bird** seeks -- and finds -- revenge and control in **Steps.**
He poisons the villagers' children and then gazes "boldly
into my persecutors' eyes, provoking their assault and
maltreatment. I felt no pain. For each lash I received
my tormentors were condemned to pain a hundred times
greater than mine. Now I was no longer their victim; I
had become their judge and executioner" (p. 36). The children
become a means to an end -- never personalities in their
own right -- and are indispensable to him only because
they are instruments of his revenge (AS, p. 27). Similarly,
the university student, powerless to change the collective
"climate" in the nonfiction works, now uses the collective's
standards against itself. He ruins the career of an enemy
and improves his own position,[14] ironically by mastering
the system and working within it.

Yet in a very crucial way, **Steps** is different from all of
Kosinski's earlier works. The vignettes or episodes do not

follow the time sequence of the traditional novel, with an integrated movement of incidents so as to form a coherent action; they appear, instead, as a group of panels or tableaux in a juxtaposed simultaneity of recollection and fantasy. "The relationships among the panels of incident are," writes Howe, "apparently not meant to be 'spatial,' that is, to be perceived as if on a flat surface and thereby freed from the obligation of incremental narrative. Sequence is broken, causality dissolved, coherence imperiled."[15] Or, to use Frederick Karl's analogy, the episodes of **Steps** are like numerous, seemingly random, still photos, and the dimensions of the novel become the worlds of the photographer, who snaps "at each act of imbecility, bestiality, self-indulgence, as it passes before his camera."[16]

In **Steps,** form is content: the shattering of conventional narrative provides a clear parallel to the shattered self and the chaos and fragmentation caused by modern society. The opening vignette, for example, describes an orphan girl freed from her poverty by the narrator, who takes her as his companion. Brief as this introductory episode is, it nevertheless provides a sort of summary of -- or introduction to -- Kosinski's thematic concerns in **Steps:** metamorphosis, ritual, sex, commercialism, the search for identity, the ease with which the self can be usurped, the need for control. The nameless orphan is a familiar character type, reminiscent of the boy in **The Painted Bird,** and as recognizable as her aimless companion, the errant yet rootless traveller who shapes the destinies of others as well as his own. Seeking to escape her servitude, she ironically begins another servitude, both sexual and commercial, to a new and perhaps harsher master who controls her fate and by that control defines her happiness. Through him, she hopes to acquire an identity, a sense of being -- but she merely relinquishes her self. In her journey from innocence to awareness (neatly conveyed by her waking from sleep during her trip from her small village to a more metropolitan town), she is suspended for a moment between two nightmares: the sleeping nightmare of her past and the waking nightmare, with all of its uncertainty, of the future.

(Similarly, in a later episode, the narrator -- still travelling, though this time from his European home to his new world, America -- feels for one interminable moment "suspended forever between my past and my future" [p. 107]. Later still, while working as a trucker, the narrator must drive his truck through the dense streets, "my attention shifting from what lay ahead to what was happening in the rear" [p. 121].) Transformed, metamorphosed from a shabby village orphan to the well-heeled city companion of a man seemingly as wealthy as a "soccer player or movie star ... even a prelate" (pp. 6-7), the girl appears before the narrator as she thinks she ought to be. Her pose largely the result of her wardrobe -- her disguise -- she defines her new identity in terms of her man (much the way the woman in the dialogue scenes which punctuate the narrative episodes in **Steps** does). She has abandoned her self and her past and assumed -- uncomfortably -- the identity the narrator has given her.

Even more than his orphan companion, the narrator is journeying to self-awareness and discovery. The opening lines, "I was travelling farther south" (p. 3), suggest an inward movement and provide a referent (or one "objective correlative," as Kosinski -- borrowing from Eliot -- terms it in **The Art of the Self**) for the reader. "The beginning of **Steps** ... creates the place for the reader's entry into the book; as it now opens, the reader immediately becomes the wanderer. His own wisdom might lead him to suspect that in an age of limited and fixed purposes iconoclasm could well be the last gesture available before indifference" (AS, p. 14).

The various episodes which constitute the plot are thus reflexive; simply told and tightly controlled, they can stand alone -- unlike the separate vignettes in the nonfiction books which are much more dependent on the larger context in which they appear and are much more interesting as interrelated parts of a larger theme (the exposition of collective life and the debate between whether man is freer in the controlled society, where his goals are clearly

marked out for him, or in the totally free society, where
he must discover and set his own goals) than as distinct
units. Likewise, the vignettes in **The Painted Bird** all push
forward to the telling of a story of the boy's learning to
be a man and finally a human being despite the dehumanizing
circumstances of his society and his world.[17]

But the episodes in **Steps** are brief and largely self-contained.
About a man in search of his individual self, of simplicity,
of control, each provides a single step toward that self-
discovery. Perhaps for this reason, Kosinski himself feels
that **Steps** "facilitates the act of reading less" than do
any of his other works. "It offers 'steps,' but refuses to
tell whether it is a 'staircase' -- and if it is one, where
does it lead."[18] Indeed **Steps** forces the reader to discover
and then to make the connections -- just as the narrator
attempts to make the same connections -- by internalizing
and individualizing the experiences. Like the vignettes
of another great experimental work, Hemingway's **In Our
Time**, Kosinski's episodes require the reader to provide
an emotional correlative since they themselves betray
no response or judgment.

In the notes he made during the writing of **Steps,** Kosinski
stated that "'Steps' has no plot in the Aristotelian sense.
In Aristotle's terms for the revelation of action, the end
fulfills the beginning and the middle determines the end.
But the aim of **Steps** precludes such an ordering of time.
The relationship of the characters exists in the fissure
between the past and the present. And it is precisely between the past and present of the incidents of **Steps** that
the projected struggle takes place" (AS, p. 13). Since each
incident in **Steps** is "morally ambiguous," the reader can
be guided only to an area of experience. With "a hint of
recognition, an intimation -- no more," he must sift and
refine and ultimately digest the experience for himself.
Yet, continues Kosinski: "Given the reader's experiences
(in daily life they constitute the reader's armor in any encounter with a stranger), the reader may perceive the work
in a form of his own devising, automatically filling in its

intentionally loose construction with his own formulated experiences and fantasies.... This reception runs counter to that of the conventional melodrama which gains its effects from predetermined emotional group responses" (AS, p. 13). Kosinski's theory of the novel as it concerns **Steps** closely parallels Alain Robbe-Grillet's ideas on the new novel. Robbe-Grillet's cinematic hero, for example, dreamed of the existential self, constantly creating itself in the act of writing, but made sure that act -- doubling, repeating, modifying -- finally denied itself fixity and refused to permit a story, a past, or a history to accumulate.[19] Of his novel, **Jealousy** (1957), Robbe-Grillet wrote: "It was absurd to suppose that in the novel there existed a clear and unambiguous order of events, one which was not that of the sentences of the book, as if I had diverted myself by mixing up a pre-established calendar the way one shuffles a deck of cards. The narrative was on the contrary made in such a way that any attempt to reconstruct an external chronology would lead, sooner or later, to a series of contradictions, hence to an impasse. There existed for me no possible order outside that of the book. The latter was not a narrative mingled with a single anecdote external to itself, but again the very unfolding of a story which had no other reality than that of the narrative, an occurrence which functioned nowhere else except in the mind of the invisible narrator, in other words of the writer, and of the reader."[20] Extending the theory of his novel to the new novel as a whole, Robbe-Grillet states that: "Far from neglecting him, the author today proclaims his absolute need of the reader's cooperation, an active, conscious, creative assistance. What he asks of him is no longer to receive ready-made a world completed, full, closed upon itself, but on the contrary to participate in a creation, to invent in his turn the work -- and the world -- and thus to invent his own life."[21]

It is little wonder that Kosinski's fiction is often compared to the novels of Robbe-Grillet -- and to those of other experimental, new, or anti-novelists such as Sarraute in France, Gunter Grass in Germany, William Golding in

England, and John Hawkes, Donald Barthelme, and John
Barth in the United States. As John Aldridge and other
critics have demonstrated, Kosinski's work cannot be fully
understood in isolation from that of those other modern
novelists.

Yet while many parallels may be drawn between Kosinski
and other new novelists, it is especially interesting to note
some of the structural and thematic resemblances between
Steps and Barth's **Lost in the Funhouse,** also first published
in 1968. The latter, like **Steps,** is a collection of short
stories and episodes -- thirteen to be exact -- with a thematic
unity and a narrative chronology which depicts the protagonist Ambrose's search for identity as an individual and as
a writer.

The title symbol of the funhouse, like Borges' garden of
forking paths and Kosinski's steps, is a metaphor for the
labyrinths of existence. But unlike Borges, whose perfect
designs are intended as analogues of defective myth and
the metaphysical systems of cosmic order, Barth seizes
upon the mirror room of the funhouse, and on Ambrose's
"coming of age" there, as a rendering of modern man's
search through the distortions and "endless replications
of his image in the mirrors" for ontological confirmation
of his existence. Like Kosinski, Barth assumes a persona
who wants to find in the form of his story a sign, of sorts,
of his ontological security.[22]

Yet Barth's mirror room, a kind of collective nightmare,
can only reflect the appearance of the person presented
to it. Ambrose's perception, instead of winding "around
on itself ... like the snakes on Mercury's caduceus," moves
outward. The world lies all before him, few memories
behind him.[23] The funhouse itself offers no answers; "though
he would rather be among the lovers for whom the funhouses
are designed," Ambrose must "construct funhouses for
others and be their secret operator." By contrast, Kosinski's
narrator's perception moves both outward and inward; he
is able to see in others a reflection of himself so that all

selves mirror his own. But, as Ambrose must, he finds
his way out of the funhouse -- the mirror maze of modern
society -- by becoming the secret operator of the funhouses
he constructs for others. In his seduction of young girls
with his credit card wealth, his feeding of ground glass
and fishhooks to children whose parents have wronged him,
and his stoning of the old watchman, he forces others to
play a game according to his rules. "In the face of faith
lost and in a universe unmasked in its indifference, collective
values" are enforced, writes Kosinski in **The Art of the
Self.** "The protagonist of **Steps** is aware of this and to
him the most meaningful and fulfilling gesture is negative;
it is aimed against the collective and is a movement towards
the solitude" of the real self. So the protagonist, going
to the edge of despair, seeks the "true gesture outside
the society" and creates his own reality (AS, p. 40). Not
content with superficial reflections, he penetrates his own
and others' psyches in given situations of his own creation.
("I covertly watched the woman's face reflected in mirrors:
her face split into fragments" [p. 141], the narrator tells
us. Another time, he makes love to a woman in a mirror,
never physically touching his partner or being touched
by her [pp. 16-17]. His lovemaking is psychological, imagined
-- and therefore strangely more gratifying.) He is more
mature than Ambrose, more sexually aware, haunted by
memories which Ambrose lacked -- but, while sometimes
equally unsure of his psychological reality, he is more ready
to act. The steps he takes are (like Barth's funhouse) clever
fictional conceptions, inventive objective correlatives
of a pointless universe -- an almost Borgian labyrinthine
universe peopled by men who are fallible, impermanent
and shadowy, and without inviolable selfness or persistent
personality; a universe infinitely vast but regressing ad
infinitum in time, in space, in human history.[24] The steps
do not lead the reader up or down, inside or out -- merely
round and round, like the author's reflexive images (the
octopus feeding on its own flesh, the copulating man-beast,
the homosexual prostitute) or the narrator's photographs.
They become Kosinski's equivalent of Barth's Moebius strip
in "Frame Tale": "Once upon a time there was a story that

began once upon a time there was a story that began once upon a time...."

Kosinski has clearly been energized by the post-avant-garde iconoclasm of writers like Robbe-Grillet or Barth, and there are elements in his work that undoubtedly would not be present if it were not for the influence of the black humor and French New Novel schools of writing.[25] Yet, as Aldridge observes, Kosinski "differs from both in the important respect that his vision is primarily philosophical. Kosinski is interested not in making a satirical indictment of modern society ... nor in attempting to explore in the French manner the various possible ways of dramatizing individual consciousness. He is concerned rather with understanding the nature and meaning of the human condition, the relation, quite simply, of human values to the terms of existence in an essentially amoral and surely anarchistic universe."[26] Thus, concludes Aldridge, whereas Kosinski may have learned something of value from those of his contemporaries who work experimentally with the novel form, his greatest teachers appear to be Kafka, Camus, Sartre, and possibly Dostoevsky, men who possessed not only unusual creative power but the ability to deal directly with concepts of being -- in the largest sense, with ideas -- and to use them in their fiction as concrete modes of dramatic action. "This has always been the strength of the later European novel: that in it ideas are as important as physical sensations and may even be experienced with all the force and acuteness of physical sensations. And this also is a quality the American novel has almost completely lacked, if only because it is a part of our frontier mythology to believe that ideas belong to one sphere of perceptions and sensations to another -- ideas to pallid and passive thought, sensations to the life of real men in the real world of robust action."[27] Though Kosinski claims he feels little literary kinship with Kafka ("I hate Kafka," he exasperatedly told one European reporter),[28] certain clearly existential qualities define his protagonist and ally him to the characters created by Kafka as well as by Camus, Sartre, and Dostoevsky.

Like the young boy in **The Painted Bird** and almost all of
the protagonists in the later novels, the narrator of **Steps**
is trapped in a world of dissolving meaning in which there
are few fragments to shore up against his ruin.[29] Even
in this darkly irrational universe, he is an outsider. In his
native land, the narrator believed in the importance of
the individual, and his search for self-awareness and realization placed him apart from the collective. In America,
he is still a stranger in a strange land, and his American
dream becomes a nightmare. As an immigrant unfamiliar
with the American language, customs, and mores, he is
unable to assimilate himself into his new environment,
which thus becomes as hostile to him as the one he left
behind. At one point in **Steps**, the narrator describes the
fur coat he has brought with him from Europe. The long,
clumsy coat becomes a marvelously apt Gogolian symbol
of his feelings of strangeness and isolation. Just as the
coat deteriorates (its skin cracks, its fur becomes matted),
so his past life begins to appear remote and useless.[30]
Just as Turkey in Melville's "Bartleby" is unable to work
comfortably in the waistcoat which his employer provides
for him, Kosinski's narrator's coat is as inappropriate and
as burdensome as the past from which he wishes to sever
himself, yet which clings as tenaciously to his present as
do "the gummy particles of paint, growing stiffer and heavier
by the hour" to his fur (p. 112).

"Everything and the only thing that the protagonist of **Steps**
is aware of," writes Kosinski in **The Art of the Self**, "is
his self, and that is ephemeral. He knows himself by hints,
by allusions; he approaches and steps away from himself;
he looks for himself in others" (AS, p. 16). Therefore, he
seeks out new situations and acts always with the fullest
comprehension of his own awareness. He is, in Kosinski's
words, "anti-acting in the sense that he creates each situation
rather than being a reactor in it" (AS, p. 16).

For a while after his arrival in the United States, the narrator
attempts to lose himself. He imagines a variety of escapes.
Looking into the porthole of an old ship whose rusty paint

he is scraping, he wishes for a sea flight and a sea change (typical of fellow Pole Joseph Conrad's protagonists). "I longed to be the only passenger on that deserted ship, protected all about by steel walls, able to sleep and then awaken to some faraway sea, my identity gone, my destination uncharted" (p. 112).

Socially disenfranchised yet wishing to belong, to identify with another group, he travels into the black ghettoes where he "wait[s] for the midnight" (p. 134). The dark of night parallels his personal crisis, his moment of existential midnight. Desperate to escape the impersonality of mass civilization as well as his own cluttered, oppressive past,[31] he imagines himself metamorphosing into a black. "If I could magically speak their language and change the shade of my skin, the shape of my skull, the texture of my hair, I would transform myself into one of them. This way I would drive away from me the image of what I had once been and what I might become; would drive away the fear of the law which I had learned, the idea of what failure meant, the yardstick of success; would banish the dream of possession, of things to be owned, used, and consumed, and the symbols of ownership -- credentials, diplomas, deeds. This change would give me no other choice but to remain alive" (p. 133).

Thus transformed, he would "hold my knife against the back of a doorman, yawning in his gold-frogged uniform, and force him to lead me up the stairs, where I would plunge my knife into his body. I would visit the rich and the comfortable and the unaware, and their last screams would suffocate in their ornate curtains, old tapestries, and priceless carpets. Their dead bodies, pinned down by broken statues, would be gazed upon by slashed family portraits." And in the morning -- only in the morning, like the characters in Hemingway's "A Clean, Well-Lighted Place" -- he would sleep, "smiling in the face of the day, the brother of my enemy" (pp. 134-135).

As a Polish Jew who survived the Nazi Occupation, Kosinski
surely feels a spiritual kinship with Black Americans as
an oppressed minority class and relates to them because,
through their heritage and experiences, they understand
alienation. (William Styron draws a similar parallel in
Sophie's Choice. Stingo, the young writer loosely based
on Styron, is able to "buy" the freedom to write as a result
of his inheritance -- a legacy of slave profits, much like
Ike McCaslin's legacy in **Go Down, Moses.** The issue, blacks
enslaved by whites, parallels the emerging story of Sophie's
life, shaped by the enslavement and persecution of Jews
and Poles under Hitler and the impossibility of breaking
with a past which haunts and torments her.) Frederick
Karl suggests another analogy: the hunted Jewish boy in
Eastern Europe as a counterpart of the hunted black in
Richard Wright's South Side of Chicago.[32]

But whereas the narrator merely imagines metamorphosing
into a black, other metamorphoses are actual. Possibly
the most significant way that he achieves so many
transformations is by changing languages -- and, at times,
by surrendering language completely. Wronged by a fellow
student at the university, he adopts the special language
of the State. Using the voice of his military commander,
he telephones the student, who is temporarily in charge
of the guard, and orders him to attack a city arsenal. The
student obeys and is arrested for his action.[33] Later in
the book, after arriving in America, the narrator has a
fantasy: he wishes to be "magically" transformed and able
to wage war against the city, its "libraries," its "clever
networks of pipes and cables and wires," its "communication
stations." He would make the city his victim (as the city
has made him its victim) by capturing its language: "I would
lift the steel lids from the gutters and drop explosives
into the black pits. And then I would run away and hide,
waiting for the thunder which would trap in mute telephone
wires millions of unheard words, which would darken rooms
full of white light and fearful people" (p. 134). The unheard
words, trapped in telephone wires suddenly made mute,
would become his prisoners.[34]

Though he is unable to render the whole city mute, he manages to become silent himself. He discards language entirely to assume the pose of a deaf mute. No longer the involuntary response of a victim to his hostile environment (as in **The Painted Bird**), the narrator's voluntary mutism is liberating. "The abandonment of linguistic expression signifies his desire to rely on the power of gesture; his destiny is thus made and not expressed. This secession from language," explains Kosinski in **The Art of the Self**, "performs a further function in **Steps:** it increases the moral ambiguity of the work in which the reality is always manipulated and seldom judged" (AS, p. 19). Whereas for others deprivation of language is a sign of victimization (the speechless woman in the cage, the "Philosopher" who philosophizes only in his toilet temple),[35] for the narrator it is a form of control. He even seeks out victims who will be taken in by his muteness. One woman, who hires him to perform domestic labor, eventually becomes his lover and so comes under his silent dominance. The narrator thus "masters" still another language -- the pent-up eloquence of the woman,[36] who feels free to speak only because she believes her words cannot be heard: "In her last outpouring she broke into a language I could understand, and spoke of herself as a zealot entering a church built long ago from the ruins of pagan temples ... she cried out again and again and again, as though trying to detach into speech what had been fused with her flesh" (p. 142). The woman's passionate flow of words constitutes the self she has kept hidden until this moment, but she does what the narrator always avoids -- she exposes her identity by her language and becomes, unknowingly, a victim of this master of all of her words.[37]

Yet, while it often affords him control, the narrator's quest for self sometimes reveals his incompleteness. As Kosinski remarked in a 1975 interview with Geoffrey Movius, "Awareness of the self must eventually lead to an awareness of one's deformities -- physical and psychological. Each of us is deformed; nobody is 'perfectly average.' Sickness deforms us; age deforms us. Social conditions, employment, accidents -- all work specific distortions."[38] Thus, contemporary fiction often uses the disease motif, especially a wasting disease, to reflect the social and spiritual malaise. Because "the bourgeois self is so caught up in abstract existence, so barely possessed of itself, so diseased," says Kosinski, "it is continually tempted to relinquish itself altogether and to let the remnants of its social awareness wither away" (AS, p. 30). For Camus, this malaise took the form of the plague; for Sartre, nausea; for Gunter Grass's deformed narrator in **The Tin Drum,** dwarfishness; for the "fictional-nonfictional" contemporary American novelists, it is the dark desires and perverse fantasies which erupt in violence. In **Steps,** Kosinski uses consumption. The sanatorium episode, writes Kosinski, "profiles the curious symbolic mating of the professionally healthy (the ski instructors) and the chronically unhealthy (the tubercular patients). In embracing the diseased, the instructors embrace the primordial human predicament. They manifest the intrinsic relationship of the erotic and the heinous, of sex and death." But since, in their desires, the instructors are sadists and the patients masochists, there can be no sense of the "heightened self" which results from the "willing relinquishment" of two single selves, "simultaneously subject and object" (AS, pp. 30-31).

Occasionally, the deformity takes other forms -- for example, a consumption more spiritual than literal. While acting as an archeologist's assistant, the narrator finds himself stranded and penniless on an island; he is forced to beg help from two women. "Folds of gray, heavily veined fat hung from their thighs and upper arms; their full, pendulous breasts were squashed in outsize brassieres" (p. 10). Prostituting himself for food -- as he had earlier prostituted the orphan girl with his credit card purchases -- he is soon virtually consumed by the women, "buried beneath their heavy bellies and broad backs," his arms pinioned and his body "manipulated, squeezed, pressed, and thumped" (p. 11). Another time, as overwhelmed by curiosity as the village peasants are consumed by lust, he watches a young girl copulate with an animal. "The peasants, still refusing to believe that the girl could survive violation, eagerly paid again and again" (p. 21). (A similar curiosity allows him to observe -- but not to release -- the deranged woman confined for the sexual pleasure of villagers.) While visiting an aquarium, he observes an octopus nibbling "at its own tentacles, consuming them one after another" and "slowly killing itself" (p. 22). Later, unable to make love to a beautiful mistress, he approaches a thickly painted and shapeless woman who makes love to him as he would make love to himself. His partner turns out to be a man; the pleasure no longer the same, he realizes "All we could do was to exist for each other solely as a reminder of the self" (p. 24). Young soldiers willingly risk mutilation for life during a game of "Knights of the Round Table." When they become aware that they have been cheated, the "knights" take their guilty comrades into the woods and slowly crush each of their victims' parts between two rocks until the flesh "bccame an unrecognizable pulp" (p. 25).

In **Steps,** freedom equals power, control. Like the narrator himself, the equation assumes many disguises in the narrative experience: murderer and victim; seducer and seduced; master and servant; photographer and subject; hunter and prey; sniper and victim.[39] The equation exists even -- perhaps especially -- in his amorous adventures. The narrator begins as lover, but his love becomes possession: he becomes a cannibalizing self, a hyena of sorts (as the nun in the sanatorium calls him), preying upon the women he beds. In seduction as in mating, he never loses his being; rather, he consciously uses the experiences to define, illuminate, and expand his sense of self (and -- in the final episode -- to expand his partner's sense of herself) and pursues his beloved like a scientist after a specimen.[40]

Kosinski claims that "from the viewpoint of the protagonist of **Steps,** the only truly satisfying relationship, then, is one of growing domination, one in which his experience -- a certain form of the past -- can be projected onto the other person" (AS, p. 20). The narrator becomes intimate with one of the "strangers" in his apartment after installing listening devices and monitoring her voice. Once privy to her past, he controls her. "When the narrator has become so intimately involved with this woman that he has succeeded in unburdening himself and grafting his past onto her, when the relationship no longer has any valid function," writes Kosinski, "then he no longer needs her, since the forms of his past and her effort to discard them were the basis of his need." So the woman becomes part of his past, which he must discard. "Since his past has transferred to another being, he assumes that its cancerous action will continue in the other person. It was a necessary act because his past was crippling him, preventing him from acting fully in the present" (AS, pp. 20-21).

Sexual encounters assume a gamelike quality throughout **Steps,** but love is only one of the many games in which the narrator participates or which he observes. As an especially imaginative being, the narrator becomes conscious of the need to engage himself deliberately "in games that will not only shock his inherited moral sensibility but also, as a consequence, nudge him toward a deeper appreciation of the processes of his being."[41] In the game of "Knights of the Round Table," soldiers conceal their pain behind a mask of heroism. But their heroism is false, as false as the rules by which "King Arthur" plays. Their maimed organs mock the notion of knighthood and the sexuality associated with it.[42] Their heroism is therefore reduced to mere prostitution, like the young girl's copulation with an animal before a crowd of peasants. (In that episode, colored bows, an inch apart, are tied to the animal's erect organ, and the peasants must pay for each additional inch of the animal's involvement. But in actuality the girl's sexual stunts, reminiscent of the well-rehearsed routine of the trapeze artist in a later scene, are less bestial than the mock heroics of the knights -- and her pain probably less genuine than theirs.) Wisely, the narrator is not a participant in but merely an observer of these incidents.

Interspersed among all the vignettes are italicized conversations between an unnamed man and woman. These conversations, always relayed in the present tense, occur just before or just after their acts of sex. Each dialogue is no more than a fragment, yet in their totality the fragments tell a story: they chronicle the progressive developments in the relationship between the two. They also relate -- though sometimes in a subtle way -- to the episodes which constitute the major action of the volume. For Kosinski, the dialogues and episodes work together; he writes, "The passages of dialogue within the novel abbreviate and articulate the action, insinuating visual and emotive activity. These fragments of conversations may be viewed simply as one more example of the protagonist's past, as his recall of verbalized imtimacies. Or they may be considered another self's reactions to what the narrator said in the book. In either case they indicate why the narrator-memorist selects certain incidents from his life, and what impact he expects to achieve -- or has already achieved -- as a result of telling his story" (AS, p. 19).

In the first of these italicized conversations, the woman questions the man about his circumcision. She ponders the cruelty of such "mutilation" and suggests that circumcision is responsible for making men less sensitive and responsive. A topic not usually appropriate for social discussion, Kosinski intentionally focuses on it only, to use the narrator's later analogy, to study it as a scientist would an experiment, to observe and to record and to analyze it until it ceases to be a mystery. This situation occurs again when the man and woman discuss sex during menstruation -- and yet again when the woman speaks of oral sex. She recalls being warned against such sex when she was a schoolgirl:

> I was taught that if a woman did it, some dreadful punishment, a foul disease or a deformity, would befall her: some of my friends claimed the taste of it was horrible, oily, slimy, lumpy ...

and besides, it was degrading, almost like eating living flesh. (p. 82)

She remembers also going to confession to receive absolution from the priest and confessing her guilt over the <u>thoughts</u> of fellatio while remaining unrepentant for the <u>acts</u> of oral sex in which she had engaged. This semantic game -- confessing the thought but not confessing or regretting the act -- is typical of her self-deception and her restriction by both language and custom.

Her word play continues when she discusses her involvement with another man during the narrator's absence. Arguing that she had an obligation to know herself better, apart from the self which the narrator had brought her to know, she acknowledges that she "spent time" with a man but that, as a result of this brief acquaintance, she is sure of her love for the narrator. She hid the truth about the relationship from him until now but no longer wants "to be separated by an experience" he knows nothing about. He, too, admits to hiding something: during her liaison, he had had her under surveillance. Her every contact had been monitored, including the nights she spent with the other man. Although her deception is exposed, she still rationalizes and protests that sleeping with the other man was not making love. It was merely a test, she claims: "An act of intercourse is not a commitment unless it stems from a particular emotion and a certain frame of mind. It wasn't an act based on love; but I had to make sure, in order to discover myself, whether it would lead to love" (p. 46). Pretty rhetoric perhaps, but the indiscretion, rationalized as an act of self-awareness, is just the contrary; it is a deception and, more importantly, a self-deception. Moreover, when the tables are turned and the narrator admits to her his own relationships with prostitutes, she is jealous and does not understand his need for such sexual attachments.

But possibly the most disturbing passage in the book is a conversation about designing concentration camps. Like the narrator's liaison with a prostitute and the woman's involvement with another man, this conversation is a test -- possibly the ultimate test -- of neutralization, of demystification. Describing his friend's work, the narrator explains: "He designs highly functional buildings where style is secondary: hospitals, schools, prisons, funeral parlors, clinics for animals." The architect's first assignment after graduating university was to draw up plans for a concentration camp. It was indeed a difficult project, not because of the camp's hideous purpose but "because there were so few precedents," which made the task "all the more challenging."

> Nevertheless, it was just a project. You could look at it from many points of view: in a maternity hospital, for instance, more people leave than arrive; in a concentration camp the reverse is true. Its main purpose is hygiene.
>
> Hygiene? What do you mean?
>
> Have you ever seen rats being exterminated? Or, better -- do you like animals?
>
> Of course.
>
> Well, rats are also animals.
>
> Not really. I mean they're not domestic animals. They're dangerous, and therefore they have to be exterminated.
>
> Exactly: they have to be exterminated; it's a problem of hygiene. Rats have to be removed. We exterminate them, but this has nothing to do with our attitudes towards cats, dogs, or any other animal. Rats aren't murdered -- we get rid of them; or, to use a better word, they are eliminated; this act of elimination is empty of all meaning. There's no ritual

in it, no symbolism; the right of the executioner is never questioned. That's why in the concentration camps my friend designed, the victims never remained individuals; they became as identical as rats. They existed only to be killed. (pp. 63-64)

The narrator is obviously using words in a way far more clever and devastating than his companion did in rationalizing her love affair. He is using them to reduce -- or to neutralize -- the horror of the concentration camp exterminations. Rats, he argues, are not useful to society; thus they are eliminated. The man who succeeds in building a better mousetrap -- or, in this case, the more efficient rat trap -- performs a worthy social service. If certain undesirables are not useful to Nazi society, they are eliminated. The man who succeeds in providing a more efficient and effective means of disposing of such undesirables also provides a worthy service. Furthermore, since his task has few precedents, his accomplishment is that much more exemplary; the architect's design is a tribute to his "exceptional vision." By this reasoning the builder of camps is no more a murderer than the good soldier who performs well in battle by eliminating the enemies of his land. From Kosinski's perspective, then, "the test of the passage is whether the reader possesses enough imagination to accept, if only momentarily, the physical neutrality of the camp as an architectural project. Such acceptance is important, for it allows the reader, much like the viewer of minimal sculpture in the 1960s, the opportunity to reconsider the 'grammar' of his own perception and thus the textual character that grounds his very self."[43]

Undoubtedly, it is the narrator who is the real gamesman of the pair; his games, though, go beyond words. His ongoing game with the woman is a function of his desire to season her perspective, to educate her with the privileged insight he possesses, to encourage her toward increasingly sophisticated moments of demystification and neutralization[44] which she has not reached on her own. He tries to provide

her an opportunity to turn her own life into a game where
the object is not only to sabotage the old rules of language
and context but also to make the acts of sabotage the basis
for a deeper and more sophisticated understanding of
herself.[45] Yet it is he who is the controlling force. In
addition to employing detectives to watch her (just as he
had eavesdropped on the lives of his fellow tenants in his
apartment house), he considers introducing her to drugs
so that she might become addicted, "might free herself
from what she had been. She might emerge as a very
different woman, and though I retained possession of her,
my knowledge of what she had been would have no more
value. A new relationship would begin ... she would expand
and develop in unpredictable directions" (p. 130). He
encourages her to touch and to stimulate herself while
they make love, to become more aware of her body. She
does what he bids, but she protests that "all you need me
for is to provide a stage on which you can project and view
yourself, and see how your discarded experiences become
alive again when they affect me" (p. 131).

Once she is under his control -- in love with him -- she
(like the woman in his apartment building) ceases to be
a mystery; she no longer has a function in his life. He
becomes increasingly impatient with her inability to make
the quick adjustments that match up with the configuration
of his own perspective. Eventually, having failed in a series
of gamelike gestures to impress upon the woman her need
for a larger and more sophisticated grasp of the essential
human predicament, he comes to regard his very departure
as the one last available gesture that might create the
necessary impact.[46]

> When I'm gone, I'll be for you just another memory
> descending upon you uninvited, stirring up your
> thoughts, confusing your feelings. And then
> you'll recognize yourself in this woman. (p.
> 146)

His departure might reflect a mere pique of frustration, but in the context of the subsequent and final episode of **Steps** a better explanation becomes apparent. Having exposed the woman to a number of his games of demystification and neutralization, the narrator probably also suspects that upon his departure she will be unable to return to the easy sentimentality of her past.[47] For him, then, she becomes the ultimate game.

In the last episode of **Steps,** the only scene in the book which is recounted in the third person rather than in the first person, and also the only scene in which the woman and not the narrator is the focus, she discovers that the narrator has left the hotel in which they were staying. His message to the hall porter was simply that he won't be back. Alone, unsure of whether to stay on or to leave as well, she finally undresses and goes for a swim in the ocean. She swims deep, well beneath the surface. "On the bottom a shadow glided over the seaweed, lending life and motion to the ocean floor. She looked up through the water to find its source and caught sight of the tiny leaf that had touched her before" (p. 148).

The focus, now shifted from the narrator, is on the woman. Is she drowning? Is she symbolically exploring the recesses of the self, submerged under rotten and rotting layers of language and tradition? Is the tiny leaf that had touched her before symbolic of the awareness which the narrator had sought to share with her? Ultimately, the reader must interpret the action for himself -- this being, one could argue, precisely Kosinski's intent: to stimulate in the reader the woman's sense of self-discovery.

But Norman Lavers suggests that the final scene is a suicide. Noting that Kosinski was severely traumatized by water as a child, when he was pushed under the ice of a river, Lavers assumes that the final sentence of **Steps** shows the woman diving under the water after being deserted by her man -- in other words, committing suicide. He cites a passage from **The Art of the Self** on suicide as "an act

of the present. In performing it a man chooses to escape
from his future and from his past, thus overcoming the
knowledge that he will die. By suicide, he takes over a
natural function. To die in nature's time is to accede to
a denial of man's dignity: to die in one's own time is to
affirm that dignity."[48] Since suicide is a choice, by choosing,
the woman has acted. Thus, for Lavers, the ending is positive:
a freeing of herself from the narrator's domination and
an assertion of the primacy of her self.[49]

Kosinski, however, claims that the passage on suicide in
The Art of the Self was a philosophic digression not related
to the situation in the ending of **Steps**. Moreover, the final
dive was not a suicidal one. Says Kosinski:

> I have not intended to portray or even to insinuate
> a suicide here. Indeed, I see it as the heroine's
> reaffirmation of her independence from the
> "steps" she has "walked" till now. Taking a
> deep breath (a sign of control, of life, isn't
> it?) she dives beneath the surface (merely beneath
> the surface -- does not throw herself in the
> depths!) -- she then looks up to find the source
> of the shadow and finds it above (read behind)
> her: nothing more than a tiny leaf that had
> touched her before -- but does not touch her
> anymore. Hence, she is free, her past a source
> of perceivable impression -- but no more than
> a shadow lending life and motion![50]

Steps is the first of several of Kosinski's books to end on,
in, or near water, an element which has long fascinated
Kosinski -- and proved fearful to him. More recently, though,
Kosinski seems to have mastered it. As he writes and demonstrates in photographs for **Life** magazine, it is now possible
for him to levitate in water for hours at a time. He acquired
his new skill while vacationing in Bangkok and observing
a middle-aged Thai enter a swimming pool and "float upright
as if standing on a transparent shelf."

The anecdote, from this point, sounds almost apocryphal and certainly reminiscent of Kosinski's own fictions, especially of one of the episodes in **Steps.**

> "Excuse me," I asked perplexed. "Why don't you sink?"
>
> "Why should I?" said the man. "I don't want to."
>
> "Then why don't you swim?"
>
> "I don't want to swim," said the man.
>
> "What do you do to buoy yourself like that?" I asked.
>
> "Can't you see?" said the man. "I do nothing."
>
> "But what's the trick?" I asked, watching his every move.
>
> "Being oneself. That's the trick... "
>
> "But when I'm myself and do nothing, I drown," I objected.
>
> "To drown is to do something," said the man. "Do nothing. Be yourself!"
>
> "Easily said! Is there a place where I could learn it?" I asked.
>
> "There is," he replied, a bit impatient. "Water."[51]

If Kosinski has come a long way, from fearing water to mastering it, so also has his protagonist come a long way, from fear of his environment to near mastery of it. No "mere disembodied voice howling in some surrealistic wilderness,"[52] as one critic has suggested, the narrator of **Steps** is finally a contemporary Everyman, metamorphosing as he climbs the winding stair in search of an elusive self. Relying on no external morality, no group, only on himself, he quests to understand that self, a self at once cunning, murderous, perverse, erotic, detached.[53] His steps are almost balletic, as he moves expertly "through the anarchy of cruelty, barbarism, appetites, which constitute modern life."[54] Without those steps, though, he would be only a victim; with steps, he can command his own presence, counterattack, and observe.[55] The young boy, victimized so often in **The Painted Bird**, has grown to manhood in **Steps** -- and will be a victim no more.

ENDNOTES TO CHAPTER FOUR

1. John W. Aldridge, "The Fabrication of a Culture Hero," **Saturday Review**, 24 April 1971, p. 25.

2. Irving Howe, "From the Other Side of the Moon," **Harpers**, March 1969, p. 102.

3. Arthur Curley, rev. of **Steps, Library Journal**, 15 Sept. 1968, p. 3156.

4. Jerome Klinkowitz, **Literary Disruptions** (Urbana: University of Illinois Press, 1975), p. 91.

5. Jerzy Kosinski, **The Art of the Self: Essays à propos Steps** (New York: Scientia-Factum, 1968), pp. 40, 22. Hereafter referred to as AS, with page number, in the text.

6. Ivan Sanders, "The Gifts of Strangeness: Alienation and Creation in Jerzy Kosinski's Fiction," **The Polish Review**, 19, Nos. 3-4 (Autumn-Winter 1974), 176.

7.   John J. McAleer, rev. of **Steps, Best Sellers,** 1 Nov. 1968, p. 316.

8.   Howe, p. 105.

9.   This is a situation which recurred with the writing of **The Devil Tree,** originally published in 1973 and revised and expanded in 1981. In his "Author's Note" to **The Devil Tree: Newly Revised and Expanded Edition** (New York: St. Martin's Press, 1981), Kosinski explains: "When I wrote this novel initially, I felt restricted by the proximity of its story to the environment and events of my recent past decade. This might account for the cryptic tone of the novel's first version." But, "Now, years later, in this revised and expanded edition, I have felt free to reinstate all the additional links that bound Jonathan Whalen to those whom he loved."

10. Norman Lavers, **Jerzy Kosinski** (Boston: Twayne, 1982), p. 58.

11. Ibid., p. 60.

12. Klinkowitz, pp. 91-92.

13. Jerzy Kosinski, **Steps** (New York: Random House, 1968), pp. 36-37. All subsequent references to this edition will be made by page number in the text.

14. Klinkowitz, p. 92.

15. Howe, pp. 102-103.

16. Frederick R. Karl, **American Fictions: 1940-80** (New York: Harper and Row/Colophon Paperbacks, 1985), p. 405.

17. Lavers, pp. 60-61.

18. Ibid., p. 58.

19.   Jack Hicks, **In the Singer's Temple** (Chapel Hill: University of North Carolina Press, 1981), p. 228.

20.   Alain Robbe-Grillet, **For a New Novel: Essays on Fiction**, trans. Richard Howard (New York: Grove Press, 1965), p. 154.

21.   Ibid., p. 156.

22.   Max F. Schultz, **Black Humor Fiction of the Sixties** (Athens: Ohio University Press, 1973), p. 33.

23.   Ibid., p. 35.

24.   Ibid., pp. 36, 133-34.

25.   Aldridge, p. 25.

26.   Ibid.

27.   Ibid., p. 26.

28.   William Kennedy, "Who Here Doesn't Know How Good Kosinski Is?" **Look**, 20 April 1971, p. 12.

29.   Daniel J. Cahill, "Jerzy Kosinski: Retreat from Violence," **Twentieth Century Literature**, 18 (April 1972), 121.

30.   Sanders, p. 176.

31.   Ibid.

32.   Karl, p. 84.

33.   Paul R. Lilly, Jr. "Jerzy Kosinski: Words in Search of Victims," **Critique**, 22, No. 2 (1980-81), 73.

34.   Ibid.

35. Ibid., p. 72.

36. Ibid., p. 74.

37. Ibid.

38. Geoffrey Movius, "An Interview with Jerzy Kosinski," **New Boston Review**, 1, No. 3 (Winter 1975), 4.

39. Hicks, p. 232.

40. Ibid., pp. 229, 232.

41. Paul Bruss, **Victims: Textual Strategies in Recent American Fiction** (Lewisburg: Bucknell University Press, 1981), pp. 190-91.

42. Ibid., p. 188.

43. Ibid., pp. 184-85.

44. Ibid., p. 192.

45. Ibid., p. 193.

46. Ibid., pp. 193-94.

47. Ibid., p. 194.

48. Lavers, p. 75.

49. Ibid.

50. Ibid.

51. Jerzy Kosinski, "How I Learned to Levitate in Water," **Life**, April 1984, p. 130.

52. Samuel Coale, "The Quest for the Elusive Self: The Fiction of Jerzy Kosinski," **Critique**, 14, No. 3 (1973), 28.

53.   Kennedy, p. 12.

54.   Karl, p. 405.

55.   Ibid.

CHAPTER FIVE

BEING THERE: HIT OR MYTH?

"Language requires some inner triggering; television doesn't. The image is ultimately accessible,
i.e., extremely attractive. And, I think, ultimately deadly because it turns the viewer into a
bystander...."
                              Jerzy Kosinski, **Paris Review**

Jerzy Kosinski's third novel, **Being There**, is more than
an ironic version of the great American success story;[1]
it is a "knuckle ball of a book delivered with perfectly
timed satirical hops and metaphysical flutters,"[2] "a tan-
talizing rebus, the **Waiting for Godot** of the seventies."[3]
Different in form and tone from his earlier novels, **Being
There** may at first seem slight, almost anecdotal. Yet,
with its deliberately spare but taut prose and sharp but
simple images, it is both a fairy tale and a frighteningly
real symbolic abstraction of life, a satire on American
society which exists simultaneously on the levels of fiction
and fact, fantasy and contemporary history.[4] Furthermore,
Being There is now possibly Kosinski's best known work,
especially since its transcription to film, a medium ironically
close to the one lampooned in the novel, and its movie
premiere on network television.

Kosinski's first truly American protagonist in an American
setting (with the exception of the closing pages of **Steps**),
Chance initially appears to be a much different hero from
the active, judgmental, often avenging protagonists of
the first two novels. Yet he is in many ways their rightful
heir. In **Being There**, as in **The Painted Bird**, Kosinski is
concerned with the innocent and helpless victim -- in the
first novel, a lost child; in the third, a lost man with the

mind of a child -- who is destined to become the object
of what Henry James (like Kosinski) saw as the worst human
atrocity: the usurpation by others of the privacy and integrity
of the individual self. John Aldridge writes that "**The Painted
Bird** was primarily a parable of demonic totalitarianism,
of that form of Nazi bestiality which is not a politics but
a violence of the soul and blood. **Being There** has to do
with a totalitarianism of a subtler and much more fearful
kind, the kind that arises when the higher sensibilities of
a people have become not so much brutalized as benumbed,
when they have lost both skepticism and all hold on the
real, and so fall victim to those agencies of propaganda
which manipulate their thinking to accept whatever the
state finds it expedient for them to accept."[5] This "fascistic
enslavement of the will" is accomplished through television's
mass brainwashing, and **Being There** makes it clear that
while Kosinski dreads the all-pervasive hypnotic power
of television, he, like most Americans, is unable to get
over its magic.[6]

Chance, like the boy of **The Painted Bird** and the protagonist
of **Steps,** is thus a victim of collectivism, the danger already
decried by Kosinski in his nonfiction works. Yet while
the boy and the **Steps** protagonist survive the oppression
by implementing their own great lyric power, Chance is
conversely a passive character,[7] an antihero elevated by
the dead souls surrounding him. Moreover, while the
protagonists of both **The Painted Bird** and **Steps** attempt,
in their respective ways, to become invisible men, the
antihero of **Being There** begins as an invisible man[8] -- and
becomes arguably the most influential but certainly the
most visible character in all of Kosinski's fictions.

Like Kosinski's earlier protagonists, Chance is an outsider.
While his assimilation problems do not spring from his own
foreignness (though EE does, at one point, say to him that
he is obviously "European" in his lovemaking) or from philosophies or traditions which are alien to him, Chance is
nonetheless estranged from the society of **Being There.**
Isolated in his rooms and his garden, he is never fully a
part of the Old Man's home. In the Rand's inner circle,

he is neither the businessman nor the presidential advisor
he is assumed to be; he is merely a gardener in search of
a real garden, not the metaphoric garden of Wall Street
with its changing climate. Chance is further estranged
linguistically; he is incapable of true communication with
anyone, from Louise to EE, from the lawyer to the President.

Words mean something different to Chance than they do
to others. When Mr. Franklin asks Chance to sign a legal
document, Chance says, "I can't sign it ... I just can't."[9]
It is Franklin who assumes that he refuses to withdraw
his claim against the Old Man's estate; Chance simply means
that he literally cannot print and therefore is unable to
sign anything. When Chance tells Ben, "all that's left [for
me] is the room upstairs" (p. 40), he literally refers to the
bedroom which he occupies in the Rand home, not the more
heavenly room on Ben's mind. When he says to EE, "I like
to watch" (p. 114), he means just that: he enjoys watching
television. It is EE who assumes that he is interested in
kinky sex and who obliges him -- and herself -- by mastur-
bating while he watches. When he says to a reporter, "I
do not read any newspapers" (p. 96), he is not commenting
on the intrinsic worth of the print media; he means exactly
what he states, that he cannot read and thus does not read
the news but watches it instead on TV. It is the reporter
who interprets his remark as a judgment that TV news
is better than news in print and who hails his candor in
striking a blow for television. When Skrapinov says to
him that "We are not so far from each other," and Chance
responds literally, "We are not... Our chairs are almost
touching" (p. 89), his response is greeted as a fine metaphor
when in fact there is no subtlety to it whatsoever. Sometimes even his silences have reverberations. When the
Soviet Ambassador speaks Russian to him and Chance raises
his eyebrows in bewilderment at the strange sounds,
Skrapinov interprets his gesture as one of understanding
and approval. Soon Chance is admired for being a
multilinguist.

Kosinski has written often of his own linguistic estrangement and of his appreciation of the individual word, especially words in his acquired languages. Ivan Sanders suggests a parallel between Chance and his creator:

> In one sense, Chance is an interesting projection of the author himself. Kosinski has often talked about the liberating influence of an adopted language where every word is a new adventure and clichés have real meaning. "Once you begin to write in another language," he has said, "you discover how much freer you are, because the new language disconnects you and requires from you -- because you do not know all the clichés yet -- some of your own." Chance, like Kosinski, experiences his clichés very profoundly; language to both of them is something external, a contrivance, a game, like television. The image ... of a rootless, pastless, totally unaffiliated man who sees everything as though for the first time must have fascinated the author.[10]

This newness of his experience makes Chance an Adamic prototype and gives the whole novel a biblical dimension (a dimension more clearly conveyed in the film version, especially in the closing image). A number of critics have called the book a parable, a morality tale for our age; others have interpreted the Old Man as God. Some have even claimed that Ben Rand, the second "Old Man" Chance encounters, is another godlike figure, since it is to his garden that Chance returns after his expulsion from his first home. And of course there is the presence of EE, or Eve, who tries to seduce the innocent Chance and who, like Anna the mental patient raped back into purity in Walker Percy's **Lancelot**, violates herself into a new innocence, and the spiritually dead society of postlapsarian men into which Chance is thrust after his own expulsion and violation. The novel's structure of seven parts and its time frame of seven days, within which Chance shapes not simply his own future but also the world's, may parallel the biblical creation.[11] As still others have argued, in this "loosely cosmogenic parable and satiric creation story about a new sort of telegenic being and generation," TV literally becomes the creator and Chance its creation. The new theology "centered around the almighty TV" is further suggested by the chronological distinction Chance makes between "before television" and "after."[12]

The "before" and "after" distinctions recall similar dichotomies in earlier American fiction, especially in Nathaniel Hawthorne's works. Giovanni Guasconti, a dreamy yet melancholic student, is eventually poisoned by the experimentation of his neighbor, the black magician Rappaccini, but not before enjoying an idyll in the garden with Beatrice. Donatello, the title character in **The Marble Faun,** is another innocent; once corrupted by experience, he cannot return to the beauty and wonder of his prelapsarian existence. Both are "Adams," new men in a new world, just as Chance is Kosinski's "American Adam."

The eternal Adam in his New World Garden has in fact been the central myth in the American novel for more than 150 years;[13] it appears not only in Hawthorne's romances but also in the works of Cooper and Melville; continues with realists Twain, Howells, and James, and naturalists Norris, Crane, and Dreiser; reappears in the lost generation of Hemingway and Fitzgerald and the southern traditions of Faulkner and Warren; and still informs the writing of contemporaries like Mailer, Baldwin, and Bellow. R. W. B. Lewis explains the genesis of "the American Adam":

> [Following separation from Europe] The new habits to be engendered on the American scene were suggested by the image of a radically new personality, the hero of the new adventure: an individual emancipated from history, happily bereft of ancestry, untouched and undefiled by the usual inheritances of family and race; an individual standing alone, self-reliant and

> self-propelling, ready to confront whatever
> awaited him with the aid of his own unique
> and inherent resources ... the new hero ... was
> most easily identified with Adam before the
> Fall. Adam was the first, the archetypal, man.
> His moral position was prior to experience,
> and in his very newness he was fundamentally
> innocent. The world and history all lay before
> him. And he was the type of creator, the poet
> par excellence, creating language itself by
> naming elements of the scene about him.[14]

Radically new, emancipated from history, bereft of ancestry,
and unburdened by inheritance (so much so, in fact, that
the combined forces of the CIA, FBI, and KGB can turn
up little more about him than the name of his tailor),
Kosinski's Chance possesses all of the qualities of the
American Adam defined by Lewis. He is an innocent (perhaps
permanently so, by freak of birth); emerging from his idyllic
(some critics have insisted "prelapsarian") surroundings,
he is also a type of the creator who gives voice to the new
society.

Seen this way, the childlike and uncomprehending gardener
of the novel's opening pages, Chance -- the American Adam
-- is expelled from the insularity and serene peace of the
Old Man's home. Uprooted, he seeks a new world garden,
finds a new benefactor in Ben Rand and a new helpmate
in Eve, and takes new root in the imaginations of those
who see and hear him; his fresh appearance and crisp outlook
provide a sharp contrast to the reality of the American
wasteland (another popular theme, especially in recent
American literature). This new American hero, for whom
a small garden was once his whole world, finds that the
whole world has become his garden.

Jack Hicks recognizes "Chance's evolution as a biblical
fable and creation myth" and identifies Chance as the modern
American Adam (though he incorrectly dismisses **Being
There** as "a minor work in both conception and execution").

According to Hicks, Chance has fallen from the garden but has not been compensated by any of the "benefits" of that fall. "He possesses neither sexuality, nor consciousness, nor pride, nor imaginative will." This "failure of the passive imagination" is evident in his "loss" of sexual innocence -- a loss which is never replaced by any experience.[15]

If Chance's fall is incomplete, as Hicks argues, perhaps it is because Chance's garden -- modern American society -- is corrupted before the fall. Chance, the brain-damaged messiah, cannot save society; it is too far gone to be saved. "It's too late," Kosinski remarked when asked about TV's influence and the hope he had for the future of viewers. "Television has already done its work on an entire generation."[16] A product of society's self-willed brainwashing, Chance is thus the voice of his generation. A redeemer from the ranks, he cannot deliver the world from its evil but can merely lead it into further videocy. His voice is worse than the nada of an earlier lost generation; it is an echo from the wasteland.

So while Chance is the American Adam, Kosinski's tale is actually more video nightmare than American dream. As John McAleer writes, "Part of the grim fun of **Being There** is that it spoofs the American dream of success. With no materialistic aspirations, Chance soars to affluence and renown with a speed that must leave gasping all Horatio Alger dreamers."[17] He soars with no substance, though; his enigmatic eminence[18] is the result of his nullity. He is only what others want him to be, the "quintessential screen,"[19] more echo than oracle.

The echo image suggests a second significant mythic perspective in **Being There**, that of the Narcissus myth. According to legend, Narcissus was a youth so handsome that every young woman who saw him longed to be his. Yet he scorned all of them. As punishment for his arrogance, Nemesis caused him to see his own reflection in a pool of water, and he became so enamored of the image that he gradually pined away (and metamorphosed into the flower which bears his name). Echo, the fairest of the wood nymphs, had been punished by Hera never again to use her tongue except to repeat what was said to her. She too fell in love with Narcissus, but when he spurned her, she hid in a cave, never to be confronted, and wasted away from her unrequited longing. Only her voice remained.[20]

Being There is a retelling of the Narcissus myth, also popularized by John Barth, especially in the last two stories of **Lost in the Funhouse** (1968). According to the Narcissus myth, the symbols of the garden and of water are duplicating archetypes, and -- as archetypes -- are infinite and can never be finally identified, but recur according to some pattern. Within **Being There**, the garden assumes its traditional and familiar meaning of the soul, the unconscious; it represents the wholeness which dissipates when differentiation or fragmentation occurs. When this wholeness is broken, when the primordial unity is destroyed, expulsion is the natural consequence.[21] Like his archetypal predecessors, Adam and Eve and Buddha, Chance achieves wholeness within the confines of his garden at the home of his original benefactor and protector, which is dissolved when the Old Man dies and Chance is expelled from the estate. But Chance continues to seek a new garden in which to work -- and his garden imagery has a continuing appeal to the American people, who desire a similar "natural" security and harmony through his simple wisdom of changing seasons and cyclical growth.

Although **Being There** has a controlling pastoral motif through the use of the garden, Kosinski has replaced the symbolic pool of water with a television set, a synthetical symbol which offers the same ultimate meaning. Like Narcissus, who is drawn to his own reflection, Chance is drawn to his own image, reflected on the television screen. "Though Chance could not read or write, he resembled the man on TV more than he differed from him. For example, their voices were alike" (p. 6). Like Larry in Leonard Cohen's **Beautiful Losers,** who reassembles himself after his disintegration by way of identification with celluloid cinema images, he cannot define his existence apart from the McLuhanesque medium; he is as inextricably linked to his television as Narcissus was to his pool and he looks to it as one would to a wise mentor for a code of behavior. For him,

> Everything on TV was tangled and mixed and yet smoothed out: night and day, big and small, tough and brittle, soft and rough, hot and cold, far and near.... By changing the channel, he could change himself.... By turning the dial, Chance could bring others inside his eyelids. (pp. 5-6)

People "began to exist, as on TV, when one turned one's eyes on them. Only then could they stay in one's mind before being erased by new images" (p. 14). When he is thrust into the world outside the garden, Chance is "bewildered: there was clearly no place to which he could run away. He searched his mind and recalled situations on TV...." (p. 76). When he is approached sexually by a male guest at a party, "he tried very hard to recall seeing something like this on TV but could remember only a single scene in a film in which a man kissed another man" (p. 110). After EE enters his room and asks Chance to make love to her, he feels that "EE should no more have wanted to be touched by him than should the TV screen have wanted it" (pp. 113-14). His life revolves around TV: he falls asleep by it each evening, watches it while travelling from point to point in Rand's car, and even judges people by their resemblance to television images which he recalls. He becomes one of a generation of "watchers," men whose minds are picture pasteboards -- video without audio -- all reception, no perception, part of a society suffering a Big Brother dependency on TV.[22]

In **Being There**, "the hero's reliance on television is a perfect symbol of our removal from the real."[23] Yet Chance is not the only one who identifies strongly with TV images.

The other characters in the novel -- and by implication all of modern American society -- hail television, with all of its artificiality, as the ultimate reality. They see Chance only as an attractive and well-groomed man who consorts with politicians, travels in proper social circles, and projects the right image. Never mind that he says nothing of substance or that he rarely answers even a simple question directly; after all, he looks and sounds good. Just as EE is convinced by Chance's appearance that he is a wealthy businessman and the President assumes by Chance's presence at Rand's side that he is a financial expert, so modern society is duped -- brainwashed -- by the collective fantasy of television. Resembling the politician Kosinski stereotyped in "The Lone Wolf" as "a mere television image, a product of his own public relations men,"[24] Chance, a kind of human void, fills society's collective void. Yet he is in reality "an absolute blank of a person who is elevated to power by the narcissistically reflected dead souls around him."[25] Those dead souls are no more than mere receptors -- echoes to Chance's Narcissus.

Narcissus serves as an ideal prototype for Chance in many ways. According to Marcuse's definition, Narcissus in myth and as symbol illustrates the denial of all repression in society; he stands as the absolute challenge to social values, a figure who opposes by showing another way, who challenges simply by "being there."[26] Unlike Barth's Narcissus, who himself becomes a fabulator regressus ad infinitum, recounting his tale which involves multiplicity and winds back to the incontrovertible source of being, Chance cannot be cured of self-absorption by saturation;[27] he is too much of a "blank page" (which was Kosinski's working title for the book).[28] Instead, Chance harks back to the Ovidian Narcissus, whose very existence is a passive rebuttal to social values. Furthermore, throughout the novel Chance remains a passive character, not acting but being acted upon. This "reflection" or "echoing" of the values which others lack in themselves but ascribe to him, this spiritual narcissism, is conveyed by the numerous mirror images. (Chance himself becomes a trick done with mirrors, an image created by a television screen.) Chance relates well to the plants in his garden because "Plants were different from people ... there is no mirror in which the plant can recognize its face" (pp. 3-4). People, however, are less familiar to him unless they reflect TV characters; Chance even defines his own image via television: "The figure on the TV screen looked like his own reflection in a mirror" (p. 6). After the Old Man's death, Chance remembers their last meeting. On that occasion -- "There was no TV then" -- he caught "sight of his reflection in the large hall mirror" (p. 7). With the Old Man dead, Chance has no home and no identity, reflected or otherwise; he observes the shrouded furniture and "the veiled mirrors" (p. 7). At the Rand home, just before the President arrives, Ben cautions him to hide his mind, since the President's security officers often confiscate "sharp objects." Wondering about Ben's remark and almost coincidentally with the assumption of his "new" identity as Rand's advisor and confidant, he looked at the mirror, "liked what he saw," and "turned on the TV" (pp. 48-49). Before appearing on the THIS EVENING show, Chance sits in front of a mirror as a man makes him up with a layer of powder (just as the nurse had earlier disguised Rand's near deadness). "Chance was astonished that television could portray itself; cameras watched themselves and, as they watched, they televised a program. This self-portrait was telecast on TV screens facing the stage and watched by the studio audience ... only TV constantly held up a mirror to its own neither solid nor fluid face" (p. 63). At the novel's end, caught up in the blur of EE's society friends, he is blinded by "the blaze of photographers' flash-guns" (pp. 139-140) and seeks his own image once again in the garden. It is ·mirrored in a pool of rain water just beyond the glass door.

Chance also serves as a mirror for other characters in the novel. For EE, "there were innumerable selves that he evoked in her" (p. 74) as he showed her how truly to be free. On the television talk show, "the viewers existed only as projections of his own thoughts, as images," just as "Chance became only an image for millions of real people"

(p. 65). There is discussion that Chance soon "may fill Rand's place" (p. 93). Many of the predominant images in the novel are related to the visual; besides the very concretely visual medium of television, there is much importance attached to what characters see and how they are seen; to the appearances of Rand, the President, and others; to the act of watching others; to being in the public eye; etc.

Kosinski's nature child, a noble savage in TV's jungle,[29] a Candide in reverse[30] -- Chance is the modern Narcissus. As the reflection of society's superficial values, he holds Kosinski's critical mirror up to a medium based on and a government run by narcissism.[31] Kosinski himself called Chance "a character beyond self-definition ... lost in the passive pursuit of an outside source. He has lost any sense of becoming ... incapable of self-reflection, of acquiring self-knowledge. He is a human plant, a point zero."[32]

As an idiot-savant figure in literature, Chance has many precedents. In Kosinski's native Polish literature alone, one is reminded of Boleslaw Prus's "Michalko" about an illiterate young peasant newly arrived in Warsaw. Michalko, described by Czeslaw Milosz as "a little like a Steinbeck hero,"[33] although strong and hardworking, is by city standards so immensely naive that he is considered no more than a fool. Yet it is he who saves a man from being crushed by a wall on a construction site, totally unaware of his very heroism. Similarly, in Prus's novel **Placowka** (The Outpost), two of the lowliest creatures -- by village standards -- emerge as bearers of the most lofty ethics of selflessness:[34] a wandering Jewish peddler who befriends Slimak ("Snail"), the protagonist, and who shares his misfortune as though it were his own; and Slimak's half-witted farm hand, who rescues an abandoned baby, carries it to his own miserable quarters, and takes it under his permanent care. (Thus the legacy of the future is in the half-wit's hands -- as in **Being There**.)

Jozef Wittlin, in his **Sol ziemi** (Salt of the Earth, 1936), describes another idiot-savant, his protagonist Piotr Niewiadomski (Peter "Unknowing"), a simple and naive Polish mountaineer without education or political orientation who -- by mere chance -- is drafted into military duty. Removed from the primal security and safety of his mountain dwelling, Niewiadomski is at a loss to understand the new world surrounding him, the world of war. He cannot comprehend why he should bear arms against other men so much like himself, why he should shoot at people said to be "enemies" yet who have never brought him any harm. He is perhaps a simpleton, perhaps a philosopher, perhaps only an ordinary man lost in a strange environment. According to Manfred Kridl:

> The war ... is seen through the eyes of a simple "Hutsul" peasant of Polish-Ukrainian origin. This man lives in a state of neverending bewilderment; everything he sees appears puzzling, mysterious and paradoxical to him: mobilization, militarization of railways, medical examination, evacuation. The strangeness of the world, as reflected in the soul of Piotr Niewiadomski, becomes a forceful means of artistic expression. Facts and phenomena grow into the symbols of important and weighty problems. The experiences of this simple man assume a universal significance, become the common experiences of every man oppressed by the monstrous conditions of life... [35]

Piotr is the pawn of fortune (or, more accurately, misfortune); preferring the pastoral to the political, he is thrust into an alien world and will always remain a stranger to its ways.

Another memorable idiot-savant is Nikodem Dyzma, the protagonist of Tadeusz Dolega-Mostowicz's bestseller, **Kariera Nikodema Dyzmy**. An aggressive though stupid dirty trickster, Dyzma is an unemployed postal clerk who leaves his small town to seek employment in Warsaw. Hungry, he finds an invitation to a reception at the prime minister's palace and decides to attend. At the reception, he is shoved by an impertinent dignitary who knocks Dyzma's food to the floor and leaves without apology. The still-hungry Dyzma, angered by the loss of his meal, assaults the aggressor who turns out to be not simply boorish but also hated. For his reckless abandon, Dyzma becomes the hit of the party; his new friends assume he is an important powerful newcomer in the government (who else would confront the dignitary in such a haughty and unfearing way?) and welcome his straightforward stupid remarks as excellent jokes. With the help of Dyzma's own contacts, his popularity rises and his bad manners establish him as a man of strong conviction. Ultimately depriving his benefactor of both his wife and his fortune, Dyzma emerges a national hero.

His idiotic witticisms are the core of the novel. When a society woman asks how "one comes up with a good business idea":

> Nikodem shrugged his shoulders. "It's simple. One sits down, one thinks, and gets an idea." To illustrate his words, he leaned his head on his hands. The gesture started a stream of laughter.
>
> The lady in the gray frock who, until now, silently observed Dyzma through her lorgnette, nodded with approval. "Mr. Chairman, you really are terrific. Your humor reminds me of Buster Keaton: an immobile mask enhances a joke."
>
> "You are malicious," said Countess Lala, showing a grimace. "I only asked if it is difficult to find such an idea."
>
> "No," said Dyzma, "very easy. You have to have a little..." He could not remember the right word. He had to finish the sentence.

"A little ... intention."

Again a general laughter and the gray lady
said to hostess: "Jeanette! Your Chairman
is charming!"

"And what esprit d'apropos," added the girl
with the scalped eyebrows.

* * * * * *

They talked about Mrs. Przeleska. The baroness
was sure she was absolutely over fifty; the
count asserted that she hadn't even hit forty-five
yet. Nikodem considered it only fair to straighten
this matter out. "Mrs. Przeleska is just thirty-
two."

Everyone looked at him with astonishment. The
bald count asked, "How do you know that, Mr.
Chairman? Isn't that estimate rather low?"

"By no means," answered Dyzma angrily. "It
is a very accurate one. She told me that herself."

He said it in all honesty, and was surprised
that the entire room again exploded with laughter.
Mrs. Koniecpolski repeated for the tenth time,
"He is malicious!"[36]

Many "divine idiots" or idiots-savant appear in recent American fiction: in Kurt Vonnegut's **Slaughterhouse-Five**, James
Purdy's **Malcolm**, Walker Percy's **The Last Gentleman**.
Yet few have had the pervasive influence or enduring effect
on the American public that the telegenic Chance has.

When he wrote **Being There**, Kosinski searched for a media
device to encompass Chauncey Gardiner's existence. First
he considered music, but that posed a problem since readers
could not "hear" what Chance was hearing. He then consider-

ed photography or painting as an analogy for Chance's vicarious life, but that would have required illustration of some sort for the book. With the inspiration of television, a medium everyone shares, the story just flowed.[37]

Does Kosinski himself like television? **WATCH Magazine** writes, "He says he does. He says a TV set is constantly on when he's at home. But he has no favorite shows, for that would be succumbing to the medium. He claims to care only about the total video environment. During a lengthy discussion he finally drops hints about what he doesn't like, the docu-dramas that purvey inaccurate details of history."[38] In **Comment**, Kosinski claims that "My own attitude toward television is neutral. The danger is in the use we make of it. I'm involved with TV the way I am with the motor car. The motor car has been with us for over 50 years, but it is only recently that we learned its exhaust pollutes our very environment."[39] In an interview for **Media and Methods**, Kosinski stated that "For me, the word 'beneficial' doesn't apply to television. TV is simply a part of contemporary life. I must confront it, think about it, accept it, or reject it." He elaborates by calling the medium "overwhelming" and asking "How do you judge its role in our political life? The impact of its commercialism? Of its ordering of time? Of its ranking what's important (therefore visible) and what's not (therefore left out)?" He confesses, however, that for him "imagining groups of solitary individuals watching their private, remote-controlled TV sets is the ultimate future terror: a nation of videots."[40]

The medium of television is one of ultimate disinvolvement. Kosinski adds, "As media ... television takes the initiative: it does the involving. It says, 'You, the passive spectator, are there. Stay there. I'll do the moving, talking, acting.' Frenetic, quick-paced, engineered by experts in visual drama, everything from a thirty-second commercial to a two-hour movie is designed to fit into neat time slots, wrapped up in lively colors and made easily digestible."[41]

Whereas the reader is tempted to venture beyond a text, to contemplate his own life in light of the book's personalized meanings, TV demands no such inner reconstruction. Everything is already there, explicit, ready to be watched.

> While viewing, you can eat, you can recline, you can walk around the set, you can even change channels, but you won't lose contact with the medium. Unlike theater or cinema, TV allows, even encourages, all these "human" diversions. TV's hold on you is so strong, it is not easily threatened or severed by "the other life" you lead. While watching, you are not reminded (as you would be by a theater audience, for instance) that you are a member of society whose thoughts and reactions may be valuable. You are isolated and given no time to reflect. The images rush on and you cannot stop them or slow them down or turn them back.[42]

The greatest danger of television for Kosinski lies in the diconnection which it causes. TV gives a viewer a sense of being there:

> The viewer knows that he is not Columbo or Captain Kangaroo. He is separated from the stars not only by his patently different identity, being here while they are there, but also -- and this is far more important -- by the very process of watching, of having been assigned the role of spectator. In this process, the spectator occupies one world, while what he views comes from another. The bridge between the two is TV's absolutely concrete nature. Every situation it portrays is particular: every descriptive detail is implied, no blank spaces are left for the viewer to fill in.[43]

"Being there" is not simply the title of Kosinski's novel (and later of the movie), but also the central concept. As a colloquial expression, "being there" suggests a variety of meanings -- the right place at the right time; making it to the top; even a sense of shared experience.[44] Yet while Kosinski must have considered these, he seems to have had a particular meaning of "being there" in mind. "TV," he says, "is itself the only experience. The world only exists as it appears here and now on television." TV allows the viewers to be a part of the world and -- at the same time -- outside of it. "This inside/outside process is a very complex one," Kosinski observes. It encourages remoteness. "If the world is so horrible, it's better to watch than to be a part of it. Thus, the medium not only by example teaches how we should behave in the real world. It also encourages us not to go out in the world. Better we should stay in front of our TV sets."[45] TV therefore discourages involvement and endorses passivity like Chance's. It deemphasizes "being here" and emphasizes "being there," especially "the indefinite 'there' of packaged consciousness."[46]

Some of Kosinski's opinions seem borne out by his experiences. To validate his ideas Kosinski tried several experiments, which he called "ad hoc sessions, crude attempts to find out a bit more about the young."[47] On one occasion, he set up TV monitors in a classroom; a closed circuit TV fed the monitors. He arranged for an intruder to rush into the room during a class session and to pick a fight with him. He found that the majority of children in the room watched the fisticuffs on the monitors instead of watching the men actually fighting in the room. Later, the children explained that they could see the attack better on the screens -- the close-ups of the attacker and Kosinski, the attacker's hand on Kosinski's face, the attacker's expression (all the details they wanted) -- without being frightened by "'the real thing' (or by the necessity of becoming involved)."[48]

Another time, Kosinski told students they could stay in class and watch TV or leave to go into the hallway, where something "really incredible" was happening. "I repeated,

'You know what's outside is really fantastic. You have never seen it before. Why don't you just step outside and take a look?'" Almost every student preferred TV to taking a chance on reality. "There it was: they were already too lazy, too corrupted to get up and take a chance on 'the outside.'"[49]

On yet another occasion, he interviewed a number of children in Johnny Carson-like surroundings. In typical conversations before the cameras started rolling, the young people felt awkward and were hesitant to talk. These same youngsters -- so long as they knew the camera was on them -- became poised, confident, blasé. Even when questioned about such topics as masturbation and shoplifting, they performed in familiar talk-show style. "Their manners typified the easy warm 'openness,' the total frankness, they've learned from TV,"[50] Kosinski recalls. Like Chauncey Gardiner, the kids felt comfortable with TV mannerisms.

Kosinski sees a particular danger in TV's influence on children and points out that a number of teachers have commented to him about the resemblance of their young students to Chance. "A child begins school nowadays with basic images from 'his own garden' -- television."[51] He learns that all things are equal, "neither bad nor good, neither pleasant nor painful, neither real nor unreal, merely more or less interesting, merely in better or worse color. It is a world without rank,"[52] one which is there only to entertain the viewer. If it doesn't entertain, the viewer simply switches the channel. Problems are solved in thirty or sixty or ninety minutes; victims rarely bleed; heroes don't die but rise again for next week's episode; prostitutes find love; justice prevails; and fantasies are fulfilled, by the omnipresent game show hosts or soap opera heroes and heroines.

The danger occurs when a child grows older and leaves the "TV room." Accustomed to controlling his environment by channel-changing, the child is often threatened by real people. By the teenage years, "he is easily depressed and beaten down ... challenged and outranked ... instead of

coming of age, he's coming apart."[53] Often he returns
to the collective fantasy of TV to escape reality. Therefore,
it is little wonder, as Kosinski notes, that the average
working American watches 1,200 hours of TV per year
but spends only five hours per year reading books.[54]

Television controls both Chance and the millions of other
people who come under its pervasive, all-embracing
influence. As an institution, it becomes as threatening
as the military-industrial complex which usurps man's power
over his own life in Joseph Heller's **Catch-22,** or the Red
Bull in Peter Beagle's allegorical **The Last Unicorn,** who
is "raging ignorance," the immense, shapeless agency which
unfits all opponents and makes them docile, or any of the
various other institutions which deny the hero of the sixties
and seventies his vitality and prerogative to exercise free
choice. Kosinski's concept of the inherent power of television
to formulate and control mass thought anticipates the
frightening possibility of an "Ultimate Computer" like
WESCAC in **Giles Goat-Boy,** guiding a civilization of men
as moronic as the employees of the Rosewater Foundation
in Kurt Vonnegut's **God Bless You, Mr. Rosewater** or the
denizens of the asylum in Ken Kesey's **One Flew Over the
Cuckoo's Nest.** (The last novel has some interesting similarities
to **Being There.** McMurphy attempts to rebel against the
authoritarian momism of Big Nurse, an agent of the
"Combine," and receives an asylum-administered lobotomy,
yet his struggle redeems Chief Bromden. The meaning
of his fight -- if one exists at all -- is that in a world in
which the normal is perverted and reason becomes madness,
the only hope for salvation lies in the nonrational or the
downright irrational. With Kesey as with Kosinski, the
inmates have taken over the asylum.)

Central to the book because he is Kosinski's symbol for
the programmed contemporary man, Chance is benumbed,
brainwashed, bewildered in the world of "here" and always
searching for escape by "being there." (A major network's
recent promotion of its fall season, which appealed to the

videot in all of us by urging us to "BE THERE," is proof of Kosinski's vision.)

Lacking self-definition, lacking even a self to define, Chance is a created persona, a vacuum adored rather than abhorred. The prototypical nobody, he becomes a somebody -- a somebody with the potential for great power (like Hitler and Mussolini, other notable nobodies who, according to Kosinski, were also able to manipulate the media).[55] It is hardly surprising, then, that Kosinski called **Being There** possibly "the saddest book I ever wrote. After all, there is no redemption for Chauncey Gardiner. It is also a cruel book, because it purposefully distorts and mocks what is so dear to most of us: innocence and celebrity fused into American sainthood."[56] Ultimately, **Being There** is a searing indictment of a society which celebrates the collective "virtue" of passivity and elevates appearance over substance.

ENDNOTES TO CHAPTER FIVE

1.   Paul Delany, "Being There," **The New York Times Book Review**, 25 April 1971, p. 7.

2.   R. Z. Sheppard, "Playing It by Eve," **Time**, 26 April 1971, p. 93.

3.   John J. McAleer, **Best Sellers**, 1 July 1971, p. 173.

4.   John W. Aldridge, "The Fabrication of a Culture Hero," **Saturday Review**, 24 April 1971, p. 27.

5.   Ibid., p. 26.

6.   Ivan Sanders, "The Gifts of Strangeness: Alienation and Creation in Jerzy Kosinski's Fiction," **The Polish Review,** 19, Nos. 3-4 (Autumn-Winter 1974), 179.

7.   Jerome Klinkowitz, **Literary Disruptions,** (Urbana: University of Illinois Press, 1975), p. 97.

8.   James D. Hutchinson, "The 'Invisible Man' as Anti-Hero," **The Denver Quarterly**, 6, No. 1 (Spring 1971), 87.

9.   Jerzy Kosinski, **Being There** (New York: Harcourt Brace Jovanovich, 1970), p. 24. All subsequent references to this edition will be made by page number in the text.

10.   Sanders, p. 179.

11.   For a fuller discussion of the biblical allusions, see Norman Lavers, **Jerzy Kosinski** (Boston: Twayne, 1982) and Ivan Sanders, op. cit.

12.   Sanders, p. 180.

13.   See David W. Noble, **The Eternal Adam and the New World Garden: The Central Myth in the American Novel Since 1836** (New York: Grosset and Dunlap/Universal Library, 1968).

14.   R. W. B. Lewis, **The American Adam: Innocence, Tragedy, and Tradition in the Nineteenth Century** (Chicago: University of Chicago/Phoenix Books, 1967), p. 5.

15.   Jack Hicks, **In the Singer's Temple** (Chapel Hill: University of North Carolina Press, 1981), p. 236.

16.   Gary H. Arlen, "From the TV Viewer's Perspective," **WATCH Magazine**, March 1980, p. 57.

17.   McAleer, p. 173.

18.   V. S. Pritchett, "Clowns," **New York Review of Books**, 1 July 1971, p. 15.

19.   Klinkowitz, p. 96.

20.   Edith Hamilton, **Mythology** (New York: New American Library/Mentor Book, 1942), pp. 87-88.

21.   For a good discussion of the garden as archetype, see Joseph Campbell's works on myth.

22. McAleer, p. 173.

23. Martin Tucker, "Being There," **Commonweal,** 7 May 1971, p. 222.

24. Jerzy Kosinski, "The Lone Wolf," **The American Scholar,** 41, No. 4 (Autumn 1972), 517.

25. Klinkowitz, p. 97.

26. See Herbert Marcuse, **Eros and Civilization: A Philosophical Inquiry into Freud** (Boston: Beacon Press, 1966), pp. 165ff. for a discussion of Narcissus and the concept of "being there."

27. For a discussion of the Narcissus myth in the works of John Barth, see Max F. Schulz, **Black Humor Fiction in the Sixties** (Athens: Ohio University Press, 1973).

28. George Plimpton and Rocco Landesman, "The Art of Fiction: Jerzy Kosinski," **Paris Review,** 54 (Summer 1972), 200.

29. Tucker, pp. 222-23.

30. Peter Glassgold, "Taking a Bad Chance," **The Nation,** 31 May 1971, p. 699.

31. Pritchett, p. 15.

32. Martin L. Gross, "Conversation with an Author: Jerzy Kosinski," **Book Digest,** Nov. 1980, p. 19.

33. Czeslaw Milosz, **The History of Polish Literature** (London: Macmillan, 1969), p. 294.

34. Ibid., p. 295.

35. Manfred Kridl, **A Survey of Polish Literature and Culture** (New York: Columbia Slavic Studies, 1956), pp. 500-501.

36.   Tadeusz Dolega-Mostowicz, **Kariera Nikodema Dyzmy** (New York: Roy Publishers, 1950), pp. 179-80, 181. My translation.

37.   Arlen, pp. 54-55.

38.   Ibid., p. 57.

39.   Jerzy Kosinski and National Broadcasting Co., Inc. From **Comment** program, 3 September 1972.

40.   David Sohn, "A Nation of Videots," **Media and Methods,** April 1975, p. 52.

41.   Ibid., p. 25.

42.   Ibid.

43.   Ibid.

44.   Arlen, p. 57.

45.   Ibid.

46.   Hicks, p. 236.

47.   Sohn, p. 30. Also reported in Arlen, p. 56.

48.   Sohn, p. 26.

49.   Ibid.

50.   Arlen, p. 56.

51.   Sohn, p. 25.

52.   Jerzy Kosinski, **Comment** program.

53.   Sohn, p. 56.

54.   Ibid., p. 52.

55.   Geoffrey Movius, "A Conversation with Jerzy Kosinski," **New Boston Review**, 1 No. 3 (Winter 1975), 3.

56.   Gross, p. 20.

CHAPTER SIX

ROOTING FOR THE AMERICAN DREAM:
THE DEVIL TREE

"[After the death of Mary Hayward Weir] I
had lived at the roots of the Protestant ethic
and now I wanted to see the branches, to know
the whole tree. I wanted to see where the sons
and daughters of the Protestant ethic went
to school and what became of them."

Jerzy Kosinski, **Los Angeles Times Calendar**

The Devil Tree, like Kosinski's third novel, **Being There,**
is a contemporary American fable of power. The central
character is Jonathan James Whalen, a poor little rich
boy whose money can buy him everything except happiness.
Whalen is, in many senses, the incarnation of the American
dream: the heir to one of the largest industrial empires
in America, he exists on a huge monthly trust allowance.
His adventures in the course of the novel find him flunking
out of Yale, running through whores and mistresses on
several continents, participating in group therapy, and
engaging in a variety of other nefarious activities.

Unlike Chance, who never acquires an identity and instead
merely mirrors and reflects the attitudes and values of
others around him, Whalen is most definitely a character
in search of self. Yet the self he seeks is a fragmented
and elusive one, and he is able to discover it only in pieces,
which he must gradually put together into a meaningful
whole -- a process which parallels the sections of Kosinski's
narrative. Jonathan's search, in fact, can best be described
in one of the novel's images: it is like looking into a kaleido-

scope, whose many splinters form a colorful mosaic of life (or, in Jonathan's case, the mosaic of a colorful life).

The Devil Tree begins as Jonathan returns to the United States; with his parents both dead, he comes home to claim his inheritance. His first act is to charter a helicopter from "Executive Heliways" (which his corporation later buys) and fly over archaic skyscrapers on Wall Street, which once housed his father's office. Jonathan recalls: "My father's office was on the top floor there. When I visited him as a kid, I used to stand there and look down at the other buildings. But it is a strange feeling to be above it looking down."[1] Jonathan has spent a lifetime "looking down" on others, just as his father spent a longer lifetime looking down on Jonathan and other subordinates. But now, in the absence of his father, Jonathan finds himself on top of the corporate world. No longer forced to look up to his father, he can look down on the building which stands as a symbol of the elder Whalen's towering wealth.

Jonathan's chartering of the helicopter is no arbitrary or capricious gesture: it is a sort of declaration of his personal independence, a heralding of the new position which he -- somewhat reluctantly -- is assuming. Almost twenty-one and only hours away from his financial "coming of age," he is back in New York, the heart of corporate America, which is itself a land of corporate trusts and bonds.

As his rented helicopter hovers for a moment over Wall Street, Jonathan is temporarily frozen, suspended between past and future, between a world which he has rejected and a world to which he aspires. The familiar objects and events from his past assume a different perspective. Like the narrator of **Steps**, in flight between his old world homeland and his new world future, or Joseph Novak of the nonfiction works, he must shed one identity in order to assume another.

The principal stockholder in his father's industrial empire, Jonathan returns not simply to a corporate bank; he must

also confront a personal bank -- of memories, of a past
replete with broken trusts and severed bonds. In the metaphor of corporate America, he must divest himself of his
father's interests and develop new principles to sustain
him.

Of the "basic components" of the novel -- "the plight of
the young man, which again typifies countless similar situations among my students at Princeton and Wesleyan and
Yale; the family trust, a very common middle class institution by now in the United States; the history of drug use
and abuse perhaps -- the young people going to Europe
or the Middle East or to Africa to use it as a playground
for exposure to drugs which they cannot that easily purchase
here; the group therapy proliferating over the nation" --
Kosinski has said, "I think the major issue is the inability
of the young to fulfill the trust imposed on them by their
parents while living off the financial trust their fathers
or mothers established for them. The ambiguity even of
the very idea of trust -- 'I trust you, and yet you will live
off that trust, financially, so to speak.'"[2]

Except for the financial, little trust existed between
Jonathan and his father. Horace Sumner Whalen was a
successful businessman, a "lone wolf" in American industry.
He had faith in no one and even divided people into unusual
categories: the wets, who sweated and therefore could
be caught in lies, and the drys, who never sweated and
thus could not be trusted. Content with the importance
of his actions and not with the pursuit of the real self behind
the gesture, Horace Whalen was a mere half-man. The
corporate world became his collective, the corporation
his very language, so that he finally was incapable of any
genuine expression. "The ultimate tragedy of Whalens,"
noted Kosinski, is "that they refuse to make themselves
accessible through imagination." The senior Whalen, like
all corporate men, was the "offspring of a very tragic tree
in which the imagination has never been allowed to emerge
as a meaningful way of communication."[3] Thus, Horace
can dictate -- but not even bother to read -- a letter to

his son at camp, a letter devoid of feeling but full of financial etiquette (travel first class; tip the porter one dollar). He can fire a faithful family servant for changing a razor blade too soon and thereby betraying his faith in the American steel industry -- though the blade, like Horace himself, needed changing. He can dispassionately kick his son's helpless dog until he breaks its spirit and teaches it who the master of the household is. And, in his dying moments, he can insist that his mistress clothe him in bathing trunks and walk him to the shore so that his death can be attributed to accidental drowning rather than purposeful indiscretion.

Unlike Benjamin Rand, chairman of the board of the First American Finance Corporation in **Being There**, Whalen is no benign or benevolent paternal figure; he is, instead, a faceless visage whose specter looms large throughout the novel,[4] a haunting reminder to Jonathan of his own inadequacy. Kosinski's portrait of Whalen (and, to some extent, of Rand) is based on the multimillionare industrialist, Ernest T. Weir, who died in 1957 and whose widow, Mary Hayward Weir, Kosinski married in 1962.

Weir, chairman of the National Steel Corporation and one of the founders of the modern American steel industry, was a curious model for the autonomous self.[5] Born poor on Pittsburgh's North Side in 1875 -- a generation after Mellon, Carnegie and Rockfeller -- he found employment at the age of fifteen with the Braddock Wire Company, "doing work, as Weir recalled, that nobody else wanted to do."[6] Though with Braddock he earned a mere three dollars a week in salary, he rose quickly through the ranks of industry, first as chief clerk in the Monongahela Tin Plate Mills and later as general manager of Monessen Mills, both subsidiaries of the American Steel and Tin Plate Company. But "no matter where he turned in Pittsburgh, he saw the chimneys rising as monuments to that sturdy breed of men of achievement,"[7] and by 1905 he joined with J. R. Phillips in the reorganization of a decrepit tin plate company in Clarksburg, West Virginia. When Phillips died a few months later, Weir took over as the company's president. The

company -- soon renamed Weirton Steel -- in the town
-- soon renamed Weirton -- grew and prospered; and by
1929, through a series of successful mergers, Weirton Steel
became the National Steel Corporation.

As independent in his political allegiances as in his industrial
ties, Weir fought bitterly with F. D. R. and the New Dealers.
In "The Lone Wolf," Kosinski's essay on Weir in **The American
Scholar**, Kosinski writes that "F. D. R. once called Weir
'that feudal lord of Weirton' and that later in his life Weir
would not visit any foreign capital that erected a monument
to F. D. R. or named one of its streets after him."[8]

Obviously, Weir was a lone wolf in many ways. Kosinski
seems especially interested in Weir as an old warrior who
refused pointless battle, recognized impossible struggles,
and contained his powers -- like the wolf -- in silent movement around the adversary. In an epigraph to his essay,
Kosinski quotes Richard II -- the Duke of York's "I do remain
as a neuter" -- as Weir's message to cold war America.[9]
A man "who would give in only to time,"[10] Weir lived nearly
eighty-two years, married three times (the last time to
a woman fifty years younger than he), and died as he had
lived: alone. He ordered a bare service with no eulogy
and no pallbearers.[11]

For Kosinski, Weir's story was the American dream of success, and Kosinski's very personal connection to Weir --
by marriage to his widow -- brought him, too, to the pinnacle
of that dream. Yet Weir's self-creation and rugged individualism, like Horace Sumner Whalen's, was a formula of
upward mobility appropriate only for a bygone age; the
same formula which helped Weir -- and Whalen -- succeed
brings disappointment, not triumph, to the next generation.
Thus, Jonathan Whalen, who comes of age in the 1970s,
is not simply a generation removed from his father; he
is separated seemingly by lightyears. The difference between
them is the difference between splitting a rail and splitting
an atom. As so, throughout the novel, the father's success
becomes the son's failure,[12] a failure compounded by the

fact that virtually all of Jonathan's freedom is the result of the same family inheritance which restricts and binds him.

To his credit, though, Jonathan cannot be content in the role of his father's second self; he needs and wants his own identity, apart from the financial and psychological legacy of his father. Yet the break he tries to make is no simple one. In fact, the more he attempts to rebel against his father's values, the more he is compelled to confront (and, in some cases, to assume) them.

As a boy, Jonathan read biographies of great leaders and envied them because there was no mention of their fathers; they became their own "event," as Jonathan seeks to become his. (Younger Whalens, Whalens who are fourteen, fifteen, today look at contemporary rock stars with exactly the same feeling. Says Kosinski, who examines the problem of self in the rock world in **Pinball:** "they are liberated from the family ethos, producing their own sound, which is a non-language." They define themselves through their medium -- like Chance in **Being There** or Goddard in **Pinball.**)[13] But all events occur in sequence, just as Jonathan is both biologically and psychologically the consequence of his father's actions. So Jonathan is unable to separate himself from the larger "event," which is the Whalen legacy.

For all of his intention to be his own person, Jonathan consistently and conveniently falls back on his family connections. To prove his own physical power and ability, Jonathan hires a champion skier to help him learn to master the sport. He succeeds, but only through the most mechanical -- and costly -- of means, available to him solely because of his vast and inherited wealth. He picks up a black woman in a bar and takes her to his abandoned family home; there he engages in sexual relations with her -- the greatest act of defiance he can think of.[14] Yet his attempt to desecrate his father's memory is not wholly successful. When he is arrested for breaking and entering, he informs the police chief that he is "Jonathan Whalen.... My father, Horace Sumner Whalen, founded this town.... My family's

portrait is hanging on the front wall in the main lobby of
the Town Hall. I am Jonathan, the boy between Katherine
and Horace Whalen" (RDT, p. 154). The rebellious young
man is reduced to the helpless child, dwarfed by the towering
figure of a father, now dead but still powerful. (This scene
typifies the relationship between Jonathan and his father.)

Similarly, Jonathan's own language is an insufficient guide
for him; it affords him little self control. He languishes
in the psychobabble of his encounter group, as deadening
in its own way as the language of corporate America. He
keeps notes of his experiences in Burma, India, and Africa
so that he will have "something tangible" from his past
to help himself -- and Karen -- understand it. But language
belongs to everyone, and whatever is captured in words
"becomes a fictional account" (RDT, p. 31), and so even
his diaries become mere fictions. However, as he comes
of age and seeks self-definition, Jonathan still turns somewhat instinctively to his father's words. He buys his father's
old letters from a collector, thus consciously or subconscious-
ly preserving the link to a man he purportedly rejects.
But his father's scrawl on the actual documents is indecipher-
able -- and as incomprehensible to him as the elder Whalen's
Calvinist ethic. (Years earlier, as a boy, Jonathan had
collected the cork tips from his father's cigarettes, believing
that they contained his unspoken words and feelings.)

It is only at the end that Jonathan appears to make a break
from his father and all that he represents: in the killing
of his godparents, the symbolic surrogates for his own parents
and emblems for America's corporate greed. When Walter
Howmet, acting in loco parentis to Jonathan, tries to shake
him out of his counterculture pose and bring him into the
sphere of business where he can take up his rightful place
as director of the company, Whalen pretends to accede.
He cuts his hair, dons a suit, joins a Masonic order that
Howmet insists on -- and then, in seeming gratitude, invites
Howmet and his wife to a private resort, where he murders
them.[15] As the tide is about to come in, Jonathan leaves
the couple to go chase sea-snakes; stranded on a sandbar
without their dinghy, they are swallowed by the tide.

The sea-snakes call up the archetypal snake who corrupted Eden and thus are associated with the diabolic and self-centered conduct of the Howmets. The snake image also allies the Howmets to the novel's central image of the baobab tree ("the devil tree"): "the devil once got tangled in its branches and punished the tree by reversing it. To the native, the roots are branches now, and the branches are roots. To ensure that there would be no more baobabs, the devil destroyed all the young ones" (RDT, p. 199). The pointed aspect of this passage, writes Paul Bruss, "is clearly the association of the perversion of the natural (and its ultimately sterilizing effect) with the Howmets' world of capitalism where human affairs and concerns have gotten turned upside down. The successful Howmets, even if somewhat unwittingly, are much like the devil who destroys the young. Because their acts of murder are so deadly, in fact, Whalen feels that he must resort to his own act of murder ... in order to free himself of the Howmets' influence and to begin the process of righting the difficulties of the derelicts"[16] -- and of his own derelict self.

Jonathan too is caught in a societal devil tree. But, like the curiously self-perpetuating and self-regenerating sea-snake, he reenacts rather than repudiates many of his father's excesses. And the ongoing dialectic between the dead father and his deadened son becomes a ghostly struggle between root and branch.[17]

In the absence of a meaningful definition of the self and in the absence of meaningful relationships, what surfaces most in Jonathan's life is -- as Kosinski puts it -- "not who I am, and not who the others are, but who I am in relation to others. In other words, to what degree I can push them around, so to what degree they can push me around." Being "incapable of creating a lasting and meaningful relationship of any kind, either with his own past even, or with his future, so to speak, which dwells in him," Jonathan resorts to "the most elementary sort of game playing."[18]

Such "game playing" explains his relationship with Barbara in Rangoon and his cruel joke about the murder of their hostess, Mrs. Llewellyn. It explains Jonathan's liaisons with his prostitutes and mistresses, like the actress, Louise Hunter, with whom he plays out a scenario of passion in London, as well as his behavior with the former family servant, Anthony, whom he humiliates. But most of all, it explains his role in the encounter group and in his very schizoid relationship with Karen, both of which ironically prevent him from discovering any true sense of self.

Of the former, Kosinski has written: "And what is the encounter group? Isn't the encounter group the ultimate game playing? It is of interest that we finally object, ... that we feel that manipulating Barbara in Rangoon is manipulating, but playing one's line in front of an encounter group, somehow is not."[19] Jonathan realizes quickly that the encounter group is interested not in theory but in the stage upon which its members enact their carefully rehearsed -- or calculated -- roles, and the sessions become not helpful avenues toward self-understanding but naive games that mirror the relentless games played out in his own mind.[20] Yet he intensifies his own inadequacy by not confronting the others or questioning their hypocritical and contradictory postures; he remains part of the group, lacking the authenticity of his own self that he needs and convinced only of the dishonesty of people around him. In fact, the encounter group in **The Devil Tree** reigns collectively supreme (as television did in **Being There**)[21] and becomes the only acceptable admission in the modern world of one's total depravity.

The relationship with Karen is even more gamelike. Throughout **The Devil Tree**, Jonathan and Karen jockey for positions of dominance in their relationship.[22] But, ironically, "Whalen's indulgence becomes his punishment";[23] and he moves so far backward that the sexual act precedes rather than culminates his attempts to establish a relationship.

Karen is dull and lacking in spontaneity; in her relationship with Jonathan she responds with the old clichés of sex so that she can avoid confronting her real self. Instead of extending herself and her horizons, she merely contents herself with the search for an ultimate climax. Never escaping the trammels of language that have always been hers,[24] she deceives herself with the "profundity" of her banal platitudes and falls victim to each successive popular -ism.[25] "You know what pleases me: my modeling, being the best and the highest paid, travel, chocolate chip cookies, fucking someone I love" (RDT, p. 20), she says in all seriousness -- not realizing that her remarks sound ludicrously like the "turn-ons" from **Playboy's** Playmate of the Month.

She accuses Jonathan of playing Whalen games: "get on your clothes, I don't want you anymore, you're getting out; sorry, I do need you, you're staying on; no, you're not staying, you're leaving now" (RDT, p. 20). But it is Karen who can't commit herself to anything or anyone. Jonathan recognizes that she is gloss without substance: "fascinated by her own surface. She is a perfect symbol of our visual age" (RDT, p. 45). But for too long he is content to bask in her reflected glory.

At one point, Jonathan wonders: "Why did I choose a woman who cannot give of herself, whose love triggers in me a sense of competition and then makes me want to retreat?" (RDT, p. 42). He answers his own question by recalling his experiences with a whore who slapped him after he told her she wasn't worth the asking price: "she gained sexual control over me as a compliant woman never could, and I desired her even more" (RDT, p. 43). And "because Karen is what I want, she holds the secret of who I am" (RDT, p. 101), claims Jonathan; yet by seeking to understand Karen, he fails to comprehend who he is. He reduces himself to a one-dimensional stance against the world; frozen in his emotional rigidity, in the familiar rituals and repetitions which allow him the mentally-induced state of numbness he seeks, he draws no nearer to self-identity but manages instead to avoid confronting any developing self awareness.[26]

Unlike the dialogues between the man and woman in **Steps,** the games Jonathan and Karen play do not lead to self-discovery and are, like their relationship, at best sophomoric. Though to casual observers Jonathan and Karen appear to be the American dream couple, beneath their bionically beautifully capped teeth and baby-soft tanned skins, they are in actuality hollow shells who inhabit a land more wasteful than T. S. Eliot's.

In the original version of **The Devil Tree**, there is no real resolution of their relationship: on again, off again, it remains the one constant facet of Jonathan's inconstant self. But in the revised **Devil Tree**, Jonathan, having exercised control over the Howmets, is able to control Karen as well. From a letter she has written to him, it seems clear that Karen finally recognizes her real feelings. In that letter, she recalls a passage from Rilke that they both had read together: "We discover, indeed, that we do not know our part: we look for a mirror; we want to rub off the paint, to remove all that is artificial, and to become real. But somewhere a bit of masking that we forget still clings to us. A trace of exaggeration remains in our eyebrows; we do not notice that the corners of our lips are twisted. And thus we go about, a laughingstock, a mere half-thing: neither real beings nor actors." But, concludes Karen, "Now with you, I'm not a laughingstock, a mere half-thing.... I'm secure in the knowledge that our love will always bring me back to you. The loss of you would be a wound for which I have no balm" (RDT, p. 204).

Curiously, Karen's admission of love for and dependence on Jonathan -- the very expression he had earlier sought -- comes too late. Jonathan has already discovered that his attraction to Karen is prohibiting, not liberating, and that their shallow affair contained rather than enlarged his sense of self. In the next-to-last fragment in the book (the one immediately following Karen's letter), Jonathan catches a reflection of himself and Karen locked in a sexual embrace. "He saw himself and Karen doubled up, clutching each other, thrusting, the mirror as a witness of the last moment of his intoxication, of his useless passion " (RDT, p. 205). He looks away and withdraws. Then he stands up, strikes her -- first with his hand and then with his fist -- and without looking back he walks across the room into his study, shutting the door behind him. The relationship is over, but this time it is he who has initiated the break.

Surely that break, combined with the break from his parents (represented by his murder of the Howmets) -- in short, his break from his youthful past -- in turn causes his breakdown in the final passage.

The ending (reminiscent of **Steps**) is, however, an optimistic one. Although some critics, like Norman Lavers,[27] mistakenly assume that Jonathan's final act is a suicide, the ending is actually an opportunity for reconciliation and renewal. Like the protagonists of **The Painted Bird** and **Steps,** Jonathan, in order to forge a future, must come to terms with the present by understanding his past. Only when he is able to overcome his own stinging memories of rejection and to restore his own trust by avenging his parents' and godparents' breach of trust is Jonathan able to confront the past -- and, in confronting it, to face the future. The confrontation occurs significantly on the shores of Lake Geneva. According to Kosinski, the experience in Geneva is **The Devil Tree's** "specific story progression," a "move from the roots to the branches."[28] At the novel's end, Jonathan "longed for change, and he knew that the longing itself was a prelude to recovery" (RDT, p. 206). One night he walks to the edge of the shore, smells the moss and the dew, and watches the fog lift. Ahead of him lie the blinking lights of Geneva.

Since Jonathan is looking back at the origin of his entire metaphysical journey, the final scene provides "a resolution of sorts." Kosinski writes that "if there is some point in the book, maybe that's the point: that somehow we all should find out what is the source of what oppresses us, or what is the source of what gives us joy, and confront it directly.... I think his going to Geneva may feasibly mean he's coming to terms with the ideological roots of his being."[29]

The Painted Bird appeared, with some changes, in three different editions; the first edition, published by Houghton Mifflin in 1965, which excised portions of Kosinski's original manuscript; the first paperbook edition, published by Pocket Books in 1966, which restored those portions deleted in the first edition; and the second edition, published by The Modern Library in 1970, which included some minor textual changes and a new introduction. **The Devil Tree**, however, is the first -- and to date the only -- one of Kosinski's novels to appear in two distinctly different versions: the original novel, published by Harcourt Brace Jovanovich in 1973, and **The Devil Tree: Newly Revised and Expanded Edition**, published by St. Martin's Press in 1981. Since the revision contains most of the original characters and situations, it naturally invites comparison with the earlier version; and such comparison reveals that the new **Devil Tree** is a better fiction which deserves separate critical consideration as well.

In reviewing the original **Devil Tree**, some critics argued that, while "Kosinski has tried to transplant whole the terrifying consciousness of Nazi-occupied Europe between 1939 and 1945 to the United States during the 1960s,"[30] the novel failed to create the horror which was central to his earlier and more successful novels, **The Painted Bird** and **Steps**. Kosinski himself stated in an interview that "I see no essential difference between World War II and any other traumatic reality. For example, I know many people whose childhood in the United States was in its own way just as traumatic as that of millions of Central Europeans."[31] Yet Jonathan's "traumatic reality" is the opposite of that experienced by the narrator of Kosinski's first novel. The boy of **The Painted Bird** is discriminated against because he is different; he is abused and misused because people fear him for his magical gypsy ways (or fear sheltering him, since he is a Jew). In the barren and bestial atmosphere of war, he is given nothing except what he takes for himself (his comet, the wisdom from Comrades Gavrila and Mitka). By contrast, because he is different, Jonathan is revered and admired. Since people fear his affluence and power, he is able to abuse and misuse others. In the materialistic "me-generation" of the sixties and seventies, he is given everything by virtue of his surname and as a result is able to do or to achieve almost nothing on his own. Whereas the boy of **The Painted Bird** tried to withdraw from the ugly reality of his world by sleeping,

Jonathan -- unable to find himself or to accept the real world around him -- attempts to create new worlds for himself. "I learned to retreat to a world of fantasies in which I was always the victor" (DT, p. 36), he states. The fantasizing takes several forms -- drugs, sex, travel -- all of them providing only a temporary escape. His erratic dabblings in the drug culture, reminiscent of Burroughs' **Naked Lunch**, for a time dispel his inhibitions; the use of drugs "gives me something to blame things on later." Yet this too ultimately proves unsuccessful. Withdrawing from his addiction, Jonathan realizes that "once more [he was] creating an artificial system of guilt from which there was no escape" (DT, p. 73). Sex provides another distraction; through sex, Jonathan feels he can assert power and thus assume a new role. "It's all right if I don't love you," he claims, "but I can't stand your not loving me, because then I don't have any power over you" (DT, p. 67). The sex-power theory also fails; he cannot control Karen and ends up in the company of escorts and prostitutes, who ironically wield power over him by charging for their services. Like the Henry Miller hero of the fifties, Jonathan literally makes his way through several continents yet never succeeds in satisfying himself psychologically.

So Jonathan is turned into a walking and vapid cliché of modern alienation and the youth culture,[32] who blames his parents for their rejection and indifference, Karen for her resistance to commitment, the encounter group for fostering alienation, and the world at large for its hostility and tendency to instill paranoia. In its treatment of Jonathan's rationalizing, the early **Devil Tree** is therefore a weak novel, which often dissolves into the psychobabble of analysis and the esoterica of popular Freudian psychology without ever having produced any motivation for Jonathan's decadent behavior or solution for his rootless deviltry.[33] As Robert Alter writes: "**The Devil Tree** is a dismal disappointment because from beginning to end it is a loose web of stylistic and cultural clichés drawn from the popular culture of psychotherapy. Jonathan's vocabulary infected by this involvement instead of bringing us closer to the particular feel of his individual experiences is a cloud of vapid cliche's from the new American world of the psychologically oriented. He constantly mouths the most worn therapeutic formulas about acceptance, insecurity, sense of unworthiness, exposing the real self, being 'aware of my reaction'; he is not above the most barbaric therapoid jargon, as when he talks about 'not structuring my feelings to gain another's approval.'"[34]

Frederick Karl, in discussing **The Devil Tree** and the later fiction, argues that there can be no denying that the novels which followed Kosinski's remarkable achievements in **The Painted Bird** and **Steps** are far less daring and interesting: "One reason, I think, is that Kosinski moved too rapidly into a literary cultural scene, became too rapidly his sole subject matter, and then found he could not distinguish between subject and object. Egomania dominates the later Kosinski canon, but it is insufficiently perceived by him to be a metaphysical principle. He remains so connected to himself that he functions with masks and personae which lack differentiation or variety, associated as they are with overlapping obsessions. With all his European sophistication and historical awareness, he became American too rapidly."[35] In **The Devil Tree**, Kosinski becomes so carried away by the possibilities of individual freedom "that he has failed to give either individual or context a valid container" and "has lost all touchstones for behavior." Jonathan is driven by narcissistic impulses through a kind of lunar landscape, and he moves without enthusiasm. "The resultant novel is a narrative based on an ego meditating with itself," and the meditation is a rather boring one.[36]

Although, like Kosinski's other protagonists, Whalen is an outsider -- the typical, alienated anti-hero in search of inner peace -- he disintegrates somewhat as a character in the original version of the novel. As Ivan Sanders observed, "Compared to the experience of the boy in **The Painted Bird** or the narrator of **Steps**, his vicissitudes seem like a series of meaningless charades. He is trapped in his own jaded, utterly decadent sensibility."[37] His flatness as a character, compounded by his narcissism, senseless brutality, and sterile materialism,[38] hardly makes his problems seem compelling. Furthermore, that flatness, combined with the static characters (almost caricatures) around him, results in the reader's inability to achieve or maintain the suspension of disbelief[39] which is necessary for this fairy tale of the super-rich.

There is, however, a considerable stylistic and psychological distance between the original novel and the revised one. As Kosinski himself comments in the "Author's Note": "When I wrote this novel initially, I felt restricted by the proximity of its story to the environment and events of my recent past decade. This might account for the cryptic tone of the novel's first version. Now, years later, in this revised and expanded edition, I have felt free to reinstate all the additional links that bound Jonathan James Whalen to those whom he loved" (RDT, n.p.).

By Kosinski's own acknowledgment, most of his fiction is based on personal experience, and **The Devil Tree** was no doubt inspired, at least in part, by Kosinski's coming of age in America among the jet set acquaintances of Mary Weir and his subsequent sense of physical and spiritual exile from his Eastern European roots. "The random succession of pain and joy, wealth and poverty, persecution and approbation [in] ... his own life, often as eventful as those of his fictional creations,"[40] is similar to the paradoxes with which Jonathan must come to terms. There are additional biographical and personal experiences in the novel, especially in the revised version: Jonathan gives Karen the notes he wrote while he was abroad so that she can better understand him, just as Kosinski wrote his first novel to explain to Mary Weir the sad events of his childhood in Eastern Europe. Mary appears by name in the revised **Devil Tree** as the former employer of Monsieur Bernardot, whom Jonathan hires as his cook, and several anecdotes from Kosinski's relationship with Mary are fictionalized as well. (For example, in the novel Jonathan learns from his mother's former companion that they had frequently travelled together -- until the man's savings were depleted merely by tipping personnel in "restaurants, nightclubs, taxis, garages, ships, trains, airports, inns, spas, clinics

-- wherever" (RDT, p. 130). This is a situation Kosinski himself experienced; he claims in the course of his early years with Mary tipping alone completed exhausted the considerable amount of money he had made from his first books.)[41] Kosinski even manages to bring in allusions to his other fiction: two friends meet on a show called **Blind Date**; Jonathan and Louise Hunter have dinner at a restaurant named Baobab and later disco at Cockpit; a midwestern professor, a former lover of Karen's best friend, writes his dissertation on passion plays. And the references to Karen's visuality and to the effect of television on the American public clearly recall **Being There.**

In the revised edition, Jonathan has more motivation for his behavior and therefore, in context, becomes somewhat more plausible as a character. His search for the self emerges as the novel's significant central motif and unifies the initially diverse fragments of Jonathan's experience into a whole -- though a rather precarious whole. Like Abraham Joshua Heschel, quoted in the book's epigraph and again on the concluding page, Jonathan grows conscious of "the most important ingredient of self-reflection, the preciousness of [his] own existence," and he struggles to gain control of the seemingly uncontrollable environment. His adventures, seen this way, become less random and discontinuous than they did in the original; instead, they seem like deliberate and progressive attempts to impose an order on existence. (Jonathan therefore is consistent with other Kosinski heroes: the young protagonist of **The Painted Bird**, who learns to control in order to survive; the narrator of **Steps,** an outsider who is an exile in his own land and later an exile in a new land; the passive media messiah of **Being There,** who unknowingly becomes the agent for order in a weak and chaotic society; Tarden of **Cockpit,** for whom surveillance and manipulation provide superiority; Levanter of **Blind Date,** who sees himself fated to act as an avenger of society's wrongs; Fabian of **Passion Play,** whose quest is for order amidst the confusion of modern morality.)

Jonathan's quest is for awareness and an understanding of the chance elements which surround him and sometimes threaten to engulf him. Yet the very nature of his quest often prohibits its success. For if Jonathan's life -- and modern life in general -- is like the devil tree, with its confusion of roots and branches, pasts and futures, there can be no realization of actions, no linear progressions. Only circles exist, like the circular prophecy of Abraham Joshua Heschel or the many mirror images of the novel which "split, enlarge, and multiply images"[42] -- and reflect and regress ad infinitum. Thus, the consequence of Jonathan's action is forever the antithesis of his intention. For all of his talk of "man against himself and nature," he can never become a master skier naturally but only through the most mechanical of means: crash programs with "specially constructed devices"; a battery-powered gyroscope; and two assistants, two video cameramen, and professional downhillers available for hire. Although he considers taping Karen's conversations to monitor her actions while they are apart, he never does; instead, he gives her his diaries which ironically allow her one more way to wield control over him. His revenge on the Howmets is provoked by their earlier manipulation of his mother, of his corporation, and even of himself. To avenge those whom his godparents victimized, he makes his godparents victims; yet almost immediately after their demise, he mysteriously becomes victim to some disease. The circle continues.

Nowhere, however, is the circularity of events more evident or the symbol of the baobab more brilliantly realized than in Jonathan's slow recognition that, in trying to escape the ghosts of his family, he becomes more like them. Like his mother, who dulls herself to the pain of reality with her arsenal of drugs, Jonathan escapes his father's legacy for a time by turning to narcotics. But, as he comes of age, he returns, a stranger in a familiar land, to command his father's commanding fortune. Repeatedly, he points out the difference between the elder Whalen and himself:

> My father worked himself to death. At the
> peak of his career, his heart, unable to keep

> up with his unlimited drive to compete, stopped.
> Because my drive is limited, I could not even
> bring myself to go to war -- the epitome of
> competition -- since that would have unreasonably
> increased the chances of my death. My father's
> death seemed like destiny's corporate refusal
> to extend the loan of time he still needed to
> accomplish his task; my own would probably
> appear as an outright refusal to take out such
> a loan. Quite appropriately, Horace Sumner
> Whalen had been mourned by all who were in
> his debt. But if I, Jonathan James Whalen, were
> to die right now ... no one would mourn the
> loss. (RDT, p. 84).

What he fails to note, however, are the remarkable similarities. Like Horace, who forced people to conform by buying
their souls or breaking their spirits, Jonathan uses his name
and his wealth to effect changes. He demands that the
police chief exact immediate retribution on a police officer
who struck "a Whalen"; he punishes Karen for her indiscretion
by paying an actress to pose as his companion abroad; and
he humiliates Anthony -- far more than his father ever
did -- with shocking stories of lewdness and violence ("I
don't know why, but perversely I continued until I was sure
he realized that my life was beyond his experience" [RDT,
p. 104]).

As the many Calvinist references (several of which were
added to the novel's second version) suggest, Jonathan
is predestined to inherit his parents' sins along with their
wealth. Despite his attempts at total depravity, he is nonetheless elect to the American dream of success and money,
twisted though it may be -- like the devil tree -- and unable
to provide him with the spiritual satisfaction he craves.
Paradoxically, as Jonathan says, he is an exile from that
same dream. Yet this seems to be precisely Kosinski's
point: such paradox is inherent in the American dream[43]
itself and implicit in modern American society.

The structure of the new **Devil Tree** ignores the conventional narrative in favor of a montage effect of images and impressions, through which Kosinski creates a kind of verbal photography. Each literary passage is like a still frame, intense and unique, yet simultaneously a fragment of a larger cinematographic sequence. In this way, Kosinski is able to convey the sometimes disjointed but intricately interconnected movements of Jonathan's mind as he seeks to define his sense of being.

Though much of the pop-cultism which Kosinski taps in **The Devil Tree** is intentional parody, there is just too much banality in both Karen's and Jonathan's cliches, even in the revised edition. Especially disturbing is the astonishing rapidity with which both principals can move from the self-centered platitudes of the "me-generation" to the profound wisdom of Rilke and Marx -- and back again -- without real awareness of any philosophy. In the end, Karen's actions are just too uncaring and Jonathan's wailings are just too shrill. Because they are too rich and too beautiful to be true, they do not sufficiently engage the reader's attention and, as characters, they remain even more disengaged from reality than does the allegorical Chance.

Nevertheless, the new **Devil Tree**, vastly superior to the original, is an entertaining story, an interesting though flawed novel, and an important link in the cycle of Kosinski's fiction.

ENDNOTES TO CHAPTER SIX

1. Jerzy Kosinski, **The Devil Tree: Newly Revised and Expanded Edition** (New York: St. Martin's Press, 1981). All subsequent references will be made by page number in the text and will be either to this edition (RDT) or to the first edition (DT), **The Devil Tree** (New York: Harcourt Brace Jovanovich, 1973).

2. Daniel J. Cahill, "The Devil Tree: An Interview with Jerzy Kosinski," **The North American Review**, 9 (Spring 1973), 57.

3. Ibid., p. 61.

4. Jack Hicks, **In the Singer's Temple** (Chapel Hill: University of North Carolina Press, 1982), p. 237.

5. Ibid.

6. Jerzy Kosinski, "The Lone Wolf," **The American Scholar,** 41, No. 4 (Autumn 1972), 514.

7. Ibid.

8. Ibid.

9. Hicks, p. 238.

10. Kosinski, "The Lone Wolf," p. 513.

11. Hicks, p. 238.

12. Ibid., p. 239.

13. Cahill, p. 61.

14. Norman Lavers, **Jerzy Kosinski** (Boston: Twayne, 1982), p. 86.

15. Ibid., p. 88.

16. Paul Bruss, **Victims** (Lewisburg: Bucknell University Press, 1981), pp. 179-80.

17. Hicks, p. 244.

18. Cahill, p. 60.

19. Ibid.

20. Bruss, p. 175-76.

21.   Samuel Coale, "The Cinematic Self of Jerzy Kosinski," **Modern Fiction Studies,** 20, No. 3 (Autumn 1974), 366.

22.   Lavers, p. 86.

23.   Stuart Hirschberg, "Becoming an Object: The Function of Mirrors and Photographs in Kosinski's **The Devil Tree,**" **Notes on Contemporary Literature,** 4, No. 2 (1974), p. 15.

24.   Bruss, pp. 176-77.

25.   Lavers, p. 82.

26.   Coale, p. 367.

27.   Lavers, p. 89.

28.   Cahill, p. 57.

29.   Ibid.

30.   Phillip Corwin, "Evil Without Roots," **Nation,** 30 April 1973, p. 568.

31.   George Plimpton and Rocco Landesman, "The Art of Fiction: Jerzy Kosinski," **Paris Review,** 54 (Summer 1972), 190.

32.   Coale, p. 366.

33.   Corwin, p. 567.

34.   Robert Alter, "The Devil Tree," **The New York Times Book Review,** 11 February 1973, p. 3.

35.   Frederick R. Karl, **American Fictions: 1940-80** (New York: Harper and Row, 1985), p. 502.

36.   Ibid., p. 504.

37.   Ivan Sanders, "The Gifts of Strangeness: Alienation and Creation in Jerzy Kosinski's Fiction," **The Polish Review,** 19, Nos. 3-4 (Autumn-Winter 1974), 181.

38.   J. B. Kiley, Review of **The Devil Tree, Critic,** 31 (May-June 1973), 80.

39.   Alter writes: "He scarcely exists as a realized character, and the human figures among whom he moves are no more than crude cartoons" (p. 2).

40.   "On Kosinski," in Jerzy Kosinski, **Pinball** (New York: Bantam, 1983), p. 306.

41.   Lavers, p. 6. Also noted in Wayne Warga, "Jerzy Kosinski Reaches Down Into Life and Writes," **Los Angeles Time Calendar,** 22 April 1973, p. 54.

42.   For a fuller discussion of mirror images in **The Devil Tree,** see Stuart Hirschberg, op. cit.

43.   Corwin, p. 568.

CHAPTER SEVEN

THE FLAME ISN'T WORTH THE CANDLE:
COCKPIT AND BLIND DATE

"Why won't you remain in Paris? All the life-
support equipment is here."

Monod looked at him steadfastly. "To be hooked
up to life through a machine?" he asked abruptly.
"The flame isn't worth the candle."

Jerzy Kosinski, **Blind Date**

Published in 1975, Kosinski's fifth novel, **Cockpit**, is a chilling
vision of our times "in which the picaresque hero has
been stripped of his ordinary motivations -- lust, greed,
desire for excitement -- and made into Tarden, a fugitive
from an unnamed totalitarian state, a former secret agent
of this his adopted country, who recites the episodes of
his life manipulating others with a god-like detachment."[1]
A contemporary invisible man twice over,[2] he is, like earlier
Kosinski protagonists, both ruthless and rootless in his
overwhelming desire to control.

A complex character, at once predictable and protean,
Tarden endeavors to realize and reconcile his many identities and to attain the freedom the realization of those
identities would confer upon him.[3] Having quit the Service
(a select agency comparable to the CIA), he becomes the
only secret agent, or "hummingbird," never to have been
successfully tracked. But to maintain an "active cover
life"[4] so as not to be eliminated (as he himself had eliminated
a former treasonous agent) -- and to expand his knowledge
of himself and his control of others -- he begins a life of
concealment, numerous disguises, and elaborate security

measures. Like Tarden himself, the novel metamorphoses; it moves "with a kind of dreamlike arbitrariness, from Kafkacsque fantasy of totalitarianism, into a spy story, and then into a series of stories about Tarden's interventions into the lives of others -- fables, rather, that end in harsh riddles rather than morals."[5]

The nameless boy of **The Painted Bird** and the narrator of **Steps** dreamed of escaping their own identities as victims; in **The Devil Tree**, Jonathan Whalen sought to discover "that language beyond words" which would liberate him from social strictures as well as from the haunting shadows of a dead father and a suicidal mother. Tarden disciplines his emotions to the point of perversion, hones his intellect to create a power of life and death, and guides his actions to defeat the faceless authority of the State, to strip the assurance of the arrogant, to play on the seeming strength of the powerful, to punish the guilty.[6] He rejects the claims of his old oppressive Ruthenian language and culture enough to master an even more potent language and to become an oppressor with a vengeance.[7]

Tarden's new language is alternately loud (like the directional microphones which he uses to create the illusion of many voices -- and the suggestion of his many personas[8] -- at his summer home) or silent (like the idiom of violence: blinding a man with a quartz watch). Controlled or withheld, it becomes a method of expanding the range of perception (p. 130). In the absence of a sufficiently strong conception of himself that he can regard as the bedrock of his experience, Tarden relies upon his mastery of this new language to free himself from the constraints inherent in any given situation, especially restrictive notions of truth or reality.[9] The possibility of going beyond the limits of others' language offers him both a challenge and an opportunity for genuinely creative experience, and the expansion of perception, played by a protean protagonist like Tarden, becomes the ultimate game.

But language is not his only tool. A kind of urban James Bond, Tarden revels in modern technology and maintains

his superiority partly because of it.[10] Living simultaneously
in a number of different apartments (all high up in modern
buildings with service elevators nearby) so that tracking
his whereabouts becomes more difficult, Tarden is never
without the numerous technological tricks of his trade,
paraphernalia which easily cripples his opponents. Forgoing
the plain, old-fashioned violence of firearms for the more
contemporary killers like needles, drugs, and sprays, "this
small, dark, unmuscular Bond ... conquers in all situations."[11]
(In one particularly prophetic episode, Tarden injects first
purple and then red dye into several food products in local
grocery stores and precipitates a national panic over tamper-
ing.)

Yet Tarden does not merely use technology; he is absolutely
fascinated by it. And having seized control of the electronic
gadgetry that so amazed the simple-minded Chance in
Being There,[12] Tarden turns each technological device
into an instrument of his own very private revenge. While
proclaiming that "I am nobody's instrument" (p. 78), he
employs his devices to engage others in the dramas that
he creates: he gains control of a young prostitute by photographing her and then "selling" back to her the photographs
she covets; he forces the young wife of a psychiatrist to
perform demeaning sexual acts by threatening to inject
her husband with a deadly poison; he makes a waxen impression of a mailman's key, which gives him access to mailboxes
all over town and allows him to intervene at will in people's
most private lives. When Veronika -- the one woman in
the novel who is Tarden's equal -- fails to honor an agreement, he pays three scabrous derelicts to abuse her sexually
while he photographs her humiliation. The second time
she reneges he exacts an even more heinous revenge by
firing off a deadly dose of radiation from the cockpit of
a test plane and tells the unsuspecting woman that "a part
of me will always be with her. Nothing would please me
more, I said, than to know that there would be days and
nights when, unable to sleep, she would recall our arrangement and how it had ended" (p. 236).

In Tarden's hands, even a telephone becomes a tool of intimidation, another weapon in his arsenal of control. As a child, he amuses himself by making random calls to townspeople and announcing in the high-pitched voice typical of the long-distance operator (and later in the gruff voice of a bureaucrat) that they must report at once to the capital for resident certification. His victims are often frightened by the strange and official request (all the more intimidating in the atmosphere of post-World-War-II Eastern Europe). Ironically, because of their meekness, he continues his cruel telephone game. Once he reaches a Jew who recently suffered a heart attack; feeling some sympathy, he considers terminating the conversation. But when he asks the Jew why he did not flee the country, the man answers that "destiny has decreed that Jews were to live in the homes of others, even if they were enemies." Enraged by his passivity, Tarden states that "destiny belonged to men, not men to destiny" (p. 115), and shapes the suffering man's destiny by insisting that he keep the appointment. As Paul Bruss notes: "Clearly what troubles Tarden in this episode, even at such a young age, is the Jew's use of the concept of destiny as a means for avoiding full responsibility for his own life. Instead of asserting his own perspective, the Jew allows a traditional language to dominate him. In the process he defuses whatever language he may have developed for himself and turns himself, at least in Tarden's eyes, into only a shell of what he might have been."[13]

Unlike the Jew he persecutes, Tarden is not content to be a mere shell, so he learns to wield control just as he learns to survive: by "order[ing] every aspect of my existence" (p. 104). And for him, memory is the most effective way of achieving that end. But even recollection is not a passive act; it too is a weapon.[14] His excellent memory of past events complements his ability to manipulate life in the present and, to some degree (as with Veronika), to create the future. A genius confirmed by tests he took as a child, he takes pleasure in circling back through images of the past: "If I evoke a single memory picture, others will spring up automatically to join it and soon the montage of a past self will emerge" (p. 13). His memories, in fact, are far more accurate and vivid than his photographs -- another way he uses to freeze and evoke a moment -- which merely hint at the wealth of recollections stored away in his mind. "All that time and trouble, and still the record is a superficial one," he says; "I see only how I looked in the fraction of a second when the shutter was open. But there's no trace of the thoughts and emotions which surrounded that moment" (p. 180). So while the chemical fantasies he creates in paper and stain are transient, his memories are not; combined with action, they exist for him in an exponential relationship -- each acknowledging and expanding the other.[15]

Recalling an old bicycle wheel which he played with as a boy, he realizes that "Each person is a wheel to follow, and at any moment my manner, my language, my being, like the stick I used as a boy, will drive the wheel where I urge it to go" (p. 148). His youthful diversions with a wheel and stick are but a prelude to his adult games, designed to heighten his own awareness as well as to control the fates of others. Some of his games are simple, like the one he plays with a barkeeper of a local tavern. Others are more complex, like the game he plays with the children and villagers at his rented estate and with the young boy whom he threatens -- in Ruthenian -- to feed like a sausage into the plane's engines. Still others are especially cruel, like his game with the retiree whom he frightens into moving into a Florida senior citizens' community (the description of which is quite possibly the most frightening scene in the book).

Like earlier Kosinski protagonists and like Kosinski himself, Tarden becomes a consummate gamesman by employing disguises, which he masters through his long apprenticeship in deception, begun in his native land and continued through his years in the Service. Disguise, he says, is "more than a means of personal liberation: it's a necessity. My life depends on my being able to ... slip out of the past" (pp. 129-30). It is difficult for Tarden to be himself, because "himself" is reviled and marked for torture and death; he must become "others" in order to survive his own self.[16]

Each disguise is a means of survival (and a metaphor for identity)[17] which allows him to create himself anew and to define his environment. (Even more than Kosinski's other protagonists, Tarden goes to great lengths to control his external environment: multiple residences; frequent moves between apartments so that no one grows to recognize him or can trace his steps; elaborate security systems including massive combination locks on his doors and various electronic devices; secret hiding places for himself and his valuables; film and tape records of others' activities.)

At one point in the novel, for example, he assumes a disguise so that he can use the totalitarian system to his advantage. Turning the State's bureaucratic confusion against itself, he invents four prominent academicians to write on his behalf recommending him for a foreign research scholarship, forwards a request for a passport application to his home-town's Provincial Passport Bureau, obtains (through further trickery) a round-trip airline ticket, and flees Eastern Europe for the United States (an episode that allegedly parallels Kosinski's own departure from Poland in 1957). Another time he successfully intervenes on behalf of -- and rescues -- an émigré removed forcibly from the free transit lounge of an airport and imprisoned by officials in his homeland.

The Service provides an opportunity both "to find a shield for the self I wanted to hide" (p. 64) and to effect change in others. Tarden joins after passing an unusual examination during which new recruits are repeatedly told to undress for a medical check-up and then to dress again. The relentless dressing and undressing is not preparation for a physical but instead an actual stress test -- and Tarden passes because he expresses "no visible emotion" and accepts the changes in orders as if he expected them all along (p. 55). This same emotionless, at times passionless, posture continues to serve him in good stead, even after he terminates his career in the Service.

Yet while Tarden learns much about deception as an agent, it is an incident with a former roommate which most expands his perceptions. Robert, a gentle man, becomes a crazed killer, turning on Tarden and assaulting him repeatedly with a large knife. Only after the police subdue and remove him does Tarden learn of Robert's unstable past from his father: "When Robert was a small boy, I gave him a dog," he said. "A big, strong animal. The kid loved it more than anything else in the world. Two years later he cut off the dog's head" (p. 48). (When Tarden later trains a hound to be used as a live bomb, he too is surprised by "his own lack of emotional response" [pp. 109-110] to the dog's death.)

Robert makes Tarden realize that no one is what he appears to be. And, "even now, whenever I become involved with others enough to expect certain patterns of behavior or to rely on them, the memory of my experience with Robert returns to alert me" (p. 48-49). Appreciating that even apparent mutual understanding can be illusory, Tarden does not permit easy familiarity like that which he enjoyed with Robert to deceive him ever again.

Instead, he probes deeply and instinctively into the existence of others around him, to know the inmost hearts of those with whom he comes into contact, to discover any potential threats, without getting close enough to allow others to know him. [18] He constantly tests people and creates his own scenarios, becoming, as he himself says, "in charge of the plot. It's my novel" (p. 169). At times, he approaches "saleswomen with legs misshapen by decades of standing on their feet, and salesmen clutching their backs when they bend down to pick out merchandise from a lower drawer," people with "faded faces" and "tired eyes" (p. 150), and plays out a familiar scene: asking to see virtually every item in their store; unsatisfied with each, leaving without making a purcahse; returning and making the same request. Only if the salespersons are unflinchingly polite and helpful throughout his test does he reward their courtesy and friendliness with a big sale and a letter to their supervisor (usually on stationery which he has somehow appropriated). Like the narrator of **Steps,** he uses specimens to conduct his experiments; but in **Cockpit** as in **Steps,** those experiments are social, not scientific.

Tarden's inherent suspicions of everything and everyone leave him unable to form close relationships, especially with women. His earliest memories are of a nanny, who hugged him to her breast -- and whom he stabbed with a small pair of scissors from her work basket (perhaps as retribution because a previous nanny had helped Tarden's father break the boy's sleepwalking habit). Even references to his mother, though infrequent, are always melancholy. After the police put an end to his telephone pranks and jail his father and tutor as suspects, he recalls his mother alternately shocked by and weeping at his deception. His later relationships are merely agreements, which he alone defines. For example, he allows Theodora, the woman who at great personal expense introduced him to the Service, to collect his sperm if she will supply him with young women for excitement. But after Theodora is impregnated by the sperm she has collected, he discredits and abandons her. And when Valerie sees through his game and realizes that by appointing himself as her liberator he actually prohibits her from shaping her existence, he secretly photographs her affair with another man.

Norman Lavers concludes that Tarden is a failure with women because "in each relationship he insists on absolute control, and he does not claim his control by the power of his person, but rather uses either money or some other sort of lever, blackmail, or some sort of contractual agreement that forces compliance with his will. He becomes, to the others, that totalitarian State which he could not endure to have over himself, and the women cannot endure it either."[19] Yet sexual identity is but another aspect of the protean self for Tarden; through his sexual encounters -- both totem and taboo -- he manipulates what once were hardening spasms of moral and social conventions. Sex -- sometimes forbidden, sometimes dangerous, sometimes repressed[20] -- is always a way of achieving a new (but not necessarily sexual) plateau of perception for himself and his partners. Hence, the title **Cockpit** alludes also to Tarden's sexploits.

As Tarden ages, his body begins to fail him: he no longer has the physical agility he once possessed; his blood pressure falls dangerously low; and, during one of his encounters with a prostitute, he worries that he might die "without leaving a trace" (p. 3). Facing the prospect of an anonymous death, he recognizes the emptiness of his own existence -- especially at the end of the novel, when he gets trapped in a broken elevator which, for more than eight hours, moves from the bottom floor to the top again, bounding and rebounding as endlessly as the rock which another existential man, Sisyphus, must push up his hill. The special devices which Tarden carries to protect himself against "hostile passengers" (p. 246) are useless. Exhausted from the heat and his own tension and paranoia, he vomits, voids himself on the elevator floor, strips himself naked -- and finally realizes he can do nothing but wait and hope that he will be rescued. "Although I have always thought of myself as moving horizontally through space, invading others people's spheres, my life has always been arranged vertically: all my apartments have been at least midway up in tall buildings, making elevators absolutely essential," he says. "Now one of these necessary devices had suddenly become a windowless cell. The forces that propelled it up and down seem as arbitrary and autonomous as those that spin the earth on its axis. Here, in the solitude of my capsule, I sense a curious time warp. Encased in a steel and rubber sarcophagus, I was completely cut off from my past: a royal mummy, safely cradled and sealed for the long voyage ahead" (p. 247).

Finally freed, he learns that "out of order" signs had been posted throughout the building the day before. But "someone had removed my floor's warning. 'Probably a child,' [the building superintendent] said, 'probably a prank'" (p. 247). And so Tarden -- the gamesman, the manipulator, the pilot in the cockpit shaping other's destinies -- becomes the random victim of a child's joke (a prank as potentially destructive as his own childhood pranks with flowerpots and telephones were), one which all of his protective techno-logical paraphernalia cannot prevent. A victim also of chance, he must concede that -- for all of his attempts to control himself and others -- he (like all contemporary men) is ultimately out of control.

The reader is reminded of Kosinski's epigraph, from Antoine de Saint-Exupery's **Flight to Arras:** "But I dwell now well in the making of the future. Little by little, time is kneading me into shape. A child is not frightened at the thought of being patiently turned into an old man. He is a child and he plays like a child. I too play my games. I count the dials, the levers, the buttons, the knobs of my kingdom." In the final pages of **Cockpit**, all of Tarden's dials, levers, and buttons fail him, and he is beaten at his own game, probably by a child who indeed "plays like a child."

The brief (two paragraph) closing episode of the novel, which immediately follows, builds on Tarden's experience in the broken elevator. Possibly while recuperating from this ordeal, he looks out of his apartment and sees the skaters gliding on the ice in the park below. Their motion becomes one rhythm, and their figures blend until "the rink appears to revolve around the skaters as they stand like frozen sculptures growing out of the ice" (p. 248). (Earlier Tarden had described how, as a child, he would toss live animals into a pond and watch them freeze in an instant: "One after another, they died, their heads cocked to one side as though listening, their eyes frozen open. When the first snow swirled down, it stuck to the animals. Throughout the winter, they sat in the frozen pond like frosted glass sculptures from the church fair" [p. 120].)

This final frozen image of the collective reminds the reader of the dominant image from **The Devil Tree** -- the baobab, whose roots become its branches and whose branches become its roots -- and triggers for Tarden yet another image, also from his childhood, of a great old army tank, hit decades ago by an enemy shell and now sunken in a shallow lagoon. The tank is a painful reminder: of fictionalized war in Tarden's Ruthenia, of actual war in Kosinski's native Poland, and of war as metaphor for modern man's continuing struggle.

Although Tarden's life depends on his ability "to instantly create a new persona and slip out of the past," at the end of **Cockpit**, there is no new persona, no escaping from the past. Tarden is, for the moment, minus all of his disguises: an aging and sickly man -- like the old army tank, a lone dead battler in a lost and forgotten war.[21] Still defiantly resisting both an actual and metaphoric frozen living death, he is nonetheless as much a victim of chance as all of Kosinski's other protagonists.

Kosinski has been quoted as saying that he considers **Cockpit** -- especially its ending -- positive. In an interview with Geoffrey Movius, he remarked, "I am astonished that so few of those who have written about **Cockpit** realized that Tarden, its main character, might generate a feeling of optimism, a sudden inner statement in a reader. Look how much Tarden does with his life."[22] Insofar as Tarden's games bring about the expansion of perception (as the narrator's desertion of the woman in **Steps** allows her a new understanding of herself) and the possibility for exploring the self, **Cockpit** is indeed optimistic.

But not all critics judge **Cockpit** so favorably. Some, like Frederick Karl, have called it "a great anal saga, dominated by a confidence man, capable of great cruelty, otherwise somewhat exhausted; a man of endless wealth and resources, all concealed." Karl also considers Tarden's extreme contempt for women, all of whom are viewed through Tarden's eyes, as a limitation of the novel. Tarden defines the moral action of the novel, and the women become mere "playthings, torments, goods, orifices."[23]

Another reviewer, Adrian Ayres, writes that "the book is basically sensationalism dealing with odd sexual practices, sado-masochistic relationships, violence, and exotic methods of killing.... One wonders what the point of all this is." **Cockpit,** he concludes, is "another in a line of alternately disgusting and depressing books ... and after awhile it all begins to wear thin."[24]

Yet **Cockpit,** a novel not only of Tarden's debriefing and exorcism of waking nightmares but also of his confession,[25] as the postscript from Dostoevsky's **The Possessed** suggests, is ultimately a largely successful work. Stylistically interesting in the way that Kosinski uses autobiography, **Cockpit** marks a development that culminates in Kosinski's most recent novels. Norman Lavers calls it a "spiritual autobiography of Kosinski himself, told by indirection"[26] -- and, by implication, a spiritual biography of modern man. As in the best of Kosinski's works, especially **Steps,** the reader must connect the random story pieces by assuming the responsibility which Tarden, through his unemotionality, avoids.[27]

Thematically, **Cockpit** is bolder than some of the novels which preceded it, just as the protagonist is bolder and more direct in the games he employs. On one level, Tarden is a familiar type in modern fiction: the undercover agent who has long appealed to the literary imagination and who appears in much contemporary literature, especially in works by Graham Greene, Anthony Burgess, and Norman Mailer and in the popular paperbacks of Ian Fleming and John Le Carre. But Kosinski's intent with Tarden is not to exploit the sensational stuff of spy fiction but rather to reclaim certain territory and experience as the rightful terrain for serious fiction concerned with morality in contemporary life. Kosinski uses the spy novel, as does Anthony Burgess, to reflect on spiritual matters, on the vagaries of personal morality and social responsibility, on the conflicting obligations to a pure self and a corrupt modern world.[28]

By contrast to the superspy Tarden, George Levanter, the hero of **Blind Date,** is no professional agent; he is a small investor, an "idea man,"[29] who works with -- but not for -- agencies like Investors International, modeled on real-life organizations Amnesty International and P.E.N. (Poets, Essayists, and Novelists Club, an international organization whose American Center's presidency Kosinski held for the maximum two-year term).

Whereas Tarden is so obsessed with power and with personal revenge that he must be in control of every aspect of his existence, assuming masks and disguises ritually and almost religiously, never exposing his true self to others, Levanter, on the other hand, is more emotionally accessible and, at times, even vulnerable. A believer in Jacques Monod's philosophies (and, like Kosinski, a close personal friend of the Nobel-Prize-winning scientist and author of **Chance and Necessity**), he recognizes that "blind chance and nothing else is responsible for each random event" (p. 86). Therefore, regardless of how careful he is with his personal investments, he knows chance will always dominate his words and deeds. In a world where Stalin's daughter, Svetlana Alliluyeva, moves halfway around the world and becomes his "ordinary next-door neighbor," Levanter -- whose friend Romarkin had years before been imprisoned for challenging Stalin's authority -- concludes that "anything can happen (p. 79). Or in a world where physical decline finally dominates mental acumen, Levanter eventually has no choice but to back off his earlier emphasis on rational control: "While his mind retained its ability to consider circumstances and issue commands, his body, which had once reacted automatically, was now frequently unable to respond as expected" (pp. 21-22).[30]

Kosinski contrasts the two protagonists this way:"Tarden perceives and lives his life as if it were a cumulative process. In **Cockpit's** opening sentence he sets up his predicament: 'Although we have known each other for a long time....' and the novel continues as a confessional <u>summa</u> of Tarden. To Levanter life is composed of moments, each commencing with one's awareness of its beginning. **Blind Date** opens with "When he was a schoolboy, George Levanter had learned a convenient routine," but for the rest of his life Levanter will rebel against routine. In **Cockpit** it is Tarden's language, his narration that is the sole dramatic agent that recasts what the protagonist claims had been his life's experiences. In **Blind Date**, objectively narrated events of Levanter's life provide the novel's outward expression."[31]

Even as a boy, Tarden uses the violence of the system against itself -- and employs the only language which the State understands: the language of intimidation. Levanter also masters the intimidating language of the State, but he employs it -- and reacts to his use of it -- in different ways. Once, while skiing, he encounters a group of vacationing Russians, probably low-level functionaries, who guess he is a Spanish laborer and criticize both his appearance and his demeanor. Levanter immediately assumes "the manner of an authoritarian Soviet bureaucrat" and addresses the Russians in their own language, reprimanding them for unmasking their "true feelings" on Spanish fascism. Yet as the crestfallen Russians sit in the ski station preparing for the investigation they are sure would await them at home, "for a moment he felt sorry for them and considered going over to apologize and tell them the truth" (pp. 19-21). But Levanter knows they would not see the joke and would only be more frightened if he attempted to explain. "Then he felt ashamed and somehow unnerved by his deception" -- feelings which never would have been stirred in Tarden -- and surprised that "the short encounter with the Soviets had resurrected a part of himself he had believed he had buried, the enjoyment of certifiable power" (p. 21). In a similar scene (alluded to earlier), after Romarkin boldly asks a challenging, unapproved question about Stalin during a party-sponsored meeting at the Lomonosov University in Moscow and is arrested, Levanter refuses to sign a state- ment labeling his good friend a subversive. "I will never sign such a statement," he said. "Never. But remember this: one day, in Siberia, I shall voluntarily admit that when I was at the university I was indeed a member of the conspir- acy dedicated to wrecking the Party apparatus. I will pro- duce facts and name names. And when I do, you -- who will probably be a captain by then -- will be accused of failing to obtain important information about the conspiracy from me during the investigation. You will be denounced for negligence. Perhaps even for being sympathetic to our cause" (pp. 45-46). Like Tarden, Levanter successfully manipulates the bureaucracy by understanding how it oper- ates. But, unlike Tarden, Levanter uses the system not to protect himself from the repercussions of his own cruel game but to protect his friend, whom he admires for challenging the party line on Stalin. (In response to Romarkin's question years later -- "Tell me, Lev, ... have you found that people are good in the West? Are they better than where you and I came from?" -- he says that people are good everywhere. "They turn bad only when they fall for little bits of power tossed to them by the state or by a political party, by a union or a company, or a wealthy mate. They forget that their power is nothing more than a temporary camouflage of mortality" [p. 8]. Levanter's perspective is more seasoned and less monotonal[32] than Tarden's rationalized revenges.)

When Tarden "sells" his photographs back to the prostitute, his motives are largely selfish. Levanter also takes photographs, which he later sells -- but he does so for a better cause. Each one of his pictures of the Deputy Minister with his beautiful companions will secure the release of an imprisoned intellectual. (After a writer whose freedom Levanter has arranged through these means complains that he feels humiliated by the bargain ["I thought that PERSAUD was torturing me for my beliefs, that they believed my ideas would spread to the masses"], Levanter reminds him that "ideas don't perish in prison cells, people do" [p. 35].)

When Levanter engages the little girl Olivia in a game about roles, it is obviously playful, unlike Tarden's more malicious deception of the young Ruthenian boy, Tomek. In the former episode, Olivia is part of the joke, and everyone laughs along with her; in the latter, Tomek -- already estranged and isolated -- is the victim of the joke (though it can be argued that he learns a very valuable lesson about life as a result of his experience). When Levanter offers to set Serena up with a three-year trust fund, it is an attempt to penetrate further the mystery which she, out of necessity, has begun to reveal -- not as a way of restricting her freedom and controlling her, which is at the root of the agreements Tarden strikes with his women. And when Levanter, watching and waiting for the minister who created the notorious

PERSAUD to be punished, imagines himself behind a missile control panel, it is to quell a bomber "on a mission of destruction" whose targets are unsuspecting men and women "in the cities, towns, and villages" below (p. 36). He is the agent for constructive or protective manipulation, not the instrument of destruction which Tarden becomes when he enters the cockpit and fires off a deadly dose of radiation at his uncooperative mistress.

From **The Painted Bird** through **Cockpit**, Kosinski's novels are packed with incident but, according to Paul Bruss, remain a fiction without content. Kosinski generally "avoids layering his fictions with specific values, and to the extent that his text is free of such value and thus challenges the reader to become aware of the processes of perception and of language in his own experience, the text -- even with its emphasis upon demystification or upon perceptual expansion -- matches up rather well with ... [minimalist] art of the 1960s. By retreating from more specific contents, Kosinski essentially forces his reader to establish a new and much more active relationship to the text. It is the reader who, in the absence of the traditional signals of theme, metaphor, structure, etc., must make the associations and relationships that give the text some coherence and significance."[33] What distinguishes **Blind Date**, then, from **Cockpit** (and from the earlier novels) is Kosinski's "increasing interest in the protagonist's relationship with other 'survivors' who have themselves discovered the necessity of understanding and exploring the limits of perception and of language that finally give shape to their experience."[34] The boy of **The Painted Bird**, accepting that he is different from others, masters only the idiom of brutality; the narrator of **Steps** observes actions almost clinically and impersonally; Chance merely watches, his mind a blank screen; Jonathan Whalen, avoiding all attachments to the past, becomes part of the very power he despises; and Tarden plays his numerous wheel games, intervening in and orchestrating the lives of others. But Levanter is the first of Kosinski's protagonists really to exhibit sympathy for those he becomes involved with and to avenge only when others have been hurt or wronged. (One reviewer calls it a "new element:

Conscience.")[35] Kosinski writes that "As a mature man, Levanter is increasingly given to acts on behalf of others -- Weston, the stockholders, PERSAUD, the tortured intellectuals, Mme. Ramoz, the imprisoned journalists, and many others. Even killing the hotel clerk is not only an act of revenge for what was done to J.P. the fencer and to countless other unsuspecting visitors from behind the Iron Curtain, but a way of breaking the chain of further denunciations and misery for them (as it was with getting rid of Barbatov, Levanter's Commander in the Army)." In neither case -- eliminating the hotel clerk responsible for incriminating so many innocent people or ridding his unit of Barbatov and his foolish quotas for reprimands to soldiers -- does Levanter take any credit for righting the injustice; and, ironically, in the latter case, he is even subjected to the ridicule of soldiers who, while envying his "better bargain" (p. 51), are unaware of what he had done to make their own daily lives easier. And "even when Levanter is blackmailed and used -- by Jolene, his out-of-town blind date, by Impton's Chief of Police, by Serena -- he does not respond with malice. He makes no attempt at revenge -- as soon as he is free, he merely steps away."[36] Perhaps because he is better able to relate to women than other Kosinski protagonists, he is also the first to marry.[37]

Kosinski himself stated that the earlier novels were part of a cycle, and "although each novel of the cycle reflects and comments upon the motifs of the others, only **The Painted Bird** and **Cockpit** concern themselves with its full archetypal spectrum. In **The Painted Bird** society refuses the individual (the Boy) a place within itself by waging war against him; in **Cockpit**, it is the individual (Tarden) who, refusing the place society insists he occupy, wages a war against the institutions of society." **Blind Date** is "a redirection of these previous concerns."[38] George Levanter is a modern character engaged in the Socratic quest to examine and assume responsibility for his own actions despite the societal framework in which they occur. "Whereas in **Cockpit**," Kosinski states, "Tarden is preoccupied with the impact of his own camouflage on others who either accept or reject his altered truth (and so does **Cockpit**

as a novel), in **Blind Date** George Levanter reveals his unful-
filled longing to be able to examine one single human being,
one single truth at a time."[39]

Even Levanter's name implies his different role. Jack
Hicks writes that "Mediterraneans know the levanter as
a damp seasonal wind that returns with the flight of birds
each spring and fall. As the name suggests, it blows from
the east, usually gathering itself from the hot eye of the
Anatolian doldrums" and is both a healing and killing wind.[40]
George (the English equivalent of the Polish name, "Jerzy")
Levanter, has -- like the seasonal levanter -- blown east
to west, away from the land of totalitarian oppression
(to which Kosinski clearly refers in his epigraph from Swift:
"Remove me from this land of slaves,/Where all are fools,
and all are knaves,/Where every knave and fool is bought,/Yet
kindly sells himself for nought; --"). But he is also aware
and critical of "the fraud and sterility implicit in the concept
of morality perpetuated by the popular culture" in his adopted
land; and his acts, too, invite the moral judgment "implicit
in any encounter -- whether with a fictional protagonist
or with a neighbor next door."[41]

Central to each of Levanter's encounters is Monod's notion
of chance, from which Kosinski's controlling image of the
blind date is derived. Somewhat disparagingly conceived
in **Being There**, chance is reimagined in **Blind Date** as a
fruitful philosophical principle.[42] So it is hardly surprising
that Kosinski chooses a second -- and perhaps even more
important -- epigraph (this one from Monod's **Chance and
Necessity**) for his sixth novel: "But henceforth who is to
define crime? Who shall decide what is good and what
is evil? All the traditional systems have placed ethics
and values beyond man's reach. Values did not belong
to him; he belonged to them. He now knows that they
are his and his alone... "

His own scientific discoveries as well as those of other
biologists led Monod to postulate a fundamental theory
that there is no plan in nature, that destiny is written concur-
rently with each event in life, not prior to it; guarding

against this powerful feeling of destiny should be the source of our new morality. Kosinski says that George Levanter is dissatisfied with Marxism because he feels betrayed by the Soviet society that preaches "'objective destiny,' proclaiming, in a travesty of scientific discourse, that Marxism offers access to the 'scientifically' established 'objective' laws of history which man has no choice but to obey, and that the State and the Communist Party have a moral duty to enforce at any cost to the population." Thus, Levanter embraces Monod's scientific postulate that forces man to acknowledge his isolation, to utilize each moment in his life as it passes rather than to dismiss it as a minor incident in a larger passage or zone of time. This philosophy, derived from and based on modern science, presupposes an ethic which bases moral responsibility upon that very freedom of choice an individual exercises in each instance of his life, an instance being dictated by chance, not necessity.[43]

Viewed this way, life is a series of blind dates (which, like the levanter wind, serve as a metaphor for the creative and destructive potentials of blind chance in contemporary life).[44] Kosinski, in an interview soon after the publication of **Blind Date**, elaborated on the title and its implication in the novel. "In Aristotle's terms, the most moving elements in human tragedy are peripeteia and anagnorisis: the first can be freely interpreted as working in blindness to one's own defeat; the second, the opening of the eyes. The American 'blind date' is, philosophically, a complex invitation to both. It presupposes an invitation relying on chance; it postulates a willingness to go through an encounter arranged by a 'third party' (who is, even if for a short moment, placed in charge of the destiny of the two other people who are about to meet); it reveals optimism -- a belief that 'the unknown' other might, in fact, become our 'partner' -- and also the fact of our isolation -- a human need for an encounter, even with a stranger."[45]

Levanter's first blind date is a chilling one. His campmate, an admitted rapist named Oscar, has devised a fail-safe way to "break the eye" of his victims. At first Levanter

finds Oscar's blind dating fascinating but forbidding --
until he spots the blond-haired girl he calls Nameless.
Feeling that he must possess her, the young Levanter rushes
her from behind in an act of anonymous penetration. The
girl is hospitalized as a result of the brutal attack. Levanter
confesses that he is responsible for the assault, but everyone
assumes that he is simply trying to cover for his friend
and Oscar is convicted. The following year, in a different
kind of blind date, he meets Nameless again. They begin
to date and he falls in love with her. When they finally
consummate their relationship, however, she recognizes
his touch, realizes that he was the one who had attacked
her so viciously, and leaves him -- in a scene at once complete and hauntingly reminiscent of their first blind date.

Another blind date occurs when his father is hospitalized
after a stroke. Expecting a status report on his father's
health from the nurse on duty, Levanter jumps out of bed
to answer the ringing phone in his mother's bedroom. He
picks up the receiver just as his mother rushes into the
room, naked and still wet from her shower. In that moment,
they become silent lovers, and their relationship continues
for years. Yet there are boundaries to their lovemaking:
they are together only in the morning, so that his mother,
who sleeps nude, never undresses just for him; they never
kiss; and he can caress nothing but her breasts. Though
they have animated discussions about the sexual proclivities
of other women and his mother introduces him to many
girls, "he never talked with his mother about their lovemaking. Her bed was like a silent, physical confessional:
what happened between them was never talked about"
(p. 10).

In ValPina, he meets another attractive woman, a pianist
named Pauline. In discussing her conservatory training,
he realizes that she studied under the same professor as
his mother had. He confides to Pauline that his mother
admitted she had been the professor's mistress. Pauline
asks, "If he were my lover too, would I be linked to your
mother?" "Yes," responds Levanter, "and if I had been
my mother's lover, I then would be linked to you." (p. 8)

Near the end of the novel, Levanter is returning to his home near Carnegie Hall when he notices that Pauline is performing there. Pretending to a spastic -- a pose Levanter (like Kosinski) sometimes assumes to get attention and immediate service -- he acquires a ticket to her sold-out concert, after which they meet. He expresses his deep longing for her, his need "to be wanted, rather then remembered. To have a fresh emotion, a sensation that isn't just a ricocheted memory. To be part of that spontaneous magic" (pp. 227-228). They return to his apartment and begin to make love. As she seems about to surrender to her passion, she cries, "I can't, I never could" (p. 229). Levanter continues to kiss and touch her; with a recording of Pauline's music playing on the stereo, he leads her to the bedroom, where he binds her with his softest ties and enters her again and again. Her moans of "No!" turn soon to whispers of "Yes!"; "and, as its sound ebbed, her body softened, freed from its own bondage, no longer struggling against any restraints" (p. 231). Levanter is also freed from his bondage; in his need-affirming sexual encounter with Pauline, he exorcises the ghosts of both Nameless and his mother. Another blind date brings him full circle again.

Perhaps the most authentic blind date is one closest to Kosinski's own experience and modeled on his first meeting with Mary Weir. After Levanter's article on the role of chance in creative investing is published, he receives an admiring note from Mrs. William Tenet Kirkland, the widow of a rich industrialist. Levanter invites her to dinner. Assuming her to be approximately the same age as her husband, who was in his mid-eighties when he died two years earlier, he plans the evening carefully: a limousine easy enough for an old woman to step in and out of, a table discreetly near a toilet lest she have stomach or bladder problems. When he arrives to collect her, he meets her secretary, Miss Saxon, who compliments Levanter on his solicitousness toward Mrs. Kirkland. She explains that Mrs. Kirkland will be delayed, and so they dine together. When it is clear that Mrs. Kirkland will be unable to join them, Levanter invites Miss Saxon first for a walk, then a drive, and finally a drink at his small apartment. A few days later he receives an invitation to a dinner party from Mrs. Kirkland and is surprised to discover that she and Miss Saxon are one and the same person.

Though "fearful that marrying her would be a step toward creating their own fate" and superstitious that if they did so "chance might turn from a benefactor to an ultimate terrorist, punishing both of them for trying to control their own lives, trying to create a life plot" (p. 220), after three years of living and traveling together, Levanter and Mary-Jane are married. (They make the decision on her plane, "The Night Flight" -- another nod to Antoine de Saint-Exupery.) But Levanter's fears soon become his reality: Mary-Jane is stricken with a terminal brain tumor. Aware of her prognosis, she cries only once -- "when she told Levanter that her illness had cut off what she saw as her mission: to expand his freedom, to offer him a life he might have lived had he inherited such great wealth himself" (p. 224). After her death he returns to the same two-room apartment in which he, unaware of her identity, had first entertained her. Now, without her, he is somewhat unsure of his own identity: "he felt he was losing his only child, becoming an orphan himself" (p. 225). All he is certain of is that he is a survivor.

One blind date alluded to throughout the novel (and treated in most of Kosinski's fiction) relates to survival, specifically to Levanter's survival of the Second World War. In another chance encounter, on his fifteenth Christmas in his new country, Levanter strikes up a conversation with his cab driver. The driver, it turns out, is from the same town as Levanter and before the war had even delivered groceries to his parents' home. "A couple lived there," he recalls, "an old professor and his young wife, a pianist. They had a boy who was sick in the head" (p. 92). The boy couldn't speak and never laughed; the maid was afraid of him because he would sneak out at night, then come back in the morning and sleep all day. Levanter replies that "He was no crazier than you or I." When the driver asks him what he means, Levanter says only "That story's for another ride" (p. 93).

Levanter, as an adult, has few remaining links to his native land: one is his friend, Woytek, whom Levanter introduces to Gibby, a wealthy heiress. Woytek and Gibby travel to California to stay with their mutual friend Sharon; and Levanter plans to fly from Europe to visit them. But the airline loses his bags, and he is forced to lay over a day in New York. Exhausted by jet lag, he is awakened the next morning by the Los Angeles Police Department, calling to inquire about Levanter's next of kin. Levanter answers that <u>he</u> is his next of kin. Apparently, the evening before -- the very evening he was expected in Beverly Hills -- the "crabs of Sunset" had committed a heinous crime, killing Sharon and all of her houseguests, a murder which Kosinski recreates vividly and evocatively in a long section of **Blind Date.** Levanter's Sharon is of course Sharon Tate; Woytek is Woytek Frykowski, Kosinski's boyhood friend and Abigail Folger's lover; and the murderous crabs are members of the Manson gang. Whether Kosinski really was expected at the Tate home that night (as Kosinski alleges) or not (as Roman Polanski, Sharon Tate's husband and Kosinski's friend, claims) is irrelevant; the lyrical murder scene (whose victims typify, for Kosinski, "the terrifying randomness of our modern existence")[46] is but another blind date for Levanter.

The strikingly beautiful woman known as Foxy Lady is yet another. Levanter becomes obsessed with her, wanting to possess her (as he earlier had wanted Nameless) and -- in an effort to understand her -- "taking pictures of her, trying to capture her expressions" (p. 142). As no woman before her had, Foxy Lady knows his sexual needs and is able to bring out his most secret lusts and longings. Returning unexpectedly one night from a business trip, he tracks her to a nightclub, where he discovers her true identity: she is a transsexual. The magic is immediately gone for Levanter. When he wonders what will happen to her, she takes him to the Menopause Room, a place every bit as depressing as the Florida senior citizens' community Tarden visits at the end of **Cockpit.** There he sees a roomful of transsexuals, in various stages of decline, members of what Foxy Lady calls "our self-made generation" who have left only memories of their brief times as "foxy ladies, young and fresh and lovely" (p. 151). Yet, she tells him, "there are still some customers willing to go on a blind date with them" (p. 151). (Transsexuals have long fascinated Kosinski. In an interview with **Penthouse**, he explained: "All my fictional characters are seekers and questers, preoccupied with self-definition. A transsexual's need for a new self-definition is far greater than most of us have. And the price a transsexual pays for redefinition is obviously very dramatic -- and often irreversible. That's why, at least twice, transsexuals have appeared among the protagonists of my fiction, and that's why I've photographed some eighty of them at various stages of their metamorphosis.")[47] In Levanter's world, where chance is the only constant, not only secret agents must live in disguise (p. 148).

Foxy Lady's argument to Levanter that, since he was her first man, with him she was really a virgin raises an important question about the integrity and use of language. (A similar question is raised by the virgin whores Tarden encounters in **Cockpit**, women who will do anything for money except "go inside.") And, as for all of Kosinski's protagonists, language continues to be significant for Levanter, especially since it remains a gauge by which he measures his experience.

Russian, in particular, becomes a reminder of the old life from which he attempts to distance himself. Just as Levanter's conversation with the Russian functionaries on the ski slope reminds him of the enjoyment of power he thought was buried in him, his meeting with a Russian actress he has long admired leaves him unable to articulate his desire for her. "His passion ran into an obstacle: the Russian language. Could Onegin possibly tell Tatyana that he wanted to eat her? Would Vronsky say to Anna Karenina, 'I want you to suck me'? Could Levanter speak such thoughts in the language of Turgenev and Pasternak to this dignified, educated woman? He could not. In Russian, the language of his childhood and adolescence, he regressed to memories of parents and schoolteachers, to early emotions of shame, fear, and guilt. Only in English could he name the nature of his desires; his new language was the idiom of his manhood" (p. 58).

For Levanter as for Kosinski, though, English as a language represents an open   field where the possibilities of experience are almost limitless. And it is for this reason that English becomes the language in which Levanter, the victim of Russian, establishes himself, insofar as possible, as the agent for shaping the nature and the quality of his life.[48] Later in the novel Jolene remarks that it is only newcomers like Levanter who "know how to change their lives overnight, how to develop new interests, take up different professions, generate fresh emotions" (p. 110). It is a shrewd comment, because the newcomer is indeed aware of the range and limits of language that he assimilates in his new territory and -- like Levanter -- enjoys a greater opportunity for becoming the agent of his own fate.[49]

Like Tarden (and like Kosinski himself), Levanter uses photography as another kind of language. But since photography "depended on imitating reality in an imaginative, subjective way," Levanter "began to evolve his own   techniques and a style that could not be readily copied" (p. 54). Even in his native land, where words were punished severely (as Romarkin demonstrated), photography becomes for Levanter another way of defying the authority of the State. One night, while photographing the image of a man walking by a fence in a field during a snowstorm -- an interesting black and white shot, nothing subversive -- Levanter is approached by a burly militiaman who confiscates and exposes his film. "We both know," says the officer in typical Soviet doublespeak, "that such a field, any field, could serve as a landing site ... a landing site for, let's say, invading paratroopers" (p. 56). In response, Levanter returns to the field the next day, waits for a man to walk by the fence, and takes his photograph.

Jolene, the imp of Impton, like Levanter, is separated from her childhood contexts (having fallen from the town's favor) and recites for him, in a kind of verbal photography,[50] the story of her life: "Snapshots from Jolene's album. Womanhood begins in grade school, age twelve. Jolene loses her virginity to a high school varsity basketball player, who also loses his. More dates. Click. Jolene discovers the orgasm. Click. High school. Meets Greg, law student. Local rich boy. Click. Going steady and bedding steady with Greg. Click. No orgasms with Greg. Click. Orgasms alone. Click. College athletes discover that Jolene puts out. Click. She gets into their games for free; they get into her games for free. Click. [After Jolene and Greg marry and split up] Jolene at the Taft with yet another stranger. Click. End of album of unique snapshots of an ordinary life. A sweet old-fashioned girl, a perfect subject for any lens to fondle" (p. 104). Much in the manner of Kosinski himself, who does not provide his texts with the qualifications and the transitions that tend to contain and thus shape the content of a traditional novel, Jolene -- not at all interested in justifying herself -- presents the episodes stripped of all subtle modifiers. Instead of trying to fix the interpretation of specific snapshots, she allows the pictures to remain in the open field, subject to Levanter's inferences. Recognizing that she possesses no means for developing convincing transitions or a web of coherence for her life, she views herself as existing within that field[51] and, as Levanter did with his photograph of the man and the fence, she defies the authority of the town with her own exposure.

Stylistically, according to Kosinski, **Blind Date** has "the order of a painting or a work of music. Its order is both circular and spiral, corresponding to the different parts of Levanter's memory."[52] Therefore, at the end, when he dies on the icy slope of the Aval on the final day of the ski season, there is a certain sense of completeness in his death. "The game was good to him, made him want to play it, yet even a solitary player needs his rest" (p. 235). He recalls the image of a young boy who wanted to hear Levanter's story but was told by his mother to enjoy the sea and not talk to strangers. The boy obeyed, stood in the water, and when "a wave rolled toward him, he assumed a fencing position and cut at it with an invisible sword. The wave washed by, lapping against the shore. When the next wave came in, he hit it twice before it flattened, foaming at his feet. Like a fencer frozen in a pass, he let the next wave swell on the sand toward him, and then the next. The waves deposited their foam on the steamy sand, one after another, one after another, and the boy, his back to Levanter, watched them mindlessly" (p. 236). A young Don Quixote -- like Levanter and other Kosinski protagonists, a picaro -- the boy tries to order the orderless waves but finally yields to their random strength.

Memories blend like the waves in Levanter's mind as he is about to die in the snow -- memories of J.P., the fencer; of "the dead German soldiers he had seen as a child during the war, their chins, noses, and ears missing, their teeth flashing through the holes in the frostbitten cheeks" (p. 233); of the black man at the arcade excelling at a game that "nobody plays ... anymore" (p. 234); of his "rebel" heart (pp. 268-69). But if, as Kosinski writes, "with a true sense of the randomness of life's moments, man is at peace with himself -- and that peace is happiness,"[53] then Levanter dies happy.

Kosinski perceives Levanter as free from "what is false within -- a man who, having learned some harsh lessons in his boyhood during World War II and as an adolescent in Stalinist Russia, has emerged greatly concerned with moral issues. As a small investor active in America, he is a classic 'permanent reformer,' preoccupied with counteracting social injustice."[54] Unlike Tarden and the protagonists of earlier novels, he is connected to his society and to other survivors -- his mother, Jolene, Serena, Foxy Lady, Mary-Jane Kirkland, Pauline, Romarkin, Woytek -- with whom he shares relationships based on mutual need and not on dominance. Thus, he becomes -- to paraphrase Monod -- a flame worthy of the candle.

ENDNOTES TO CHAPTER SEVEN

1.   Robert Kirch, "Diary of a Mad Secret Agent," **Los Angeles Times,** 24 August 1975.

2.   Richard R. Lingeman, "Fables Ending in Riddles," **The New York Times,** 15 August 1975, p. 33.

3.   Paul Bruss, **Victims** (Lewisburg: Bucknell University Press, 1981), p. 202.

4.   Jerzy Kosinski, **Cockpit** (Boston: Houghton Mifflin, 1975), p. 100. All subsequent references to this edition will be made by page number in the text.

5.   Lingeman, p. 33.

6.   Kirch.

7.   Paul R. Lilly, "Jerzy Kosinski: Words in Search of Victims," **Critique,** 22, No. 2 (1980-81), 76-77.

8.   Ibid., p. 77.

9.   Bruss, p. 202.

10.   Frederick R. Karl, **American Fictions: 1940-1980** (New York: Harper and Row, 1985), p. 504.

11.   Ibid.

12.   Lilly, p. 77.

13.   Bruss, pp. 200-201.

14.   Jack Hicks, **In the Singer's Temple**   (Chapel Hill: University of North Carolina Press, 1982), p. 245.

15.   Ibid., pp. 249, 251.

16.   Karl, p. 505.

17. Jonathan Baumbach, "Cockpit," **The New York Times,** 10 August 1975, p. 3.

18. Norman Lavers, **Jerzy Kosinski** (Boston: Twayne, 1982), p. 101.

19. Ibid., p. 106.

20. Hicks, p. 252.

21. Lavers, p. 111.

22. Geoffrey Movius, "An Interview with Jerzy Kosinski," **New Boston Review,** 1, No. 3 (Winter 1975), 3.

23. Karl, p. 504.

24. Adrian Ayres, "'Cockpit': Gray, Gloomy, Grim, and Gross," **Chicago Illini,** 8 November 1976, p. 10.

25. Baumbach, p. 3.

26. Lavers, p. 114.

27. Baumbach, p. 3.

28. Hicks, p. 245.

29. Jerzy Kosinski, **Blind Date** (Boston: Houghton Mifflin, 1977), p. 15. All subsequent references to this edition will be made by page number in the text.

30. Bruss, p. 224.

31. Daniel J. Cahill, "An Interview with Jerzy Kosinski on **Blind Date,**" **Contemporary Literature,** 19, No. 2 (Spring 1978), 134.

32. William Plummer, "In His Steps: The Mellowing of Jerzy Kosinski," **The Village Voice,** 31 October 1977, p. 78.

33. Bruss, p. 214.

34. Ibid., pp. 214-215.

35. Plummer, p. 78.

36. Cahill, p. 138.

37. John Leonard in his review of **Blind Date,** "Death
Is the Blind Date," **The New York Times,** 7 November 1977,
recognizes that Levanter's marriage "is very un-Kosinski."
But he still maintains that Kosinski's regard for women
is unchanged and concludes: "When he learns in his fiction
to respect women, he will be a fine novelist."

38. Cahill, pp. 133-34.

39. Ibid., p. 134.

40. Hicks, p. 257.

41. Cahill, pp. 141, 140.

42. Hicks, p. 259.

43. Cahill, p. 135.

44. Hicks, p. 258.

45. Cahill, p. 140.

46. Ibid., p. 137.

47. Barbara Leaming, "Penthouse Interview: Jerzy
Kosinski," **Penthouse,** July 1982, p. 130.

48. Bruss, p. 216.

49. Ibid.

50. Ibid., p. 217.

51. Ibid.

52. Cahill, p. 141.

53. Ibid., p. 142.

54. Ibid., p. 141.

CHAPTER EIGHT

NIGHTS ERRANT, KNIGHTS ABERRANT:
PASSION PLAY AND PINBALL

[He] would find himself ... a displaced person
in an uncharted landscape, an émigré to the
frontier beyond the scope of his transit.

Jerzy Kosinski, **Pinball**

"Jerzy Kosinski's heroes," according to Stefan Kanfer,
"have become dependable literary fixtures, as recognizable
as Kafka's K. or Beckett's tramps. Rootless, quixotic,
warped by an antichildhood in Holocaust Europe, they tra-
verse the American landscape like knights errant on a futile
search for purpose."[1]

In **Passion Play**, Kosinski's seventh novel, published in 1979,
the protagonist is a modern variation of the knight errant,
and his story is a reinterpretation -- of the sort discussed
by Barth in "The Literature of Exhaustion" -- of the themes
of love and combat typically found in the medieval romances.
The very title of the novel focuses attention simultaneously
on the modern and medieval worlds and emphasizes the
contemporary hero's need to quest for new values. Fabian,
a self-proclaimed "existential cowboy,"[2] an aging polo
player and sometime equitation teacher, had discovered
his aim as a boy. Astride a farm horse at full gallop, he
would play peasant games and send a ball the size of an
apple across the meadow to strike a target no larger than
a pumpkin. Since that time, his aim had not failed him;
and it was not "he who had shaped his faultless stroke,
but the faultless stroke that had shaped him." He wonders
often if some advance agent of conscious choice had determined so early his choice of polo as "the landscape of his

potency" (p. 29). In fact, especially for the aging Fabian, polo becomes quite literally the landscape of his potency: the polo field and the sexual field merge sometimes physically, almost always metaphysically, and his dominance in the former arena becomes a metaphor for his conquests in the latter.

However, polo is a team sport, with the roles of its four players clearly delineated: always forward, number one sets up the shots; number two acts as the driving force of the attack; number three, the pivot man and often the captain of the team, links attack with defense; and number four stands guard at the team's back. No one of these roles fully consumes Fabian's ability to strike and to score -- and to do so unaided. Like the medieval knight, his greatest challenges and greatest triumphs are achieved as an individual. So, while the confrontation of opposing teams, each attempting to score a higher number of goals, is the core of polo, for Fabian the game essentially becomes a one-on-one contest in which two players fight for possession of the ball. His disregard of the other three players on his team antagonizes and humiliates them, and early in his professional career he gets a reputation as a maverick. Others refuse to play with him; dropped from one team after another, he gradually slips into "the notoriety of isolation" (p. 31).

As a student, Fabian used to think that his dislike of team play emanated from a fear of being trampled to death by the mass tonnage of horses and men and from a fear of a collective strategy in which an individual destiny meant little. Like all of Kosinski's protagonists, beginning with those of the nonfiction studies, **The Future is Ours, Comrade** and **No Third Path**, Fabian abhors the collective's encroachments on the self. Later in life, he realizes that the spirit of the collective and the team bears for him another implication, less ominous but equally disturbing: "collective responsibility diluted one's faults, but it also diminished one's achievements, took away from them stature and consequence. One could no longer distinguish what was due to oneself and what to one's team; the boundaries of success and failure, victory and defeat were blurred in a tangle of humility and pride." So Fabian's brand of polo becomes "the ground of his being in the world, the only uniqueness at his command" (p. 31). Shunned by teams, he resigns himself to traveling around the country in search of one-on-one engagements, usually with wealthy opponents, during which he can fight for supremacy and submit to rules that both contestants obey, without an umpire, away from the fickleness of a public that might choose favorites. He prefers this type of contest because "The essence of competition, for him, lay not in the challenge offered by others but always in the challenge posed by oneself" (p. 33).

However, like the grail knight, Fabian is sometimes diverted from the real goal: the exploration and enhancement of the self. One such lapse occurs when he is hired by Fernando-Rafael Falsalfa, the unchallenged autocrat of a Latin American republic, to serve as his occasional polo partner. Falsalfa (a "false self") sets Fabian up by threatening to frame him for the murder of a controversial political columnist.

But, as Tarden did from his friend Robert, Fabian learns a very valuable lesson from his experience with the dictator: that in his life, he must create and direct his own scenarios rather than act out the scripts that others provide for him.[3] Later, for example, when Vanessa offers him a million dollars, he refuses to be tempted from his quest by her gift. Even though her generous check would serve as an agent of his transformation, his thoughts "unreeled the lucid image of himself, of his life and the shape of it. The reel accelerated, and he saw himself free from the chance and desperation of snaring a one-on-one game, the panic before the contest allayed, the tension of the game slackening, the easy drifting away of all that was absolute in him, all that defined the elusive order of his nature" (p. 249).

Fabian realizes that Vanessa's money is not simply a gift of life, but of a life defined both by the very nature of the gift and by the memory of the giver. To accept her

offer would be to lose the ability to create his own life's
moments; thus, to preserve his integrity as well as hers,
he declines. The whole episode provides a rather interesting
plot twist: whereas earlier Kosinski protagonists -- Tarden,
with Valerie in the opening of **Cockpit**; Levanter, towards
the end of **Blind Date,** after discovering the true identity
of Serena -- have volunteered gifts which would enhance
or restrict the freedom of others, Fabian -- ironically the
"maker,"[4] as his name suggests -- is the receiver rather
than the giver of such magnanimity.

The encounter with Vanessa, while not as physically dangerous as that with Falsalfa, is threatening nonetheless. His
face-off with Eugene Stanhope is, however, the ultimate
literal one-on-one. Fabian's friend and his chief source
of income, Eugene is the wealthy heir to Grail Industries.
(The fact that the grail has become an industry is a sign
that the modern knight must find meaning elsewhere: in
himself.) Through Eugene's assistance, Fabian is able to
purchase his VanHome and his ponies, which allow him
to be errant. Yet after Eugene's girlfriend, Alexandra
-- nicknamed the "Centipede," the counterpart to the taran-
tula in the Falsalfa episode[5] -- seduces him and lies about
it (a perversion of the courtly love triangle), Eugene challenges Fabian to a stick-and-ball game, one-on-one, during
which Fabian's fluke shot fells and kills his former friend.

Fabian acquits himself well in the combat, not because
he has injured his opponent but because he has observed
the code of the game. Like Hemingway's heroes, he has
performed with a certain grace under pressure. Still, Fabian
is pained by the loss of his friend and by the lingering doubts
which others have that Eugene's death was not entirely
accidental.

Two years later, at the Grail Industries Stanhope Polo Tournament, Fabian meets Alexandra again. She is with Costeiro,
a handsome young player, and again she contrives a match
in which she is sure Fabian will be bested. (In this scene,
she is reminiscent of Morgan le Fay tempting Accolon
to oppose King Arthur.) As he prepares for his combat

with Costeiro, Fabian feels more like a paltry clown in a carnival play than the gallant knight in a tournament of passion. Like Nick Adams in Hemingway's "Big Two-Hearted River," he measures each of his motions in what becomes a rite of purification. The impending contest is, for a moment, almost incidental; the real battle is with his own feelings about himself and Alexandra and with the regularizing of his own actions.

Once in the field, Fabian smashes a ball near Alexandra -- a wily adversary equal to Fabian; Costeiro is distracted and loses the match. (But this is not the last of Alexandra; towards the end of the novel, she mysteriously reappears at the Madison Square Garden horse show, and this time it is she who distracts Fabian and prevents him from completing faultlessly the final jump on the course.)

Fabian's win over Costeiro is due in part to the excellence of the training of his mare. That training is constant and deliberate; Fabian appreciates the fact that, in order to play his game successfully, he and his mount must perform as one. Yet, while he respects the horse, Fabian also recognizes that it is merely the vehicle for his play and that ultimately only his own skill as a rider matters.

Fabian feels a special affection for his ponies, Big Lick and Gaited Amble, which he buys at auction and successfully schools. The former, a Tennessee Walking Horse, has been trained -- in some ways crippled -- by its original owner who had applied numerous soring treatments to the horse's legs. The resulting "sore licks," open wounds that pressure from weighted boots and chains kept raw and sensitive, caused the mare to distort its prance and spring as a way of alleviating the pain. Gaited Amble, an American Saddle Horse, was similarly abused: drilled to excess in performing its exaggerated gaits, the fancy caper and the amble, and maimed by the cutting of the depressor muscles at the end of its tail. A harness forced the tail to remain erect and would not permit the severed muscles to heal; before shows, the harness was removed and galling powder was inserted into the horse's anus to enhance even further the pluming jet of the tail and the animal's elegant carriage.

He is fascinated by the horses not only because he sees their potential for the sport of polo but also because he empathizes with the abuse they suffered. Fabian remembers the cruelty he experienced. Like almost all of Kosinski's protagonists, he was himself a child-victim brutalized by war and its attendant horrors. And Fabian, like the protagonists of those earlier novels, continues to be drawn to the maimed, the deformed, and the unusual: Vanessa, the Stanhope schoolgirl whose perfect beauty is marred only by the scar from a harelip which her family judges to be a considerable deformity; Manuela, the transsexual who mirrors Fabian's own wants and desires; Stella, the former owner of Big Lick, who hides her blackness behind a facade of pale beauty and willingly submits to Fabian's special brand of love once he uncovers her secret. Perhaps this attraction occurs because, as Kosinski has noted, an awareness of self makes us aware of deformities.

If Fabian's horses give him the freedom to pursue the one-on-one polo contests he craves, his VanHome affords him a similar liberty. A virtually impregnable castle on wheels, it allows Fabian, the new knight errant, a place to prepare for his combats, to recover from his wounds, and to transport his steeds. "Like a Bedouin's tent, his VanHome went with him, and he with it, across whatever shifting landscape or mutable desert he might choose or chance upon, a place in which to bivouac or pitch camp when an unexpected oasis detained him, a companion when he bore down on the receding horizon, his thirst for what it promised never appeased, his voyage without destination (p. 5)." Fabian's VanHome bespeaks the dignity and economy of "a portable man," a phrase Kosinski proudly uses to describe himself; a veritable showplace, its beauty is like the charm of a mysterious woman who leaves her admirers wanting more. Most importantly, it enhances Fabian's own sense of reality. Not surprisingly, then, the signs he affixes to its sides (e.g., "International Wildlife Cruiser," "Quarantined," "Ambulatory") reveal more about its owner than about the van.

Fabian sees many similarities between his VanHome and his mounts. The horse, after all, had been the oldest means of voyage for man -- the only animal allowed intimate access, permitted to intercede between man and solid ground. Fabian reasons that, if once man travelled on a horse, then now, in the era of the automobile -- an even more mechanical animal -- "it was time for man to carry his horse with him" in a motor home (p. 7). So, just as he admires the horse for its stamina and utility, he prizes his VanHome for its compact and economical mobility. (The comparison between horse as machine and machine as horse is one Kosinski makes frequently throughout the novel. For instance, as Fabian drives in his VanHome across a narrow concrete bridge, he looks "down at cars streaking in whatever freedom the highway allowed, each blur a rider buckled in his plastic-covered saddle, in command of his solitary mount, his energy and surge a fusion of oil and flame, his tack and harness a cocoon of glass and steel" [pp. 36-37]. And, in the novel's brilliant concluding image, which recalls the epigraph from Don Quixote, he races Big Lick, unrestrained, down the runway, as Vanessa's corporate jet take off. As horse and plane rush along the strip, "Fabian no longer thought of Vanessa: all that mattered was his horse, freed from the oppression of the brush, ready to race." Vanessa, her forehead bent to the plane's window, would catch sight of a man dressed in white, his horse black, "the run of the horse unbroken, the rider tilting, as if charging with a lance" [p. 271].)

A nomad of the highway who often shuns the main streets for the back roads, Fabian insists not only on his privacy but also on the singularity of his name. His first name, he says, is too difficult to pronounce, so he uses Fabian, which has the ring of Plato (or of Lancelot), and implies a _faber_ or maker, a creator of his own self.[6] As the novel's deliberately ambiguous title suggests, the aging Fabian attempts to recreate himself through his frequent play; his failing, aching, wounded body surges with a new vitality each time he rides competitively. So, in passion's play, especially in his favorite game of one-on-one, he comes alive.[7] The title alludes not only to Fabian's suffering, his own personal passion, but also to the central tension of the book: passion (sex, women) and play (games and combat, horses).

Fabian treats his women as he does his horses: he finds many of them when they are young, and he trains them by shaping them to his will: "like a colt, she was to be schooled, he at the lead, she following at liberty, without rigs, harness, reins" (p. 196). Once he brands them, psychologically and sexually, they are his; he possesses them, the way Levanter wants to possess Nameless and Foxy Lady in **Blind Date.** Like **Lolita's** Humbert Humbert, another older man devoted to the pursuit of nymphets, Fabian frequently seeks out virginal girls of high school age. (As Norman Lavers notes, Kosinski's humor and language are quite Nabokovian. Kosinski playfully puns on equus. When Fabian is about to deflower one young woman, Kosinski writes that Fabian is about "to break her equanimity" [p. 161]. And just as the young girls in lepidopterist Nabokov's books are sometimes described in terms reminiscent of butterflies, those in **Passion Play** are defined in horselike ways:[8] Fabian prefers women who are "young, tall, slender, long-legged, with large eyes and thick hair, a wide mouth" [p. 110]; Alexandra has a "mane of copper-colored hair" [p. 52] and a "broad, mobile mouth framing wide teeth" [p. 68]; the young hairstylist in the barbershop "chewed gum with the monotony of a tired mare chomping on its food" [p. 1].)

Cruising the country in his VanHome, Fabian reads **Saddle Bride,** the trade journal of the horse world which also chronicles the social milieus of the tournament, turf, stable and show. (The double entendre of the publication's title, which suggests both a play on horseback riding and on sexual intercourse, is exploited fully.)[9] Of special interest to Fabian is the feature "Ladies of Horse: Who's Who Under Seventeen," which provides photographs of young horsewomen -- jumping, at the paddock, in full show regalia, in formal gowns and in riding breeches -- along with brief accounts of their rich and prominent families, medals and competitive standing, aspirations, and favorite mounts.

Once he becomes involved with the girls, his sexual encounters take on the dominant aspects of a rider with his horse. The girls become, quite literally, his saddle brides. He mounts them as he would a horse; he takes them from the rear; he forces bridles and harnesses and horse blankets on them; sometimes he even copulates in the tack room or in the stalls, and bends the girl's body against the horse so that her movements and the horse's become almost one.

In addition to being a player and a riding teacher, Fabian is also a writer, although "in twenty years, he had published only a meager handful of books" (p. 32). His volumes in equitation, while skillful, are not especially popular; in fact, "no hardcover bookstore ever carried more than one or two copies of each of Fabian's books, few of which, he discovered when he stopped in a city or large town, ever seemed to sell" (p. 177). When he questioned bookstore managers about his slow sales, they replied that the public wanted books which portrayed riding as an "easy diversion" and which were richly illustrated (p. 177); the public did not seem to want "reflections on the state of equitation," and so "Fabian's books failed as mass-market tributes to the pleasures and rewards of riding" (p. 177).

Fabian, however, feels that an excessive appeal to the sense of sight is insidious and debilitating. He resists the lulling implication that knowledge was above all what was to be seen and refuses the "passive luxury of the spectator's chair, the flattening of reality, time arrested in one angle of vision. He suspected that to submit to that vision would be to clog the active play of images that were fluent and mobile within each person, fantasy and emotion that written language alone could quicken" (p. 178). (The parallel to Kosinski's own novels is obvious. In fact, until he wrote the screenplay for **Being There**, Kosinski claimed that he would never film any of his works, arguing that "the book and the film have little in common. Movies are a much more dynamic industry; so much is done so quickly it diminishes those who write.")[10]

Fabian is not only a writer but also a reader. Just as his
VanHome provides a private trailer for his ponies and his
belongings, books -- in particular novels -- provide "a private
trailer for his mind" which permits him to travel to a reality
outside the dominion of nature, to fuse what the present
was becoming with a history of what the past might have
been, to pass weightlessly through time and place and
thought, coasting with a freedom unmatched by any
spaceship. So moved, Fabian would find himself "no longer
the solitary passenger of his VanHome, but a fugitive from
an exhausted view of himself, a displaced person in an
uncharted landscape, an émigré to the frontier beyond
the scope of his transit" (p. 127).

In sharp contrast to the world of possibilities offered by
books -- and, by implication, by the imagination -- is the
lack of creativity fostered by another medium, television
(already explored more centrally in Kosinski's third novel,
Being There). **Passion Play** nevertheless allows Kosinski
another opportunity to examine and to criticize American
videocy and its social as well as its philosophic repercussions.

When Fabian arrives in Florida to play polo at the estate
of a rich and powerful businessman, he stops first at a
local stable. There, overcome by the southern heat, his
exhaustion from the flight, and the medication he has been
taking, he passes out; in an episode that reads like a parody
of Elaine of Astolat's tending of the wounded Lancelot,
a salesgirl comes to his assistance and offers to take
him back to her apartment until he is able to move on.
Fabian stays with her for several days; becoming her lover
-- by accepting more favors than Lancelot did from Elaine
-- as well as her patient, he is struck by her incredible
passivity. Overweight and sloppy, she spends all of her
free time virtually glued to her television set. Hurrying
through the dishes each night -- Fabian could not recollect
her hurrying through anything else -- she would settle down
on cushions on the floor in front of her set and rise only
to change a channel. As "television's faithful babysitter"
(p. 145), she takes reassurance from "its world without
rank; its ordered rhythm" and "its steady punctuation of

cheering commercials that reminded her of life's arsenal of unrealized needs and wants but did not rebuke her failure to set out after them, that promised relief from pain; the unceasing parade of stars, their deaths never final; life's mysteries exposed by lovers who marry or divorce; villains murdering or being killed; diseases that consumed or were cured; wars that began and quickly ended, planets lost and regained" (p. 145). Fabian thinks of her as a refugee from some nameless war, "forgotten, still in futile wandering, searching for a place she might call her own" (p. 143).

As soon as he recovers, he leaves her and is installed at the home of his millionaire host. However, the girl shows up, without invitation, one night to see him. Unnerved and agitated, Fabian insists that she go away, but "he knew his words passed over her mind like yet another image from television" (p. 150). Claiming that she has no life apart from him, but without the romance of Elaine's inability to live without Lancelot, she refuses to leave and mindlessly repeats that she wants to be with him. A menacing presence like the "crabs of Sunset" in **Blind Date**, she continues to pursue him even though he shouts that "I'm not your TV, you can't turn me on when you want to" (p. 151). Finally he abuses her, both physically and verbally, and tells her that she has nothing to give, that her emotions are as crude as her body, and that she is deserving only of the company of her television. Later she is found hanging from a boundary post on the edge of the estate, the victim of her own failed imagination -- a pathetic play with no sequel. Her death, lacking the tragic dignity or even the true passion of Elaine of Astolat's, emphasizes the waste of mind and life that makes the modern world literally a land of waste.

What the unnamed girl lacks is precisely what Fabian seeks: a sense of self, his elusive but contemporary grail. Whereas for medieval writers the grail was an apparition, a means for salvation to be achieved outside of oneself, in a modern world where the grail has become an industry, the real quest -- as Fabian recognizes -- can only be for something within. In fact, **Passion Play's** Grail Industries, the nation's largest electronics manufacturer, is the antithesis of the spiritual ideal that the grail should represent, as false a representation of the original as Duessa was to Una in Spenser's allegory.

So throughout the novel Fabian's quest remains one for the self -- both the awareness of his own self and the realization of the self of those around him. (It is as if Fabian becomes the knight to whom Cervantes refers -- in the passage used by Kosinski as an epigraph -- "There have been some amongst them who have been the salvation, not only of one kingdom but of many.") By his involvement with Manuela, he understands the nature of his own wants and desires as he does her; they are "each an embodiment of the other's quests" (p. 119). By exposing the truth about Stella, the black woman posing as white, he sets her free and allows her to reclaim "awareness of her self." His sexual strategies -- though always brutal, always dominant -- are designed "to reveal what inhabited her most inward self"; he spares no effort "in quest of that withheld annunciation" (p. 166).

And with Vanessa, the woman whom Fabian has loved since she was a girl, he realizes that he must give her the right to confront her life on her own by unfastening the chain that bound her to him. Like the narrator of **Steps,** who engages the woman in several acts of demystification and then finally leaves her so that she can achieve a new level of the self, Fabian heightens Vanessa's awareness to the degree that she is "finally free of him, free of herself" (p. 225). Having played many roles -- as mentor, as lover, as father -- in her life, Fabian must ultimately leave and allow her to create her own dramas, her own plays of passion, without him.

It is a difficult decision for Fabian to make. Vanessa was always special to him, different from his other adolescent saddle brides; as if to preserve that unique bond between them, he never violated her youthful virginity. When he reenters her life, it is significantly as a knight on a white horse, offering her a rose as a token of his love. She, in turn, has saved herself for him. Since "the knowledge of who he was lay within her, and only by claiming her could he discover it" (p. 222), Fabian, inevitably yet somewhat reluctantly, consummates their love.

That consummation, however, leads Fabian to a growing awareness of his own physical deterioration and a realization of Vanessa's possessiveness. When he makes love to her one last time in her hometown, aptly named Totemfield, he tries again "to impel her back to herself" (p. 265) so that she can discover her own identity. Soon afterwards, fearing -- as did Ahab in Kosinski's epigraph from **Moby Dick** -- "there's naught beyond," he frantically races, in the novel's final pages, to catch up to Vanessa's plane. But as it is about to ascend, Fabian, freed from his despair by the exhilaration that comes from the speed of his mount, forgets Vanessa and returns to his struggle for the freedom of his self, like a knight "in combat with an enemy only he could see" (p. 271). This final image is a powerful conclusion to a novel which successfully uses medieval motifs to describe the struggle of a modern knight errant against a society that constantly besieges his selfhood.[11]

Like the protagonists of Kosinski's earlier novels, Fabian is also a type of the author. Kosinski has, in fact, called Fabian "my most perfect autobiographical character" and polo "an allegory of my fiction."[12] (There is a clear parallel between Fabian's works and Kosinski's. "**The Runaway,** Fabian's first book, concentrated on the trauma an accident had on riders, and it won particular praise, even though it disturbed many critics and book reviewers by what they labeled as Fabian's mistrust of the established principles of horsemanship. **Obstacles** was his second work, a detached rehearsal of the still more complex variety of potential mishaps that might ensue within the riding arena. The audacity of its technique was widely acclaimed, and even though **Obstacles** was singled out for the prestigious National Horse Lovers Award, the book further alienated a large number of critics, who chose to ignore the wisdom of its warnings ..." [p. 78]. **The Runaway** is, of course, an allusion to Kosinski's own first novel, **The Painted Bird**, about a young boy attempting to flee from some of the horrors of the second world war, this century's most awful "accident"; and **Obstacles** is **Steps,** Kosinski's second novel, a brilliant and indeed audacious work which was an even more complex examination of the self than **The Painted Bird** and which won for its author the highest literary prize of the United States, the National Book Award. The pattern of critics warning unseasoned readers to avoid Fabian's "pessimistic" works "continued with subsequent books, the critics disowning his conception of the equestrian art as too bleak, a brutal excess of case histories that passed the bounds of credibility" [p. 178]. Kosinski is again taking a playful poke at the reviewers of his own novels -- reviewers who frequently level similar charges of pessimism, excessive violence, gratuitous sex, and incredibility at his fiction.) Like serious creative writing, explains Kosinski, polo is a marginal, small-audience game; it is also a quintessential American sport, based on organized team violence, yet offering ample scope for the one-on-one individual star, who is a sort of refined version of the American cowboy.[13]

If, in **Passion Play,** polo is the allegory for Kosinski's fiction, then music -- both classical and rock -- becomes the metaphor in his eighth novel, **Pinball,** first published in 1982. Virtually everyone in the novel is musically inclined, either as a composer, performer, student, or groupie. And everyone is looking for the elusive rock star Goddard, in the same way that an earlier generation of existentialists waited for Godot.[14]

Kosinski has referred to a "cycle of novels," starting with **The Painted Bird** and ending with **Passion Play.** "Pinball," he states, "stands outside that cycle, but in a way, refers to it." In what he acknowledges is a "departure" from his other novels, instead of the more typical Kosinski protagonist, there are two: "While each of the seven novels of the cycle was a single pyramid with one central character at its top, with its two main characters, **Pinball** interlocks two such pyramids."[15]

At first glance, the two protagonists appear to be opposites: Domostroy is an older man, a composer who no longer composes, a classical musician whose works are appreciated by a very few. James (Jimmy) Osten -- in reality Goddard -- is a young electronic rock genius and a prolific composer of extraordinary popular music.

Actually, the characters are in many ways mirror images of each other. Both Domostroy and Osten have, in Kosinski's words, "by now created a 'cycle of work' -- classical music, in the case of Patrick Domostroy, rock music in the case of Goddard -- and as a result, become famous."[16] And their lives are interlinked: both have close connections to Etude Classics (Jimmy's father owns it, and Jimmy's music as Goddard supports it; Domostroy is Etude's best selling musician). Their women at times seem interchangeable (when Domostroy is living with Andrea, Jimmy is living with Donna; after Domostroy moves out of Andrea's apartment so that she can close in on Goddard, Andrea starts dating Jimmy and Domostroy begins his relationship with Donna); they know the same people (Jimmy's stepmother, Vala Stavrova, for example, was once Domostroy's girlfriend) and cross paths socially as well as professionally. Both loners by nature, they cherish their privacy and independence and at times become virtual recluses, each retreating to his own secure world (Osten to his New Atlantis, Domostroy to his Old Glory). Both suffer at the hands of supposed fans. But, most importantly, they seem to understand each other better than anyone else does throughout the novel. So when Jimmy is exposed as Goddard at the novel's end, it is Domostroy alone who appreciates the reasons for Osten's secrecy and who promises to protect his identity.

Like almost all Kosinski heroes, Patrick Domostroy is "an adrenal wanderer, ready for any existential errand."[17] A once-successful musician whose creative energies have now evaporated, he lives in a gigantic disused ballroom and banquet center in the South Bronx -- a "great shell"[18] which reflects his own emptiness -- and supports himself through small royalties and his occasional work as an accompanist in a Bronx bar called Kreutzer's (named for **The**

Kreutzer Sonata, "Tolstoy's most personal, obsessive, sexually driven novel").[19] Kosinski tells us that "Since he no longer composed, he could devote his life to his own existence rather than the existence of his music.... Freed as he was from the deceptive security of accumulated wealth and the chimera of success -- his freedom a useful by-product of his composer's block -- he rejoiced at being able to live his life as he pleased, at the time and in the place he was living it, and at being able to follow his own ethical code of moral responsibility, harming no one, not even himself -- a code in which free choice was always the indisputable axiom" (pp. 8-9).

By contrast, Jimmy Osten, the other protagonist, is forced to lead a double existence. "I wish I could invent a new me," he says, and in Goddard he does just that. But if **Being There's** Chance is a sort of trick done with mirrors, reflecting others' images of him, Goddard is a different kind of contemporary creation: an electronic marvel, created out of his amplifiers and synthesizers. Jimmy's sound is truly the language of contemporary America: loud, contrived, artificial (like the false voice he assumes in public).

Especially in its description of music and musical techniques, **Pinball** has many fine moments -- moments which rival the passionate intensity of the one-on-one riding scenes of **Passion Play.** But that intensity is not sustained, and all too often **Pinball** dissipates into scenes and episodes as vapid and contrived as the rock music and rock songs which Kosinski contends dull people's sensitivities.

The novel is also marred by strained plotting. Whereas chance is important in all of Kosinski's fiction, it is not an element used to greatest effect in **Pinball.** Bizarre incidents like the rise to prominence of Chauncey Gardiner in **Being There** emphasize the absurdity of a world controlled by chance, but the coincidences of **Pinball** are contrivances which merely weaken the plot. It is just a little too hard to believe that Jimmy Osten recognizes Domostroy's photographic technique so immediately that he associates the photograph of his stepmother in his father's apartment with the photograph of his naked -- and headless -- mystery correspondent, or that Domostroy and Andrea and Jimmy and Donna should cross paths quite so frequently and conveniently.

And just as many of the coincidences are overdone, so is some of the dialogue. Even when spoken by characters as shallow and vacuous as Andrea, many of the conversations have an unintentionally hollow ring:

> "Why do you think you like Donna Downes? Because of her wonderful talent and Juilliard schooling? Bull! You went after your tawny temptress, Mr. Whitecock, not because her music made your cock hard, not because she was your spiritual soul sister, but because she was black, and for you, and for every other white male sexist, black skin means slavery and black cunt means whoredom. You tell yourself that you want Donna because of her music and talent and other shit like that, but in fact you want to fuck the cunt of a chocolate chippie slave." (p.233)

When the supposedly distinguished and cultured Gerhard Osten (a man whose life has been devoted to promoting classical music through Etude) discusses his wife's love, the dialogue dissolves as rapidly as the edible panties Kosinski describes elsewhere:

> "They [Mood Undies] test sexuality. Each pair has a little heart sewn on the front -- you know where!" He chuckled again. "The heart is treated chemically, and as you --" he hesitated, searching for words -- "are intimate with your lady and her mood changes, so does the color of her heart! A scale next to the heart shows just how hot she feels for you! If the heart turns blue, it means she is feeling really excited; if it turns green, she's just playful; brown means she's only mildly interested; and black -- well,

she's cold about the whole thing, physically
cold, I mean. You understand?" (p. 118)

The elder Mr. Osten must understand: he admits he and
his wife have "used at least a dozen of these Mood Undies"
(p. 118). The process is very scientific, he assures his son.
"None of that Goethe and Erika stuff -- lovers finding true
love in each other's letters. As long as Vala keeps her
heart blue, I won't be blue" (p. 119).

Later in the novel, after the depth of Andrea's treachery
has been revealed and Goddard has literally almost lost
his tongue, Jimmy sums up the situation simply: "Here
I was ready to call my next record 'Andrea'!" (p. 272).

Perhaps it is Kosinski's aim in passages like these to evoke
the complete narcissism of a culture weaned on rock and
video. (Andrea is, after all, connected to the Atavists,
and her promiscuous sexuality suggests a certain atavistic
tendency.) But if Kosinski succeeds in conveying the
tenor of a world in which celebrity supercedes substance,
he fails to give us characters worth caring about.

Moreover, the frequently banal dialogue, like the mindless
lyrics of some of the rock songs described in the novel,
provides a tremendous contrast to the brilliance and eloquence of the simple verses of Joyce, Yeats, and Auden,
quoted by Goddard and others. Citing Shakespeare's
Merchant of Venice in the epigraph, Kosinski warns us
to "Mark the music" and to trust not "The man that hath
no music in himself"; yet the falsity of dialogue in **Pinball**
is closer to "treasons, stratagems, and spoils" than to the
"concord of sweet sounds" Shakespeare and other poets
envisioned.

In previous novels, Kosinski has included various autobiographical details. His courtship of and relationship with
ex-wife Mary Weir, for instance, appear in **Blind Date** and
Passion Play, and references to his childhood and wartime
experiences can be found in almost all of his works. But

in the dual protagonists of **Pinball** -- and especially in the character of Domostroy -- Kosinski seems to make more overt use of his autobiography than ever before. In what is becoming a trademark similar to Alfred Hitchcock's cameo appearances in his films, Kosinski provides a list of creations that parallel his own novels. Domostroy has composed eight "masterpieces" (p. 13), the first of which was **The Bird of Quintain.** Domostroy explains the meaning of the title: "In the Middle Ages ... a quintain was a practice jousting post with a revolving crosspiece at the top. At one end of the crosspiece was a painted wooden bird and at the other a sandbag. A knight on horseback had to hit the painted bird with his lance and then spur his horse and duck under the crosspiece before the heavy sandbag could swing around and unseat him. I thought the bird of quintain was an apt metaphor for my work -- and for my life as well" (p. 25). Kosinski is making an obvious parallel between his own first novel, **The Painted Bird,** and Domostroy's composition. Similarly, Domostroy's second work, **Octaves,** which won the National Music Award, parallels Kosinski's second book, **Steps,** winner of the National Book Award. A third composition by Domostroy, **Chance,** was voted the best film score of the year by both the Music Writers Guild of America and the British Academy of Film and Television Arts (p. 17), just as the screenplay for Kosinski's own third novel, **Being There,** won the Writers Guild of America and the British Academy of Film and Television Best Screenplay Awards. When Domostroy visits the historic Passion Play Church or performs the Baobab Concerto which he wrote, Kosinski is alluding to other more recent works of his (**Passion Play** and **The Devil Tree.**) And in her erotic midnight phone calls to strangers, Andrea pretends she is "Ludmila, Karen, or Vanessa" (paperback, p. 66), the names of women from Kosinski's other novels.

Andrea tells Domostroy that she has read numerous articles about him (including the "cover profile in **The New York Times,**" according to the paperbook edition, changed from "the profile in **The Washington Post**" in the hardback first edition) and is familiar with his connections: "You knew every big shot in the music field and the arts. I saw photographs of you with pop singers, business types, movie stars, TV anchormen, dress designers. I read the resolution the composers, lyricists, and performers of MUSE International drew up to honor you when you finished your second term as president of that organization. They said you had shown an imaginative and protective sense of responsibility towards musicians all over the world; and that the fruits of what you had achieved would extend far into the future" (p. 17). Again Domostroy's accomplishments are obviously based on Kosinski's own: the actual cover profile in the Sunday **New York Times Magazine,** which featured photos of Kosinski with various celebrities, including George Harrison, Zbigniew Brzezinski, Diane Von Furstenburg, and Mike Wallace; the resolution acknowledging Kosinski's contribution to writers worldwide, issued on the occasion of the completion of his second term as president of the PEN (Poets, Essayists, Novelists) Club.

Further parallels can be drawn: like Kosinski, Domostroy was born and lived in a totalitarian state; his mother was a classical pianist; as a boy, "he had almost drowned and ever since had been afraid of water"; as a young man, he studied in Warsaw; once in this country, he taught at an Ivy League college and even acted in films (playing "the part of a Russian composer in an epic Hollywood film" because "such an experience could only stimulate his imagination and be useful to his art" [p. 196] -- the same reason Kosinski offered for playing the Russian officer Zinoviev in **Reds).** Domostroy's habits of frequenting sexual clubs and appearing in disguise are described in "an old **New York** magazine profile of him" (p. 110). Moreover, he acts as a "free agent ... unhampered by corporate or collective considerations" (p. 32); through his art, he hopes to create "the means to outlive himself" (p. 52); and he drinks Cuba Libres (Kosinski's favorite).

Even the controversy over the authorship of Kosinski's novels generated by Geoffrey Stokes and Eliot Fremont-Smith in their **Village Voice** article, "Kosinski's Tainted Words" (discussed in Chapter One) finds its way into **Pinball.** Referring to a comparable controversy over Domostroy's music,

Andrea says that "Every serious musician can tell that only one ear -- yours! -- wrote every one and all of your music pieces! Yet, because, to guard the integrity of your work, you hand picked your own music-editors, that radical scandal sheet went after your entire reputation by alleging you didn't write your music alone!" (paperback, p. 19). Years later, people "still recall those press hatchet jobs about your 'secret' collaborators and what their headlines did to your reputation" (paperback, p. 48). Yet at no time would Domostroy "enter into a public dispute with his slanderers or ask the courts to intercede on his behalf when he was viciously libeled by the yellow press" (paperback, p. 33).

Kosinski's relationship with convicted murderer Jack Abbott also appears in **Pinball.** Through Abbott is never named, he is the "rather famous case involving a prisoner at Leavenworth" which Domostroy cites. The man had been incarcerated, on and off, for twenty-five years, beginning when he was twelve. While in jail, he started writing country and western music, whose lyrics expressed contempt for the ignorant faceless masses. Certain music critics, however, hailed him as a genius.

Barely two weeks after his release from prison and his arrival in Nashville, where he was welcomed by the establishment as if he were a Johnny Cash clone, he asked to use the washroom in a coffee shop. The counter man, a newly-married twenty-two-year-old musician, told him there was no toilet. Possibly to save face in front of the two young women who were with him, the "noble savage" knifed the young man to death.

In an interview published shortly after **Pinball's** publication, Kosinski discussed the nature of his association with Abbott, an account which helps to explain the inclusion of the incident in the novel.

> In 1973, as president of P.E.N., I reinforced P.E.N.'s Prisoners Writing Program, sponsoring, among others, reading programs among prisoners,

awards in writing fiction, poetry, essays, providing prisoners with books and magazines, facilitating intellectual exchanges between prisoners who read and write and American writers, et cetera. Coming, as I was, from Eastern Europe, where access to literature was arbitrarily censored by the Party, I, too, saw myself as a one-time "prisoner" and perhaps that's why I devoted more of my own time -- and P.E.N.'s -- to that particular program, which soon counted several hundred prisoners. Among them was Jack Henry Abbott, a convicted murderer at Leavenworth who, as a result of the program, had submitted some of his poetry to P.E.N. In 1973, P.E.N. received a letter from him, telling us that he was a Stalinist put off by the desecration of Stalin's work. But then, he wrote, "I had the distinct impression that **The Painted Bird** reflects my sentiments in the matter of Stalin, and that, as a Communist I'm very grateful to Jerzy Kosinski, P.E.N.'s President, for having written it."[20]

Kosinski began a correspondence with Abbott to disabuse him of his notions about Kosinski's works; in return he received hostile letters, in which Abbott accused him of being a "Rockefeller coupon-clipper, a capitalist entrepreneur." Later, toward the end of Kosinski's presidency, Abbott sent him some more apologetic letters. "The rest," writes Kosinski, "is history." Abbott was paroled; his book was published. Kosinski, as one of the five or six individuals most responsible for Abbott's writing career, was invited to a special dinner.

I went to that dinner even though I knew that in **The Belly of the Beast**, Abbott proposed the very view of man and society that I have always found most dangerous to life. Yet, in spite of it -- perhaps corrupted by "visibility," perhaps by curiosity, but regardless which -- I chose to go to that dinner.

> In the light of what happened after that dinner
> -- the incomprehensibly vicious murder of the
> young Richard Adan -- a writer at that -- my
> own corruption acquired a far greater, not-
> forgivable dimension. The only way left for
> me to deal with it was to try to understand
> what it was that corrupted me so easily -- and
> to make certain it won't <u>ever</u> happen again.[21]

There are aspects of Kosinski in Goddard as well. They
share the same motto (<u>Larvatus</u> <u>Prodeo</u>) and even a similar
mailing address. Both lead two existences -- one public,
one private ("His denial of a public self was therefore the
ultimate affirmation of his private self" [p. 140]); enjoy
a certain anonymity ("Osten loved his anonymity because
it guaranteed his freedom, and he loved his freedom because
it let him be anonymous" [p. 19]); and feel a need always
to create new selves, especially through their art. And
both appreciate that ultimately, as composers, only ideas
-- and not electronic assistance devices -- suffice. ("In
the last analysis, as a composer and performer, he knew
that he had to rely solely on his own ideas and emotions
and to search inside himself for the sounds and words that
would express them, both for him and for all those people
to whom his music could serve as echoes of their feelings"
[p. 138]).

If music provides a "flight from reality" (p. 50), then the
image of the pinball conveys the opposite: reality itself,
with all of its chance and random elements. Domostroy
realizes that his life had become his only art -- aimless
as the path of a steel ball in a pinball machine. After the
events at Old Glory stain his reputation and the gossip
columns bring back the past in allusions to his unsavory
conduct, his presence can only harm Donna's image. So
he decides to leave her alone. With nowhere else to go,
he heads for an after-hours club and -- in the closing scene
of the novel -- he turns to a pinball machine. The game
is "Mata Hari," and "ONE TO FOUR CAN PLAY": "He
dropped a coin into the slot. Where GAME OVER had been
a second before, BEGIN GAME now began to flash at him.

He pressed the button, and the first ball popped up into the shaft, but for a moment Patrick Domostroy could not make up his mind whether to play it or not" (p. 297).

Barbara Gelb suggests yet another dimension which both Domostroy and Goddard represent for Kosinski:

> He [Kosinski] has been worrying, lately, about running out of ideas -- a common preoccupation among writers. He voices this concern in "Pinball," which depicts Kosinski in yet another thinly veiled version of himself -- or, rather, of two conflicting selves. He is both Domostroy, the aging composer and pianist whose career has dried up, and Goddard, a phenomenally successful recording star of rock songs, who has kept his identity a mystery from his fans and whose motto is "everyone has his secrets."
>
> In "Pinball," Kosinski seems to be confronting these two selves -- his young, vital, confident self and his aging, insecure, frightened self. Is he musing about the Domostroy in him, the legitimately creative man who has run out of steam, as opposed to Goddard, the pop artist in him, the fashioner of a synthetic product compounded of electronics and hype? Does he see himself as a Goya or as an Andy Warhol?[22]

Critical reaction to **Pinball** has generally been harsh. Mara Neville observes that "the usual Kosinski character is a rootless, aimless soul, his personality shaped by incessant TV watching or by a single warped obsession, a stranger in a moral wasteland. But 'Pinball' covers the usual Kosinski territory -- the living hell that we call the 20th century -- with about as much grace and fluidity of style as a tractor trailer with three flats. It reads not like one overcooked version of some half-baked soap opera, but rather like three or four all jumbled together."[23] Benjamin DeMott in **The New York Times** writes: "One tries dutifully to attend to events and characters

-- sex partners screaming, thrashing, arising from bed to photograph each other's anguish. But in truth, taking in the action is difficult. What's most visible on any given page isn't a scene at all but the spectacle of self-imprisonment -- of a writer locked by choice in a cage through which no glimpse of the common living world can be caught. It's a pitiable sight, and a sadly unrewarding book."[24] And Stefan Kanfer of **Time** concludes that admirers of Kosinski must view this inconsistent novel and respond: "'What a premise!' 'What talent!' 'What a waste!'"[25]

Kosinski's response to the sometimes mixed and often hostile reviews of **Pinball** is to speculate:

> Edmund Wilson wrote that one of the best ways in which a book critic achieves a vicarious sense of creation is either to encourage and present a new, or previously unknown, or little known, writer -- or by putting down one that is known to have been around.... Another reason might be that **Pinball** is about the entrapments of visibility and notoriety as a creative force, and this at a time when, in the eyes of many reviews, Jerzy Kosinski has become all too visible: by playing in movie **(Reds)**, making the rounds of TV and radio talk shows, giving interviews, being profiled, et cetera, et cetera.[26]

He concludes that **Pinball** is open to many interpretations: like its title image, "it invites free play of the reader's imagination. Let the critics be as free to criticize it as I was to write it. Still, I have my reasons to have written **Pinball** the way I wrote it."[27]

Like Fabian in **Passion Play**, Goddard and Domostroy both end up losing the girl. Goddard will probably return to the isolation of his New Atlantis, Domostroy to the dead heat of his sex clubs and to his Old Glory -- knights aberrant passing nights errant. And Kosinski, one can only hope, will continue to do what he does best: to compose, "yet not to play anything with an even tone"; "to combine a variety of shading" (p. 284); and to discover the often elusive self in a world of dissolving meaning.

ENDNOTES TO CHAPTER EIGHT

1. Stefan Kanfer, "When Going Is the Goal," **Time**, 17 September 1979, p. 105.

2. Jerzy Kosinski, **Passion Play** (New York: St. Martin's Press, 1979), p. 3. All subsequent references to this edition will be made by page number in the text.

3. In this regard, Fabian is similar to Ambrose in the title story of John Barth's **Lost in the Funhouse** (Garden City: Doubleday and Company, 1968). Ambrose asks, "For whom is the funhouse fun? Perhaps for lovers.... He wishes he had never entered the funhouse. But he has. Then he wishes he were dead. But he's not. Therefore he will construct funhouses for others and be their secret operator -- though he would rather be among the lovers for whom funhouses are designed" (pp. 73, 97).

4. Frederick R. Karl, **American Fictions: 1940-1980** (New York: Harper and Row, 1985), p. 531.

5. Norman Lavers, **Jerzy Kosinski** (Boston: Twayne, 1982), pp. 148- 49.

6. Karl, p. 531.

7. Ibid., pp. 531-32.

8. Lavers, p. 142.

9. Ibid., p. 143.

10. "Press Panels: Movies -- and the Unexplained," **Publishers Weekly,** (23 June 1973), p. 49.

11. Some critics view Fabian's quest less generously. Frederick Karl, for example, calls it "a traditional one, of a narcissist in pursuit of his image, the quest Kosinski has pursued in his last four books" (p. 532)."

12. Lavers, p. 152.

13. Ibid.

14. Mara Neville, "The False Sound of **Pinball**," review of **Pinball.**

15. Regina Gorzkowska, "Jerzy Kosinski: An Interview -- **Pinball**: Aspects of Visibility," **Society for the Fine Arts Review,** 4, No. 2 (Summer 1982), 3.

16. Ibid.

17. Stefan Kanfer, "Trebles," **Time,** 12 April 1982, p. 86.

18. Jerzy Kosinski, **Pinball** (New York: Bantam, 1982), p. 7. All subsequent references to this edition will be made by page number in the text. Occasional references will also be made to the paperback edition of **Pinball** (noted as "paperback" and cited by page number in the text). According to Kosinski, the paperback edition, published by Bantam in 1983, "incorporates minor texual changes and revisions."

19. Gorzkowska, p. 3.

20. Ibid., p. 4. Kosinski makes similar comments on the Abbott affair in an interview with Barbara Leaming in **Penthouse,** July 1982, pp. 167-68.

21. Ibid. Similar comments can be found in Leaming's **Penthouse** interview, op. cit., pp. 167-68.

22. Barbara Gelb, "Being Jerzy Kosinski," **The New York Times Magazine,** 21 February 1982, p. 52.

23. See Neville's review.

24. Benjamin DeMott, "Grand Guignol with Music," **The New York Times Book Review,** 7 March 1982, p. 8.

25. Stefan Kanfer, "Trebles," p. 86.

26. Gorzkowska, p. 3.

27. Ibid.

CONCLUSION

EVERY MAN'S EVERYMAN:
KOSINSKI AND HIS PROTAGONISTS

> A writer is most useful and yields the most
> valuable truths when he writes what he has
> thought and felt and suffered. His social function
> is that of a detonator. He makes known what
> he thinks is critical and provoking, and acts
> under the assumption that because it is provoking
> to him -- and he is <u>every</u> man's <u>Everyman</u> --
> it will also be provoking to others. He is driven
> to bring an awareness of that perplexity to
> the world at large. He feels the need to arm
> and rearm them, against apathy and self-defeat.
>
> Jerzy Kosinski, **New Boston Review**

Perhaps more than any other contemporary writer, Jerzy
Kosinski has used the incredible details of his own life as
the stuff of his fiction. Therefore it is hardly surprising,
as various critics have noted, that all of Kosinski's novels
are, to a greater or lesser degree, about Kosinski. The
narrator of **Steps,** Chance of **Being There,** Jonathan Whalen
of **The Devil Tree,** George Levanter of **Blind Date,** Tarden
of **Cockpit,** Fabian of **Passion Play,** Patrick Domostroy
and Goddard of **Pinball:** all are extensions of, or metaphors
for, the nameless boy of the first novel.[1] The painted
bird of his society, the boy becomes an extension of Kosinski
himself by finding his own identity and learning to fight
effectively against the people and forces that oppress him.

But the novels are more than just autobiographical reflections; they are part of an important fictional cycle. Kosinski
has spoken often of that "cycle of seven novels that I started

with **The Painted Bird**" and ended with **Passion Play**[2] and of his eighth novel **Pinball**, which continues that cycle by referring to and commenting on it.[3] Even his two non-fiction works, **The Future is Ours, Comrade** (1960) and **No Third Path** (1962), while not actually a part of the cycle, anticipate many of the methods and techniques of the fiction. Those works also present the philosophy which is so essential to Kosinski and to an understanding of his fiction: the struggle of the self for definition against collective forces which threaten to restrict its freedom.

The protagonists of all of Kosinski's books, from the non-fiction works through his most recent novel, are existential wanderers, men who act as agents -- sometimes secret agents (like Tarden), but always agents of the self. Though considered by some critics to be socially aberrant, they are, in Kosinski's words, "self-appointed reformers of an unjust world,"[4] frequently forced to defend themselves against entrapments by oppressive societies. All outsiders (usually of Eastern European origin), familiar with death and violence, "desperate to find out who they are," they must free themselves from an outer oppression and "fend off the threat of society using complex bureaucratic means as well as camouflage, disguises, escapes, and so forth."[5] Like their creator, Kosinski's characters undergo many metamorphoses as they seek self-definition.

If there is a formula to Kosinski's fiction, it lies in the experiences which the protagonists share: "I feel that putting the individual on a constant moral and emotional alert has a positive effect in that it heightens the sense of life, the appreciation of its every moment, the sheer miracle of existence in a basically hostile environment."[6] In the nonfiction that hostile environment is the collective which demands the suppression of the creative self. In **The Future is Ours, Comrade**, Kosinski explains that "... your private life is subordinated to the life of this society" (p. 163). And in **No Third Path**, he notes that the success of Communism lies in "the total subordination of the individual to the group and ... the shift of the center of gravity from 'people' to 'aims and tasks of the commune'" (p. 222). He remembers acquaintances like the musician Peter G., who composes magnificent experimental music which he must suppress because it is too Western and therefore not approved, and recalls how art critics greeted a well-executed painting of a nude at a gallery: "How can a nude serve socialism?" they asked (p. 57).

In **The Painted Bird**, the nameless boy survives despite the disintegration of society around him. He endures innumerable atrocities at the hands of local peasants while escaping the even more unimaginable atrocities being perpetrated simultaneously by the Nazis. The subsequent Communist regime also proves disappointing to him. So, in a world devoid of values, the boy realizes he must create his own. He employs the lessons of cruelty he has learned from Jealous, Lekh, Garbos and Mitka to take revenge on those who harmed him: he derails a trainful of peasants en route to the market; he enlists the support of Soviet soldiers to punish the orphanage principal; he drops a brick on the theater attendant who will not allow him to purchase his ticket. A victim too often, he vows never to be a victim again.

The narrator of **Steps** inhabits a similarly horrific postwar wasteland; and like the boy in **The Painted Bird**, he learns that he must master the practices of his environment if he is to survive and persist in his quest for the self. More mature than the nameless boy of the first novel -- and even more scarred by his struggles -- he attempts, step by step, to discover the peace and control which elude him and all modern men. But his acts of revenge, his games, his very use of language are more sophisticated than the boy's were: the boy, for instance, was rendered mute by his ordeals, while the narrator of **Steps** chooses -- at significant times -- to withhold language entirely. The narrator must also find meaningful and fulfilling gestures to aim against the collective, against "those formerly protective agencies like society and religion"[7] which prevent the self from discovering its own reality. Like Joseph Novak, he leaves the oppression of Eastern Europe, but he arrives in his new land only to find an impersonal, technological barbarity.

Not content with superficial reflections, he penetrates his own and others' psyches in situations of his own creation and metamorphoses in several ways, some imaginary (imagining himself a black or fantasizing waging war against the "communication stations" of the city), others quite real (feigning muteness to control a new lover and allowing her to reach new sexual heights, making love to another man). He moves from victim to victimizer, seduced to seducer, servant to master, prey to hunter,[8] as he defines his identity.

Totalitarianism, the ultimate enemy of the self, finds yet a different expression in **Being There.** The benumbing medium of American television, which reduces its viewers to videocy and renders them incapable of intelligent and free choice, becomes as oppressive a force as the Eastern European collective. John Aldridge called it "a totalitarianism [in **Being There**] of a subtler and much more fearful kind, the kind that arises when the higher sensibilities have become not so much brutalized as benumbed, when they have lost both skepticism and all hold on the real, and so fall victim to those agencies of propaganda which manipulate their thinking to accept whatever the state finds it expedient for them to accept."[9] By the power of television, society's electronic mirror, Chance is transformed from a simple gardener to Chauncey Gardiner, media darling and presidential advisor. His imminent election to the Vice-Presidency (and, in the movie version, to the Presidency) is a reflection of society's vacuousness and narcissism.

For Kosinski, television's mass brainwashing is perhaps the most harmful of the many negative aspects of popular culture. He notes that "In small European communities still without television, the old people remain physically active, mixing with the young, venturing out into the real world. Here, like their young grandchildren, they sit immobilized by TV. An American senior citizen once told me that his TV set gave him a sixth sense -- at the price of removing the other five. I think that both young and old are acquiring, via television, a superficial glimpse of a narrow slice of unreality." Thus, for Kosinski, "imagining groups of solitary individuals watching their private, remote-controlled TV sets is the ultimate future horror: a nation of videots."[10] This horror is evident in several of his novels -- most directly in the persona of Chance, the new social messiah in **Being There,** but also in other characters, like the television-addicted woman who nurses Fabian back to health and later kills herself because of his rejection of her in **Passion Play** and Karen, the visually-oriented bionic beauty of **The Devil Tree.**

In **Pinball,** Goddard, the invisible rock star, plays a role similar to Chance's. He is a nobody, elevated to superstar status because of his music, which, while extraordinarily popular, is nothing more than a very elaborate combination of computers, synthesizers and "electronic Paganinis." For Kosinski, rock music is as deadening to the creative imagination as television. In fact, the children who grow up, essentially mute and unresponsive, in front of their television sets, are as teenagers "anxious to join an amorphous group -- a rock band or a film audience. The music or the film relieves them of all necessity to interact with each other -- the blaring sounds prevent communication, the screen above their heads is the focus of all their attention. They remain basically mute: sitting with each other, next to each other, but removed from each other by this omnipresent third party -- music or film."[11] Consequently, many of today's adolescents are no closer to a realization of self than Chance was: "they are liberated from the family ethos, producing their own sound, which is a non-language,"[12] and they define themselves solely through their collective medium.

Young people are not the only ones so affected. In America's corporate boardrooms and bedrooms, protagonists like Whalen, Tarden, Levanter, and Fabian find themselves entangled in societal devil trees -- on blind dates with chance. Jonathan Whalen, having fallen out of step and having lost the control of himself that the narrator of **Steps** so desperately sought, is caught in the baobab of popular culture, with its drugs, empty attachments, and cliches of psychotherapy -- but not before he gets even with his vain girlfriend, Karen; with his pompous and presumptuous godparents, the Howmets, whom he manages to murder in what he makes look like a freak boating accident; and -- by a desecration of their memory -- with his dead parents (at one point, he beds a black woman in his southern family home).

Where **Steps** was the young immigrant's coming of age in a hostile land, **The Devil Tree** describes a different rite de passage -- that of a corporate heir who inherits his father's fortune as well as his Calvinist ethics. (It is as if, in the two novels, Kosinski is exploring the American Dream from different perspectives -- that of the twenty-four-year-old immigrant, for whom that dream is elusive; and that of the twenty-one-year-old heir, born to the manor, for whom the dream is part of an inheritance which, like grace for the Calvinist, cannot be refused.)

The later protagonists -- Tarden, Levanter, Fabian, and Domostroy -- are in many ways similar. Heroes of what one critic too quickly dismissed as great anal sagas[13] heavily dependent on Kosinski's biography, they are a bit like aging Polish James Bonds, womanizers prancing from adventure to adventure, men experiencing noticeable physical decline, obsessively recalling their pasts and striking, now and then, a sentimental pose.[14]

Tarden is the most compulsive; he allows no deed to go unpunished: a writer who feigns his own death in order to increase his book sales is found -- dead, under mysterious circumstances; a woman who reneges on her agreement with Tarden meets an even more gruesome end, a slow death from radiation poisoning. Even children are not exempt from his manipulation: Tomek, the young Ruthenian, is taught never to trust what he believes to be true; the village youngsters are tricked into thinking that their antics have resulted in the death of a local Indian. Levanter is more of a righteous avenger; he retaliates only when societal injustice demands it. He avenges the persecution of his friend, J.P. the fencer, and symbolically impales the hotel clerk who betrayed him on a fencer's sword. He is also the first of Kosinski's protagonists to marry (though, like

Mary Weir, his wife dies fairly soon after the marriage, succumbing to cancer of the brain).

Fabian of **Passion Play** is also a gamesman. But where Levanter's sport was skiing, Fabian's is polo, especially the one-on-one engagement. Yet few such contests of solitary skill remain for the contemporary quester, and so Fabian must journey in search of worthy opponents. He finds diversion in his saddle brides, the young women he trains in equestrian -- and sexual -- skills. However, when his protegée Vanessa tries to bind him to her, he resists; for his freedom and for hers, he realizes he must go it alone. Similarly, Domostroy, the burned-out composer, initially assists the shallow Andrea Gwynplaine to locate the elusive rock star, Goddard. Andrea, one of Kosinski's least interesting characters, is also one of his meanest; her cruelty touches everyone who comes in contact with her. Naturally, she receives an appropriate comeuppance -- she is gunned down by a black gang leader whom Domostroy pays to protect him. But when Andrea's former classmate, the talented black pianist, Donna Downes, whom Domostroy has trained, wins the International Chopin Competition, he realizes that association with him can only sully her reputation and ruin her promising career. And so he too retreats -- to his Old Glory (the empty shell of a Bronx ballroom which he inhabits) to play his pinball games of chance, alone -- as Fabian had earlier retreated to his solitary VanHome. A little mellower than Kosinski's earlier protagonists, Fabian and Domostroy seem more reconciled to their fates -- to their aging, to their loneliness, to their declining talents -- though no less fascinated by kinky sex and by the pursuit of self-definition.

Kosinski's protagonists are all obsessed with revenge, the best way to defend themselves against entrapments by oppressive societies. Kosinski has said, "I see revenge as the last vestige of the eminently threatened self." Kosinski should know: "When I was a student at the Stalinist university," he writes, "and the party threatened me with prison unless I would reform or openly perform an act of self-criticism and repent, I warned them, 'Don't forget, if I go down, some of you will go with me.' Revenge can be a positive force -- the victim's final dignity."[15]

In brief, then, the typical Kosinski protagonist is an uninvolved, unattached individual who, either by choice or necessity, views human interaction "as an essentially one-sided affair, where the aim above all is to master a situation, to understand, to control, to possess experience -- visually, verbally, if not always physically."[16] Detached and often dispassionate, he lives at the edge of life and of society. Separated by time, space, or language from the past, he has few enduring ties in the present either. A relentless, industrious, and inventive survivor -- like Kosinski himself -- that protagonist is a Horatio Alger "of the nightmare, the first and last frontier."[17]

Unable to exist as "the sheep in the middle" of the collective herd, Kosinski's protagonists emerge instead as the solitary and brilliant painted birds of their societies. And Kosinski, like his protagonists, is a painted bird in recent American literature. With his stripped prose, his picaresque heroes, his episodic plotting which approximates a verbal photography, and his unique but sometimes sensational method of transforming fact into fiction, he has established himself as a colorful and significant force in contemporary fiction. A controversial, often brilliant writer, Jerzy Kosinski plays on our passions with his deviltry and his games of chance.

NOTES TO CONCLUSION

1.   Barbara Gelb, "Being Jerzy Kosinski," **The New York Times Magazine**, 21 February 1982, p. 45.

2.   Martin L. Gross, "Conversation with an Author: Jerzy Kosinski," **Book Digest**, November 1980, p. 19.

3.   Regina Gorzkowska, "Jerzy Kosinski: An Interview -- **Pinball**: Aspects of Visibility," **Society for the Fine Arts Review**, 4, No. 2 (Summer 1982), 3.

4. Gail Sheehy, "The Psychological Novelist as Portable Man," **Psychology Today**, December 1977, p. 55.

5. Ibid.

6. Ibid., pp. 54-55.

7. Jerzy Kosinski, **The Art of the Self: Essays à propos Steps** (New York: Scientia-Factum, 1980), pp. 40, 22.

8. Jack Hicks, **In the Singer's Temple** (Chapel Hill: University of North Carolina Press, 1981), p. 232.

9. John W. Aldridge, "The Fabrication of a Culture Hero," **Saturday Review**, 24 April 1971, p. 26.

10. David Sohn, "A Nation of Videots," **Media and Methods**, April 1975, p. 52.

11. Ibid., p. 54.

12. Daniel J. Cahill, "**The Devil Tree**: An Interview with Jerzy Kosinski," **The North American Review**, 9 (Spring 1973), 61.

13. Frederick R. Karl, **American Fictions: 1940-80** (New York: Harper and Row, 1985), p. 504.

14. Gelb, p. 45.

15. Barbara Leaming, "Penthouse Interview: Jerzy Kosinski," **Penthouse**, July 1982, p. 167.

16. Ivan Sanders, "The Gifts of Strangeness: Alienation and Creation in Jerzy Kosinski's Fiction," **The Polish Review**, 19, Nos. 3-4 (Autumn-Winter 1974), 172.

17. Elizabeth Stone, "Horatio Algers of the Nightmare," **Psychology Today**, December 1977, p. 60.

AFTERWORD

A NOTE ON THE HERMIT OF 69TH STREET

In the "Note" which precedes Jerzy Kosinski's most recent novel, **The Hermit of 69th Street: The Working Papers of Norbert Kosky** (1988),[1] an "autofiction" about a half-European, half-American Holocaust survivor and self-styled hermit, the author writes: "As this book was going to press, I discovered among Kosky's possessions a further set of footnotes and final insertions too late to incorporate in the first edition." Thus, concludes Kosinski, the reader of this brudnopis, or collection of working papers, must be rewarded with an incomplete compleat.

So too is the present critical text about Kosinski and his fiction an incomplete compleat: in press before the release of **The Hermit**, it can offer in this Afterword but a brief acknowledgement of Kosinski's ninth and newest novel. Recalling Barth's comment on contemporary American fiction, first quoted at the end of the Introduction to this work ("No turning back now, we've gone too far. Everything's finished. Name eight. Story, novel, literature, art, humanism, humanity, the story itself. Wait: the story's not finished."), it also serves to illustrate the challenge -- and the frustration -- of writing about a living author who continues to produce serious, significant fiction.

The Hermit of 69th Street, at first glance, is a different book from its predecessors. (Even the dust jacket announces that this is Kosinski "at his new and different narrative best.") Certainly the longest and most overtly autobiographical of Kosinski's novels to date, its plot, like much of the best contemporary European and American experimental fiction, is deliberately thin; by contrast, however, its language is rich -- at times overrich -- and full of allusions (to people real and imagined), quotations (from Talmudic scholars to pornographic publishers), footnotes (at times up to five per page), and puns (some as banal as Karen's dialogues in **The Devil Tree** or as empty as Chance's witticisms in **Being There**). At an Academy Awards ceremony, for example, during which Kosky must make a presentation, he is met by a page assigned to assist him. "Appropriately for our page-turning author," Kosinski writes, "the Aryan introduces himself as Kosky's official page." This affords an opportunity, two paragraphs later, for "[the author to scream] at his page" (p. 154). And, in a later scene, Kosky explains his authorial method to his companion Cathy: "'Having my own head examined is the only research I need in order to be able to write from the top of my head.' Here our literary headhunter crawls backward photographing Cathy from the point of view reserved for one about to give head, by one who is in a position to give it" (p. 226).

In fact, to summarize the plot of **The Hermit** is to state that it is precisely about Kosky's head. According to Stephen Schiff, the novel is "an attempt to portray what goes on inside a writer's mind as he composes a novel -- his sexual fantasies, the readings he refers to, the way he associates his own predicament with his character's and with the predicaments of history. It is a book of both impressive erudition and bizarre naiveté, the product of a brilliant and ambitious mind that has long since outstripped its owner's talent. It's Kosinski's unwieldy contribution to Joycean metafiction. And as far as he's concerned, he's hit upon The Next Big Thing."[2]

Kosinski loves **The Hermit** and thinks "it's the most imaginative novel I have written, and certainly the most imaginative I have read in a very long time. By far. Because it departs. **The Hermit** says to the reader, 'You don't need any other book but this. You may not want to read any other books from now on, because this book gives you basically insight to the whole genre.' **The Hermit** may not be readable, but it was sure great fun to work on it. And anything in literature that can compete in fun with polo and skiing and sex is fine with me. This was my Nirvana."[3]

The novel is, in fact, both a departure and a return for Kosinski: a departure from the simple, unembellished prose of the early fiction, and a return to the experimental style he so successfully employed in **Steps**. Norbert Kosky is quite typical of Kosinski's other protagonists, especially the narrator of **Steps**, who is scarred by his wartime memories and experiences, and the characters of more recent works (Tarden in **Cockpit**, Fabian in **Passion Play**, Domostroy in **Pinball**), who have had to confront their failing health and creative energies.

Above all, like those earlier protagonists -- and like Kosinski, for whom he is an "autofictitious" counterpart -- Kosky is a man simultaneously obsessed with his need for privacy and his desire for popularity, a man who (according to the book's jacket) is a spiritual wrestler -- "not a literary boxer -- who wrestles his rebellious Self the only way he knows: by wrestling the art of narrative tradition." A fifty-five year old Polish-Jewish, now American, writer whose previous works, like **Spinball Passion** and **Cockamamie**, play quite obviously on Kosinski's own, Kosky is a rare bird. In fact, he likens himself to that "spiritual fellow," the peculiar Hermit Thrush, who "knows more about disguises than any other bird of its kind, whether it's a painted bird or merely tainted" (p. 102).

"Tainted" of course suggests the central event of **The Hermit** as well as Kosinski's reason for writing it: the literary controversy over authorship of his works (discussed in Chapter One). This latest novel becomes an exorcising of the demons (specifically Geoffrey Stokes and Eliot Fremont-Smith, the **Village Voice** writers who initiated the scandal with their front-page article, "Jerzy Kosinski's Tainted Words") which, since 1982, have haunted Kosinski and which he believes almost ruined his career. In **The Hermit**, Norbert Kosky is a popular writer with eight celebrated novels to his credit, but his celebrity is dubiously enhanced by the accusations of local journalists from the **Courier**, who impugn his reputation and attack his credibility by charging that he is not the author of his own stories (specifically, that he cannot "float" without assistance). In the novel,

the journalists are "two slimy spiders": Thomas Carlyle,
an essayist turned columnist and a man with unexplained
hates, and Theveneau de Morande, a "graduate of the School
of Journalism in La Rumorosa, Eastern California: a literary
sports reporter with no sport to call his own." De Morande,
in particular, "finding himself without resources, dealt
in scandal, and composed gross libels, in which he defamed,
insulted, and calumniated, without distinction, all ... which
came under his pen" (pp. 324-25).

They claim that their article is "a probe into the nature
of his floating, which we believe is a crude water act --
acted out with the help of a secretly worn, and by now worn-
out, wet vest, not unlike one initially invented by Mr.
McWaters though perhaps invisible, or hidden inside his
empty testicles or sore scrotum" (p. 325). Kosky must
as a result try to restore his integrity by demonstrating
that he is a "fakir" of his sport rather than the faker he
is alleged to be and that indeed he has "an inner craft"
(p. 327) which allows him to float.

The **Village Voice** controversy and the scandal which surrounded it, Kosinski alleges, accounts for his difficulty
in getting **The Hermit** published. Delayed by several years
and rejected by at least three other publishers, **The Hermit**
was finally released in 1988 by Seaver Books/Henry Holt;
the advance, however, was only $100,000, as compared
to the $300,000 advance Kosinski received for **Pinball** and
the $250,00 he demanded from his usual publisher, Bantam,
which some three years ago first announced in its catalogue
that **The Hermit** was forthcoming.

The novel is sprinkled liberally with references to characters
from Kosinski's other works (including Chauncey Gardiner
and Patrick Domostroy); with allusions to other personae
Kosinski assumes (including Niskisko [an anagram for
Kosinski] and Jay Kay); with themes and images typical of his
fiction (the discovery of the self by various means: sex,
polo-playing, skiing, meditation in water; the fascination
with popular culture and especially the media of television
and movies; the elusive mysticism -- and mythicism --

of narrative art); and with the now standard disclaimer that all of the truths contained therein are fictions and all the fictions are truths.

Kosinski believes that **The Hermit** fuses and confuses footprints and footnotes, alchemy and religion, sex and cabala. Without doubt, this fusing and confusing makes it an interesting work. Yet for the reader unfamiliar with Kosinski's novels -- and even for the admirer of his fiction -- this new "autofiction" is a bit of an inside joke: the telling overly long, the build-up somewhat tortuous, and the punchline a little too obscure.

Yet the novel must be recognized as the clever satire and self-parody that it is. An ambitious attempt to set the literary record straight while attempting to set a new literary record, **The Hermit** is a <u>tour</u> de <u>force</u>: by so closely intertwining the minutiae of Kosinski's life and fiction,[4] it argues that no one else could have written this novel but the man responsible for all of the works in the Kosinski canon. Thus the one novel becomes the author's refutation of the allegations concerning the authorship of his many novels and a statement that they all are of one voice and from one hand -- Kosinski's -- alone. At the same time, it is a proof positive that no author -- Kosinski or anyone else -- writes without reference to a tradition and that all artists have contexts and rely on sources, whether acknowledged or not.

At the conclusion of **The Hermit,** Kosky is dragged by faceless men to the end of a pier, then lifted and tossed by them high in the air. "He flies up like a bird, but up only for a moment so short it already seems ago -- then, he starts falling down." Yet, like the painted bird of Kosinski's first novel who metamorphoses, almost phoenix-like, in the later works, there is more to Kosky's story: "He: the unsinkable Lotus Man disguised as the American Unsinkable Molly Brown" (p. 527).

In the **Hermit of 69th Street,** Jerzy Kosinski is serving notice to his admirers and detractors alike: not simply will he never sink; instead, he will swim -- and even float effortlessly -- as he continues to make literary waves.

NOTES TO AFTERWORD

1.   Jerzy Kosinski, **The Hermit of 69th Street: The Working Papers of Norbert Kosky** (New York: Henry Holt/Seaver Books, 1988). All subsequent references will be made by page number in the text.

2.   Stephen Schiff, "The Kosinski Conundrum," **Vanity Fair,** June 1988, p. 117.

3.   Ibid.

4.   In this regard, **The Hermit** is reminiscent of the styles and works of other important novelists, from James Joyce to Jorge Luis Borges and John Barth (whose recent novels, particularly **The Tidewater Tales,** similarly intertwine fiction and autobiography while commenting on the art of the narrative).

BIBLIOGRAPHY

Works by Kosinski:

Kosinski, Jerzy. "Against Book Censorship." **Media and Methods,** January 1976.

-----. **The Art of the Self: Essays à propos Steps.** New York: Scientia-Factum, 1968.

-----. **Being There.** New York: Harcourt Brace Jovanovich, 1970.

-----. **Blind Date.** Boston: Houghton Mifflin, 1977.

-----. "Charisma Camouflages Mortality." **Daily News,** 14 May 1981, p. 5.

-----. **Cockpit.** Boston: Houghton Mifflin, 1975.

-----. "Dead Souls on Campus." **The New York Times,** 13 Oct. 1970, p. 20.

-----. **The Devil Tree.** New York: Harcourt Brace Jovanovich, 1973.

-----. **The Devil Tree: Newly Revised and Expanded Edition.** St. Martin's Press, 1981.

-----. **The Hermit of 69th Street: The Working Papers of Norbert Kosky.** New York: Seaver Books, 1988.

-----. "How I Learned to Levitate in Water." **Life,** April 1984, pp. 129-32.

-----. "The Lone Wolf." **American Scholar,** 41 (Autumn 1972), 513-19.

-----. **Notes of the Author.** Third Edition. New York: Scientia-Factum, Inc., 1967.

-----. "Packaged Passion." **American Scholar,** 42 (Spring 1973), 193-204.

-----. **The Painted Bird.** Boston: Houghton Mifflin, 1965.

-----. **The Painted Bird.** New York: Pocket Books, 1966.

-----. **Passion Play.** New York: St. Martin's Press, 1979.

-----. **Pinball.** New York: Bantam, 1982.

-----. "The Reality Behind the Words." **The New York Times,** Oct. 1971, p. 23.

-----. **Steps.** New York: Random House, 1968.

-----. "To Hold a Pen." **American Scholar,** 42 (Fall 1973), 555-67.

-----. "TV as Babysitter." Transcript of NBC **Comment** program, 3 September 1972.

Novak, Joseph (pseudonym for Jerzy Kosinski). **No Third Path.** Garden City: Doubleday, 1962.

-----. **The Future is Ours, Comrade.** Garden City: Doubleday, 1960.

Selected Primary and Secondary Works:

Abbott, Jack Henry. **In the Belly of the Beast: Letters from Prison.** With an introduction by Norman Mailer. New York: Vintage Books, 1982.

Aldridge, John W. "The Fabrication of a Culture Hero." **Saturday Review,** 24 April 1971, pp. 25-27.

Amory, Cleveland. "Trade Winds." **Saturday Review,** 17 April 1971, pp. 16-17.

Arlen, Gary H. "From the TV Viewer's Perspective." **Watch Magazine,** March, 1980, pp. 54-57.

Ayres, Adrian. "'Cockpit': Gray, Gloomy, Grim, and Gross." **Chicago Illini,** 8 November 1976, p. 10.

Barth, John. **End of the Road.** New York: Bantam, 1969.

-----. "The Literature of Exhaustion." **Atlantic,** 220 (Aug. 1967), 29-34.

-----. **Giles Goat-Boy: or The Revised New Syllabus.** New York: Doubleday, 1966.

-----. **Lost in the Funhouse.** Garden City: Doubleday, 1968.

-----. **The Sot-Weed Factor.** New York: Doubleday, 1960; revised 1967.

-----. **The Tidewater Tales.** New York: G. P. Putnam's Sons, 1987.

Batchelor, John Calvin. "The Annotated 'Roman à Tease.'" **The New York Times Book Review,** 3 July 1988, p. 11.

Baumbach, Jonathan. "Jerzy Kosinski Working Out Past Imperfections." **The New York Times Book Review,** 10 Aug. 1975, p. 3.

-----. **The Landscape of Nightmare: Studies in the Contemporary American Novel.** New York: New York University Press, 1965.

Berger, Thomas. **Little Big Man.** New York: The Dial Press, 1964.

Bettelheim, Bruno. **The Uses of Enchantment: The Meaning and Importance of Fairy Tales.** Middlesex: Penguin Books, 1985.

Bilik, Dorothy Seidman. **Immigrant-Survivors: Post-Holocaust Consciousness in Recent Jewish American Fiction.** Middletown, Connecticut: Wesleyan University Press, 1981.

Blotner, Joseph. **The Modern American Political Novel, 1900-1960.** Austin: University of Texas Press, 1966.

Borges, Jorge Luis. **Labyrinths.** Ed. Donald A. Yates and James E. Irby. New York: New Directions, 1962.

Boyers, Robert. **Excursions: Selected Literary Essays.** Port Washington, N.Y.: Kennikat Press, 1977.

-----. "Language and Reality in Kosinski's **Steps**." **Centennial Review,** 16 (Winter 1972), 41-61.

Brown, Earl B., Jr. "Kosinski's Modern Proposal: The Problem of Satire in the Mid-Twentieth Century." **Critique,** 22 No. 2 (1980), 83-87.

Broyard, Anatole. "Casual Lust, Occasional Journalism." **The New York Times Book Review,** 6 Nov. 1977, p. 14.

Bruss, Paul. **Victims: Textual Strategies in Recent American Fiction.** Lewisburg: Bucknell University Press, 1981.

Buckeye, Robert. "The Anatomy of the Psychic Novel." **Critique,** 9, No 2 (1967), 33-45.

Cahill, Daniel J. "The Devil Tree: An Interview with Jerzy Kosinski." **The North American Review,** 258 (Spring 1973), 56-66.

-----. "Interview with Jerzy Kosinski on **Blind Date**." **Contemporary Literature**, 19, No. 2 (Spring 1978), 133-42.

-----. "Jerzy Kosinski: Retreat from Violence." **Twentieth Century Literature**, 18 (April 1972), 121-32.

Campbell, Joseph. **The Hero with a Thousand Faces.** Princeton: Princeton University Press, 1968.

Coale, Samuel. "The Cinematic Self of Jerzy Kosinski." **Modern Fiction Studies**, 20, No. 2 (Autumn 1974), 366.

-----. "The Quest for the Elusive Self: The Fiction of Jerzy Kosinski." **Critique**, 14, No. 3 (1973), 25-37.

Corngold, Stanley. "Jerzy Kosinski's **The Painted Bird**: Language Lost and Regained." **Mosaic**, 4 (Summer 1973), 15-68.

Coover, Robert. **The Universal Baseball Association, Inc. J. Henry Waugh, Prop.** New York: Random House, 1968.

Corry, John. "17 Years of Ideological Attack on a Cultural Target." **The New York Times**, 7 Nov. 1982, Section 2, pp. 1, 28-29.

Corwin, Norman. **Trivializing America.** Secaucus, New Jersey: Lyle Stuart, 1983.

Corwin, Phillip. "Evil Without Roots." **Nation**, 30 April 1973, pp. 566-568.

Curley, Arthur. Review of **Steps**. **Library Journal**, 15 Sept. 1968, p. 3156.

Delany, Paul. "Being There." **The New York Times Book Review**. 25 April 1971, pp. 7, 58.

DeMott, Benjamin. "Grand Guignol with Music." **The New York Times Book Review**, 7 March 1982, p. 8.

DeSalvo, Louise A. "Being There: An Introduction." n.p., n.d.

Dillard, Annie. Living by Fiction. New York: Harper Colophon Books, 1982.

Dolega-Mostowicz, Tadeusz. Kariera Nikodema Dyzmy. New York: Roy Publishers, 1950.

Eisinger, Chester E. Fiction of the Forties. Chicago: Phoenix Books, 1963.

Federman, Raymond, ed. Surfiction: Fiction Now and Tomorrow. 2d ed., enlarged. Chicago: Swallow Press, 1981.

Fiedler, Leslie. "Cross the Border, Close the Gap." Playboy, 16 (Dec. 1969), 151+.

-----. Love and Death in the American Novel. Cleveland: Meridian Books, 1962.

-----. The Return of the Vanishing American. New York: Stein and Day, 1968.

-----. What Was Literature? Class Culture and Mass Society. New York: Touchstone, 1982.

Friedman, Bruce Jay. Stern. New York: Simon and Schuster, 1962.

Gardner, John. "Lancelot." The New York Times Book Review, 20 Feb. 1977, pp. 1, 16, 20.

-----. John. On Moral Fiction. New York: Basic Books, 1978.

Gelb, Barbara. "Being Jerzy Kosinski." The New York Times Magazine, 21 Feb. 1982, pp. 42-46+.

BIBLIOGRAPHY   269

Glassgold, Peter. "Taking a Bad Chance." **Nation**, 31 May 1971, pp. 699-700.

Gorzkowska, Regina. "Jerzy Kosinski: An Interview -- **Pinball:** Aspects of Visibility." **Society for the Fine Arts Review**, 4, No. 2 (Summer 1982), 3-4.

Grass, Gunter. **The Tin Drum.** Trans. Ralph Manheim. New York: Random House, 1962.

Gray, Paul. "Dead End." **Time**, 31 Oct. 1977, pp. 104-10.

Gross, Martin L. "Conversation with an Author: Jerzy Kosinski." **Book Digest**, Nov. 1980, pp. 19-27.

Grynberg, Henryk. **Child of the Shadows.** Trans. Celina Wieniewska. London: Vallentine, Mitchell, 1969.

Halley, Anne. "Poor Boy Spreads His Wing." **Nation**. 29 Nov. 1965, pp. 424-26.

Hamilton, Edith. **Mythology.** New York: New American Library/Mentor Books, 1942.

Hand, Judson. "Down Depravity Lane." **Daily News**, 30 Oct. 1977, p. 18.

Harmetz, Aljean. "Book by Kosinski, Film by Ashby." **The New York Times**, 23 Dec. 1979, Sec. 2, p. 1.

Harris, Charles. **Contemporary American Novelists of the Absurd.** New Haven: College and University Press, 1971.

Hassan, Ihab. **Contemporary American Literature, 1945-1972: An Introduction.** New York: Frederick Ungar, 1973.

-----. **Radical Innocence.** Princeton: Princeton University Press, 1961.

Hays, Peter L. **The Limping Hero: Grotesques in Literature.** New York: New York University Press, 1971.

Heller, Joseph. **Catch-22.** New York: Dell, 1969.

Hendin, Josephine. "Experimental Fiction." In **Harvard Guide to Contemporary Writing.** Ed. Daniel Hoffman. Cambridge: The Belknap Press, 1979.

Herman, Jan. "Did He or Didn't He?" **Chicago Sun-Times Book Week,** 25 July 1982, p. 24.

Hicks, Granville, with the assistance of Jack Alan **Robbins. Literary Horizons: A Quarter Century of American Fiction.** New York: New York University Press, 1970.

Hicks, Granville, ed. **The Living Novel: A Symposium.** New York: Macmillan, 1957.

Hicks, Jack. **In the Singer's Temple: Prose Fictions of Barthelme, Gaines, Brautigan, Piercy, Kesey, and Kosinski.** Chapel Hill: University of North Carolina Press, 1981.

Hirschberg, Stuart. "Becoming an Object: The Function of Mirrors and Photographs in Kosinski's **The Devil Tree.**" **Notes on Contemporary Literature,** 4, No. 2 (1974), 14-15.

Hoffman, Frederick J. **The Modern Novel in America.** Los Angeles: Gateway, 1956.

Hollowell, John. **Fact and Fiction: The New Journalism and The Nonfiction Novel.** Chapel Hill: University of North Carolina Press, 1977.

Holman, C. Hugh. **A Handbook to Literature.** Third Edition. Indianapolis: Odyssey Press, 1972.

Howe, Irving. "From the Other Side of the Moon." **Harpers,** March 1969, pp. 102-105.

Hutchinson, James D. "Authentic Existence and the Puritan Ethic." **Denver Quarterly,** 7, No. 4 (Winter 1973), 106-114.

-----. "The 'Invisible Man' as Anti-Hero." **Denver Quarterly,** 6, No. 1 (Spring 1971), 186-192.

-----. "Retrospect: Judging a Book Award." **Denver Quarterly,** 4 (Autumn 1969), 128-35.

Jung, Carl G. and C. Kerenyi. **Essays on a Science of Mythology.** Trans. R. F. C. Hull. New York: Harper Torchbooks, 1963.

Kanfer, Stefan. "Corrupt Conquistador." **Time,** 4 Aug. 1975, p. 63.

-----. "Trebles." **Time,** 12 April 1982, pp. 85-86.

-----. "When Going is the Goal." **Time,** 17 Sept. 1979, p. 105.

Karl, Frederick R. **American Fictions: 1940-1980.** New York: Harper and Row/Colophon, 1985.

Kartiganer, Donald M. and Malcolm A. **Griffith. Theories of American Literature.** New York: Macmillan, 1972.

Kaufmann, Stanley. "A Double View." **Saturday Review,** 27 Feb. 1973, pp. 42-43, 46.

Kazin, Alfred. **Bright Book of Life: American Novelists and Storytellers from Hemingway to Mailer.** Boston: Little, Brown, 1973.

Kennedy, Adrienne. Letters Column. **The New York Times Sunday Magazine,** 28 March 1982, p. 110.

Kennedy, William. "Who Here Doesn't Know How Good Kosinski Is?" **Look,** 20 April 1971, p. 12.

Kesey, Ken. **One Flew Over the Cuckoo's Nest.** New York: New American Library/Signet Books, 1962.

Kiernan, Robert F. **American Writing Since 1945: A Critical Survey.** New York: Frederick Ungar, 1983.

Kiley, J. B. Review of **The Devil Tree. Critic,** 31 (May-June 1973), 80.

Kirsch, Robert. "Diary of a Mad Secret Agent." **Los Angeles Times,** 24 Aug. 1975.

Klein, Marcus, ed. **The American Novel Since World War II.** New York: Fawcett, 1969.

Klein, Marcus. **After Alienation: American Novels in Mid-Century.** Cleveland: The World Publishing Co., 1964.

Kleiner, Dick. "Butchered Reputations Live on After Death." NEA Syndicate, 19 Dec. 1969

Klinkowitz, Jerome. "How Fiction Survives the Seventies." **The North American Review,** 9 (Fall 1973), 69-73.

-----. "Jerzy Kosinski: An Interview." **Fiction International,** 1 (Fall 1973), 30-48.

-----. **Literary Disruptions: The Making of a Post-Contemporary American Fiction.** Urbana: University of Illinois Press, 1975.

-----. **Literary Subversions: New American Fiction and the Practice of Criticism.** Carbondale: Southern Illinois University Press, 1985.

Korn, Eric. "Alienation Effects." **The Times Literary Supplement,** 29 Aug. 1975, p. 963.

Kridl, Manfred. **A Survey of Polish Literature and Culture.** New York: Columbia Slavic Studies, 1956.

Lale, Meta and John **Williams.** "The Narrator of **The Painted Bird:** A Case Study." **Renascence,** 24, No. 4 (Summer 1972), 198-206.

Langer, Lawrence L. **The Holocaust and the Literary Imagination.** New Haven: Yale University Press, 1975.

Lavers, Norman. **Jerzy Kosinski.** Boston: Twayne, 1982.

Leaming, Barbara. "Penthouse Interview: Jerzy Kosinski." **Penthouse,** July 1982, pp. 128-30, 167-71.

Leonard, John. "Death Is the Blind Date." **The New York Times,** 7 Nov. 1977, p. 33.

Lewis, R. W. B. **The American Adam: Innocence, Tragedy, and Tradition in the Nineteenth Century.** Chicago: University of Chicago Press/Phoenix Books, 1967.

Lilly, Paul R., Jr. "Jerzy Kosinski: Words in Search of Victims." **Critique: Studies in Modern Fiction,** 22, No. 2 (1980-81), 69-82.

Lindberg, Gary. **The Confidence Man in American Literature.** New York: Oxford University Press, 1982.

Lingeman, Richard R. "Fables Ending in Riddles." **The New York Times,** 15 Aug. 1975, p. 33.

Lupack, Barbara Tepa. "Hit or Myth: Jerzy Kosinski's **Being There.**" **New Orleans Review,** 13, No. 2 (Summer 1986), 58-68.

-----. "New Tree, Old Roots. **The Polish Review,** 29, Nos. 1 & 2 (1984), 147-53.

-----. Review of **Passion Play. The Polish Review,** 25, Nos. 3-4 (1980), 116-117.

Lustig, Arnost. "Love and Death in New Jerzy." **The Washington Post Book World,** 27 Nov. 1977, p. E1.

Lyons, John O. **The College Novel in America.** Carbondale: Southern Illinois University Press, 1962.

Marcuse, Herbert. **Eros and Civilization: A Philosophical Inquiry into Freud.** Boston: Beacon Press, 1966.

Martin, Jack. "Sellers Flips His Lid After Writer Leaks His Face-lift Secret." **New York Post,** 14 March 1980.

McAleer, John J. Review of **Being There. Best Sellers,** 1 July 1971, p. 173.

-----. Review of **Steps. Best Sellers,** 1 Nov. 1968, p. 316.

McNamara, Eugene. "The Absurd Style in Contemporary American Literature." **Humanities Association Bulletin,** 19 (Spring 1968), 44-49.

Milosz, Czeslaw. **The History of Polish Literature.** London: Macmillan, 1969.

Mitgang, Herbert. "A Talk with Walker Percy." **The New York Times Book Review.** 20 Feb. 1977, pp. 1, 20-21.

Morrell, David. **John Barth: An Introduction.** University Park: Pennsylvania State University Press, 1976.

Movius, Geoffrey. "An Interview with Jerzy Kosinski." **New Boston Review,** 1, No (Winter 1975), 3-4.

Nabokov, Vladimir. **Lolita.** New York: G. P. Putnam's Sons, 1966.

Neville, Mara. "The False Sound of **Pinball.**" Review of **Pinball.**

Nin, Anais. **The Novel of the Future.** New York: Collier Books, 1972.

Noble, David W. **The Eternal Adam and the New World Garden: The Central Myth in the American Novel Since 1836.** New York: Grosset and Dunlap/Universal Library, 1968.

Olderman, Raymond. **Beyond the Waste Land: A Study of the American Novel in the Nineteen Sixties.** New Haven: Yale University Press, 1977.

Olney, Austin. Letters to the Editor. **The Village Voice,** 6 July 1982.

Orzeszkowa, Eliza. **Dziurdziowie.** Warsaw: Ksiazka i Wiedza, 1952.

Panichas, George A., ed. **The Politics of Twentieth-Century Novelists.** New York: Thomas Y. Crowell, 1974.

Penner, Dick, ed. **Fiction of the Absurd: Pratfalls in the Void: A Critical Anthology.** New York: Mentor Books/New American Library, 1980.

Petrakis, Byron. "Jerzy Kosinski's **Steps** and the Cinematic Novel." **The Comparatist,** 2 (1978), 16-22.

Pinwinski, David J. "Kosinski's **The Painted Bird.**" **The Explicator,** 40, No. 1 (Fall 1981), 62-63.

Plimpton, George and Rocco **Landesman.** "The Art of Fiction: Jerzy Kosinski." **Paris Review,** 54 (Summer 1972), 183-207.

Plummer, William. "In His Steps: The Mellowing of Jerzy Kosinski." **The Village Voice,** 31 Oct. 1977, pp. 77-79.

Podhoretz, Norman. **Doings and Undoings.** New York: Farrar, Straus and Giroux, 1964.

Polanski, Roman. **Roman.** New York: William Morrow, 1984.

Prescott, Peter S. "The Basis of Horror." **Newsweek,** 19 Feb. 1973, p. 83.

"Press Panels: Movies -- and the Unexplained." **Publishers Weekly,** 23 July 1975, p. 49.

Pritchett, V. S. "Clowns," **New York Review of Books,** 1 July 1971, p. 15.

Pynchon, Thomas. **The Crying of Lot 49.** New York: J. B. Lippincott, 1966.

-----. **V.** New York: J. B. Lippincott, 1963.

Reymont, Wladyslaw. **The Peasants.** New York: Alfred A. Knopf, 1942.

Richter, David H. "The Three Denouements of Jerzy Kosinski's **The Painted Bird.**" **Contemporary Literature,** 15 (Summer 1974), 370-85.

Riley, John. "Kosinski's Banquet of Forbidden Delights." **Los Angeles Times,** 27 Nov. 1977, p. 4.

Robbe-Grillet, Alain. **For a New Novel: Essays on Fiction.** Trans. Richard Howard. New York: Grove Press, 1965.

Rosenbaum, Lorrin P. "Jerzy Kosinski: The Writer's Focus." **Index on Censorship,** 5, No. 1 (Spring 1976), 47-48.

Roth, Philip. "Writing American Fiction." **Commentary,** 31 (March 1961), 223-33.

Rubin, Louis D., Jr. **The Comic Imagination in American Literature.** New Brunswick: Rutgers University Press, 1973.

-----. "The Curious Death of the American Novel: Or, What to Do About Tired Literary Critics." In **The Curious Death of the American Novel: Essays in American Literature.** Baton Rouge: Louisiana State University Press, 1967.

Rusch, Frederic E. "Jerzy Kosinski: A Checklist." **Bulletin of Bibliography,** 31, No. 1 (Jan.-March 1974), 6-9.

Sanders, Ivan. "The Gift of Strangeness: Alienation and Creation in Jerzy Kosinski's Fiction." **The Polish Review,** 19, Nos. 3-4 (Autumn-Winter 1974), 171-189.

Schiff, Stephen. "The Kosinski Conundrum." **Vanity Fair,** June 1988, pp. 114-119, 166-70.

Scholes, Robert. **Fabulation and Metafiction.** Urbana: University of Illinois Press, 1979.

-----. **The Fabulators.** New York: Oxford University Press, 1967.

-----. **Structural Fabulation: An Essay on Fiction of the Future.** Notre Dame: University of Notre Dame Press, 1975.

Schulz, Bruno. **Proza.** Krakow: Wydawnictwo Literackie, 1964.

-----. **Sanatorium Under the Sign of the Hourglass.** Trans. Celina Wieniewska. New York: Walker and Co., 1978.

Schulz, Max F. **Black Humor Fiction of the Sixties: A Pluralistic Definition of Man and His World.** Athens, Ohio: Ohio University Press, 1973.

Sheehy, Gail. "The Psychological Novelist as Portable Man." **Psychology Today,** Dec. 1977, pp. 54-65+.

Sheppard, R. Z. "Playing It by Eye." **Time,** 26 April 1971, p. 93.

Sherwin, Byron L. **Jerzy Kosinski: Literary Alarmclock.** Chicago: Cabala Press, 1981.

Sienkiewicz, Henryk. **Pan Wolodyjowski.** Warsaw: Panstwowy Instytut Wydawniczy, 1955.

Simpson, Louis P. "Southern Fiction." In **Harvard Guide to Contemporary Writing,** Ed. Daniel Hoffman. Cambridge: The Belknap Press, 1979.

Sloan, James. "On Kosinski." **University Review.** 18 (Summer 1971), 1.

Slotkin, Richard. **Regeneration Through Violence: The Mythology of the American Frontier, 1600-1860.** Middletown, Connecticut: Wesleyan University Press, 1973.

Slung, Michelle. "The Wounding of Jerzy Kosinski." **Washington Post Book World,** 11 July 1982, p. 15.

Smith, Dave. "Kosinski Whodunit: Who Ghost There if Not Jerzy?" **Los Angeles Times,** 1 Aug. 1982, pp. 3-5.

-----. "One Interpretation of Novelist's Words." **Kansas City Star,** 15 Aug. 1982, pp. 1-I, 9-I.

Sohn, David. "A Nation of Videots." **Media and Methods,** April 1975, pp. 24-31, 52-57.

Sontag, Susan. **Against Interpretation.** New York: Farrar, Straus and Giroux, 1964.

Steiner, George. **Language and Silence: Essays on Language, Literature, and the Inhuman.** New York: Atheneum, 1958.

Stokes, Geoffrey and Eliot **Fremont-Smith.** "Jerzy Kosinski's Tainted Words." **The Village Voice,** 22 June 1982, pp. 1, 41-43.

Stone, Elizabeth. "Horatio Algers of the Nightmare." **Psychology Today,** Dec. 1977, pp. 59-64.

Swindell, Larry. "Kosinski's Labyrinth Is No Funny Forest; But Compelling, Yes." **The Philadelphia Inquirer,** 18 Feb. 1973, p. 6-H.

Tepa, Barbara J. "Jerzy Kosinski's Polish Contexts: A Study of **Being There.**" **The Polish Review,** 22, No. 2 (1977), 52-61.

-----. "Kosinski Takes Another Chance." **The Polish Review,** 23, No. 3 (1978), 104-108.

Thorpe, Jac. **John Barth: The Comic Sublimity of Paradox.** Carbondale: Southern Illinois University Press, 1976.

Tolkien, J. R. R. **Tree and Leaf.** Boston: Houghton Mifflin, 1965.

Tucker, Martin. "Being There." **Commonweal,** 7 May 1971, pp. 221-23.

Updike, John. Review of **Being There. The New Yorker,** 25 Sept. 1971, p. 131.

Vonnegut, Kurt. **Cat's Cradle.** New York: Holt, Rinehart and Winston, 1963.

-----. **God Bless You, Mr. Rosewater; or, Pearls Before Swine.** New York: Dell, 1973.

-----. **Slaughterhouse-Five: or, the Children's Crusade.** New York: The Delacorte Press, 1969.

Warga, Wayne. "Jerzy Kosinski Reaches Down into Life and Writes." **Los Angeles Times Calendar,** 22 April 1973, pp. 1, 54.

Wolff, Geoffrey. "Last Brave Wish to Try Everything." **Book World,** 25 March 1973, pp. 3, 10.

Wright, Charles. **The Wig.** New York: Farrar, Straus, and Giroux, 1966.

Ziff, Larzer. **Literary Democracy: The Declaration of Cultural Independence in America.** New York: Viking, 1981.

Barbara Tepa Lupack holds degrees in English Language and Literature from Boston University, Boston College, and St. John's University. She has taught writing and literature at the college level for over thirteen years, most recently at Empire State College/SUNY, where she is both a mentor and an academic administrator. In 1981-82, she served as Fulbright Senior Lecturer in American Literature, first at the University of Wroclaw, Poland, and later at the Universite de Savoie a Chambery. She has authored or edited several works on composition, basic skills, and Native American culture, and has published on contemporary authors in both American and European journals, including **The New Orleans Review, The Polish Review, The Slavic Review, and Etudes Anglaises.**